RUNWAY KNITS

30 FASHION-FORWARD DESIGNS

BERTA KARAPETYAN

PHOTOGRAPHY BY
JUSTIN WILLIAM LIN

POTTER
CRAFT

POTTER CRAFT
NEW YORK

Copyright © 2007 by BERTA KARAPETYAN
Photographs copyright © 2007 by JUSTIN WILLIAM LIN

Published in the United States by Potter Craft, an imprint of the Crown Publishing Group,
a division of Random House, Inc., New York.
www.crownpublishing.com
www.pottercraft.com

POTTER CRAFT and colophon and POTTER and colophon
are registered trademarks of Random House, Inc.

Library of Congress Cataloging-in-Publication Data
Karapetyan, Berta.
Runway knits : 30 fashion-forward designs / Berta Karapetyan ;
photographs by Justin Lin. — 1st ed.
p.   cm.
Includes index.
ISBN-13: 978-0-307-33968-3
1. Knitting—Patterns.   I. Title.
TT820.K32   2007
746.43'20432—dc22   2006028067

ISBN: 978-0-307-33968-3

Printed in China

Design by JENNIFER K. BEAL

10   9   8   7   6   5   4   3   2   1

First Edition

acknowledgements

I am very grateful to the following people:
My dear friend and designer Nick Atkinson, for his advises and kindness.

My friend Irina Novick, for her help with pattern writing, and my tech editors, Jean Lampe and Peggy Greig, for being so pleasant to work with.

My husband, Raf, for his patience and support

My favorite editor, Rosy Ngo, and the wonderful Christina Schoen, for great help in every possible way.

The many knitters who have supported my ideas and my designs.

In memory of my mother, who always admired my work

cont

ents

Chapter 4: Driven

introd

When I knit, there's nothing I love more than a challenge. For the past decade, I've found that challenge designing high-fashion knitwear collections for Karabella and working as a technical knitwear developer for the best fashion houses in New York, including Donna Karan, Calvin Klein, Ralph Lauren, Club Monaco, and others. As a designer, my strength has always been my ability to master difficult techniques, and when design houses approach me, it is usually because the work involves something particularly special or complicated.

Growing up in Moscow, Russia, I began knitting at the age of twelve and haven't stopped since. I still remember the first sweater I ever knit—it was T-shaped with a simple lace pattern. When I showed it to my family, they were fascinated by my creation, but I wasn't happy with the way it fit. To perfect my skills, I started reading books about sweater construction and quickly realized the importance of math in designing well-proportioned pieces. Even today, I always tell my knitting students, "Never guess—calculate."

In 1976, I graduated from the Moscow Finance Academy with a master's degree in finance. After working for the Moscow City Department of Finance for a short time, I got married and had two children, Masha and Arthur, and I never pursued a finance career again. My passion for knitting and crocheting took over, and I discovered that I loved sharing my skills with others. I began teaching knitting and crocheting at a women's club in Moscow. My classes quickly became recognized among craft lovers in Moscow, and every fall my students and I put on an exhibition of our work that was always very well attended.

When my family and I emigrated from Russia to the United States and settled in New York in the late 1980s, I discovered a whole new world of styles and shapes. I also began to see how I could apply my talents to the fashion industry. My real entrée into the New York fashion scene began in 1995, when I purchased School Products, the largest and oldest yarn store in Manhattan and a favorite among designers and fiber artists.

Inspired by the runways of New York, as well as my Russian roots, I quickly learned to translate my technical skills into high-fashion knitwear and developed a strong fashion sensibility that you will see in the patterns I have created for this collection. In all my designs I attempt to marry texture and yarn, color and shape. At the same time, I am conscious of the actual people who are going to wear my knitwear—you. I don't want my designs to overwhelm your body; the garment should flatter you. I want my pieces not only to be tasteful but also to have a sense of adventure.

I also love interesting details, and the designs in *Runway Knits* are all unique. Sometimes I may use an unusual stitch pattern or construction method, and in other patterns it is the combination of a simple stitch and a complementing color that creates an elegant, fashionable design. Made in the Karabella line of yarns owned by my son Arthur and hand-selected by me, all of these designs exude personality; so much so that when you wear them your look will set the mood. As such, I have divided the book into four sections: Spirited, Playful, Demure, and Driven.

When you flip through the pages of this book, I want you to say, "Wow, I *have* to make that." But my greatest hope is that my designs will both inspire you to improve your technical skills and give you the confidence to take on increasingly difficult projects. Not all the patterns in this book require intermediate or advanced skills. There are some, such as the Vintage Shawl on page 26 or the Cozy Moss Shrug on page 126, that beginning knitters should have no trouble completing. The Flamingo Capelet on page 10 and Corded Sweater on page 136 may be better suited to intermediate knitters. For those of you who are looking for some real fun, try your hand at the Cabled Cardigan on page 86 and Leaf-Drop Sweater on page 162.

I have written hundreds of patterns over the years and have developed a style of pattern writing that many knitters find approachable. As the owner of two yarn stores, I get lots of feedback from my customers, and I have learned the importance of ensuring that my patterns are reliable and that they gently guide knitters through skills they may be trying out for the first time. All of these patterns have gone through meticulous testing and editing to ensure that even new knitters can proceed with confidence.

I take great satisfaction in knowing that I can share the wealth of my knowledge—challenges and all—with you in this wonderful collection. I hope that you'll enjoy the experience of both knitting these pieces, and, above all, wearing them!

CHAPTER I: SPIRITED

FLAMINGO CAPELET

This flirty cropped capelet screams for attention so you don't have to. Its vibrant color, unusual shape, eye-catching collar, and sassy front ties—perfect for that first date—will make you the main attraction. Cable-knit in one piece, starting with the ties, the Front is shaped at the sides with diagonal darts.

FLAMINGO CAPELET

SIZES
To fit S (M, L). Directions are for the smallest size, with larger sizes in parentheses. When only one set of instructions appears, it applies to all sizes.

KNITTED MEASUREMENTS
Bust: 32 (35, 38)" [81 (89, 96.5)cm]

Length: 13½ (14½, 15½)" [34 (37, 39.5)cm]

Upper arm: 11 (12½, 14)" [28 (32, 35.5)cm]

Arm length: 25½ (26, 26½)" [65 (66, 67)cm]

MATERIALS
9 (10, 11) balls Karabella Margrite (80% extra fine merino wool, 20% cashmere; about 154 yds [140m] per 1¾ oz [50g] ball): color # 8456, Hot Pink

Size 7 (4.5mm) needles, or size to obtain gauge

Cable needle

Stitch markers

Stitch holders

GAUGE
29 sts and 32 rows = 4" (10cm) over Honey Cable Pattern (HCP), using size 7 needles.

HONEY CABLE PATTERN (MULTIPLE OF 6 STS + 2 STS)
ROW 1: P2, *sl 1 to CN and hold to back, k1, k1 from CN, sl 1 to CN and hold to front, k1, k1 from CN, p2*; repeat from * to * to end.

ROWS 2 AND 4: *K2, p4*; repeat from * to * to last 2 sts, k2.

ROW 3: P2, *sl 1 to CN and hold to front, k1, k1 from CN, sl 1 to CN and hold to back, k1, k1 from CN, p2*; repeat from * to * to end.

Repeat these 4 rows for patt.

HONEY CABLE (OVER 4 STS)
ROW 1: Sl 1 to CN and hold to back, k1, k1 from CN, sl 1 to CN and hold to front, k1, k1 from CN.

ROWS 2 AND 4: P4.

ROW 3: Sl 1 to CN and hold to front, k1, k1 from CN, sl 1 to CN and hold to back, k1, k1 from CN.

Repeat these 4 rows for patt.

BACK
Note: The back is worked with p1 edge stitch at each end of every RS row, and k1 at each end of every WS row.

Increase 1—Use the backward loop (e) cast-on method to make the increases.

Cast on 100 (112, 124) sts.

ROW 1 (RS): P1 (edge st), work row 1 of Honey Cable Pattern as follows: p2, *sl 1 to CN and hold to back, k1, k1 from CN, sl 1 to CN and hold to front, k1, k1 from CN, p2*; repeat from * to * across row to last st, p1 (edge st).

ROW 2 AND ALL WS ROWS: Work sts as they appear (knit the knit sts, purl the purl sts).

ROW 3: P1 (edge st), work row 3 of Honey Cable Pattern as follows: p2, *sl 1 to CN and hold to front, k1, k1 from CN, sl 1 to CN and hold to back, k1, k1 from CN, p2*; repeat from * to * across row to last st, p1 (edge st).

Work even in established patt for 6 rows total from CO.

NEXT RS ROW: P1 (edge st), increase 1, work in established patt to last stitch, increase 1, p1 (edge st). Work new sts into the Honey Cable Pattern when possible—102 (114, 126) sts.

Repeat these increases every 6th row 6 times more—114 (126, 138) sts.

Continue working in patt as established until piece measures about 6½ (7, 7½)" [16.5 (18, 19)cm], ending with WS row and at the same time row 4 of Honey Cable Pattern.

ARMHOLE SHAPING
Bind off 7 sts at beginning of next 2 rows—100 (112, 124) sts.

Work even in established patt for 4 rows more.

ROW 7 (RS): P1, p2tog, work in established patt to last 3 sts, p2tog, p1—98 (110, 122) sts.

Work even in established patt for 5 rows more.

ROW 13 (RS): P1, sl 2 to CN and hold to back, k1, k2tog from CN, sl 1 to CN and hold to front, k1, k1 from CN,

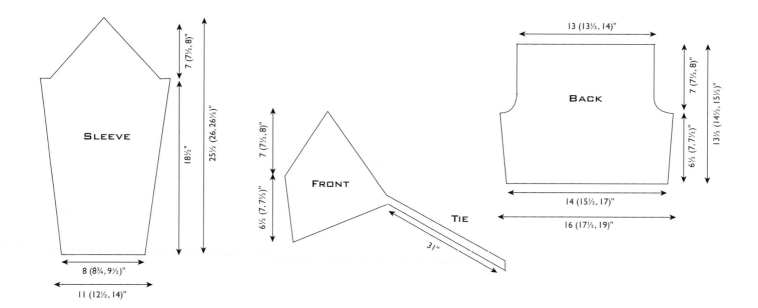

continue in established patt to the last 4 sts, sl 1 to CN and hold to front, k2tog, k1 from CN, p1—96 (108, 120) sts.

Work even in established patt for 5 rows more.

ROW 19: P1, ssk, sl 1 to CN and hold to back, k1, k1 from CN, continue in established patt to the last 3 sts, k2tog, p1—94 (106, 118) sts.

ROW 21: P1, k1, sl 1 to CN and hold to front, k1, k1 from CN, continue in established patt to the last 2 sts, k1, p1.

ROW 23: P1, k1, sl 1 to CN and hold to back, k1, k1 from CN, continue in established patt to the last 2 sts, k1, p1.

ROW 25: P1, k1, ssk, continue in established patt to the last 4 sts, k2tog, k1, p1—92 (104, 116) sts.

ROW 27: P1, sl 1 to CN and hold to back, k1, k1 from CN, continue in established patt to the last 3 sts, sl 1 to CN and hold to front, k1, k1 from CN, p1.

ROW 29: P1, sl 1 to CN and hold to front, k1, k1 from CN, continue in established patt to the last 3 sts, sl 1 to CN and hold to back, k1, k1 from CN, p1.

ROW 30: Work sts as they appear.

FOR SIZE SMALL ONLY:

Repeat rows 27–30 until Armhole measures 7" (18cm).

Bind off 92 sts for Upper Back.

FOR SIZE MEDIUM ONLY:

ROW 31: P1, k2tog, continue in established patt to the last 3 sts, ssk, p1—102 sts.

ROWS 33–35: P1, k1, continue in established patt to the last 2 sts, k1, p1.

ROW 37: P1, p2tog, p1, continue in established patt to the last 4 sts, p1, p2tog, p1—100 sts

ROWS 39–41: P3, continue in established patt to the last 3 sts, p3.

ROW 43: Repeat row 7—98 sts.

Work even in established patt until Armhole measures 7½" (19cm).

Bind off 98 sts for Upper Back.

FOR SIZE LARGE ONLY:

ROW 31: P1, k2tog, continue in established patt to the last 3 sts, ssk, p1—114 sts.

ROWS 33–35: P1, k1, continue in established patt to the last 2 sts, k1, p1

ROW 37: P1, p2tog, p1, continue in established patt to the last 4 sts, p1, p2tog, p1—112 sts.

ROWS 39–41: P3, continue in established patt to the last 3 sts, p3.

ROWS 43–62: Repeat rows 7 through 26—104 sts.

Work even in established patt until Armhole measures 8" (20.5cm).

Bind off 104 sts for Upper Back.

RIGHT FRONT (AS WORN)

Begin with tie. Cast on 3 sts.

Note: Increase 1—Use the backward loop (e) cast-on method to make the following increases.

ROW 1 (RS): Sl 1, increase 1, k1, increase 1, p1—5 sts.

ROWS 2, 6, AND 10 (WS): Sl 1, *k1, p1*; repeat from * to * to end.

ROW 3: Sl 1, increase 1, p1, k1, p1, increase 1, k1—7 sts.

ROWS 4, 8, AND 12: Sl 1, *p1, k1*; repeat from * to * to end.

ROWS 5, 9, AND 13: Sl 1, increase 1, *k1, p1*; repeat from * to * to last 2 sts, k1, increase 1, p1—(17 sts after completing row 13).

ROWS 7 AND 11: Sl 1, increase 1, *p1, k1*; repeat from * to * to last 2 sts, p1, increase 1, k1.

Beginning each row with sl 1, work even in established single rib patt for 31" (78.5cm). Increase 1 st in the next row to balance the rib and patt—18 sts.

Begin working in patt following chart I from row 1 to row 40, chart II from row 41 to row 73 for all sizes. Chart III from rows 74 to 79 for Medium and 74 to 85 for Large. When chart rows are finished, follow text instructions to complete the right front.

FOR SIZE SMALL ONLY:

ROW 74: Remove markers in this row. Bind off 60 sts (this is the right front side), work sts as they appear to end.

ROWS 75–93: Work short rows as follows:

ROW 75: Work in the established Honey Cable patt to the last 6 sts, wrap next st, turn work.

EVEN-NUMBERED ROWS FROM 76 TO 94: Work sts as they appear.

ODD-NUMBERED ROWS FROM 77 TO 93: Work in the established Honey Cable patt to the last 6 sts from the previous wrap (for example in row 77 work to the last 12 sts, in row 79 work to the last 18 sts and so on), wrap next st, turn work.

ROW 95 (SMOOTHING ROW): Note: Work wrap and purl st together as they appear. P1, * Honey Cable, p2; repeat to last 5 sts, Honey Cable, p1.

ROW 96: Bind off all sts (Raglan line).

FOR SIZE MEDIUM ONLY:

ROWS 74–79: Repeat rows 2–7.

ROW 80: Remove markers in this row. Bind off 63 sts (this is the Right Front side), work sts as they appear to end.

ROW 81: Work in the established Honey Cable patt to the last 9 sts, wrap next st, turn work.

EVEN-NUMBERED ROWS FROM 82 TO 100: Work sts as they appear.

ODD-NUMBERED ROWS FROM 83 TO 99: Work in the established Honey Cable patt to the last 6 sts from the previous wrap (for example in row 83 work to the last 15 sts, in row 79 work to the last 21 sts and so on), wrap next st, turn work.

ROW 101 (SMOOTHING ROW): Note: Work wrap and purl st together as they occur. P1, * Honey Cable, p2; repeat from * to last 8 sts, k3, Honey Cable, p1.

ROW 102: Bind off all sts (Raglan line).

CHART I, RIGHT FRONT, ROWS 1–40 (ALL SIZES)

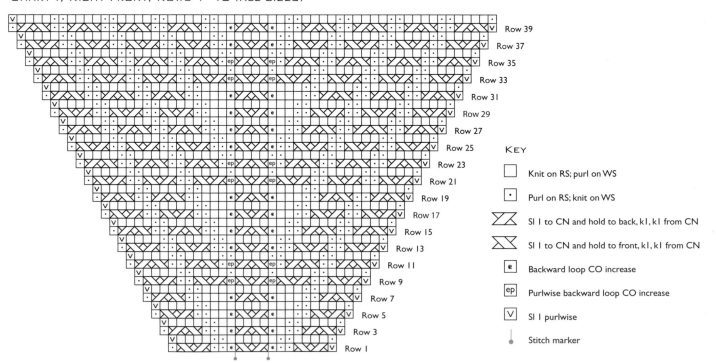

Row 39
Row 37
Row 35
Row 33
Row 31
Row 29
Row 27
Row 25
Row 23
Row 21
Row 19
Row 17
Row 15
Row 13
Row 11
Row 9
Row 7
Row 5
Row 3
Row 1

KEY

☐ Knit on RS; purl on WS

• Purl on RS; knit on WS

⟩⟨ Sl 1 to CN and hold to back, k1, k1 from CN

⟨⟩ Sl 1 to CN and hold to front, k1, k1 from CN

e Backward loop CO increase

ep Purlwise backward loop CO increase

V Sl 1 purlwise

↓ Stitch marker

CHART II, ROWS 41–73 (ALL SIZES)

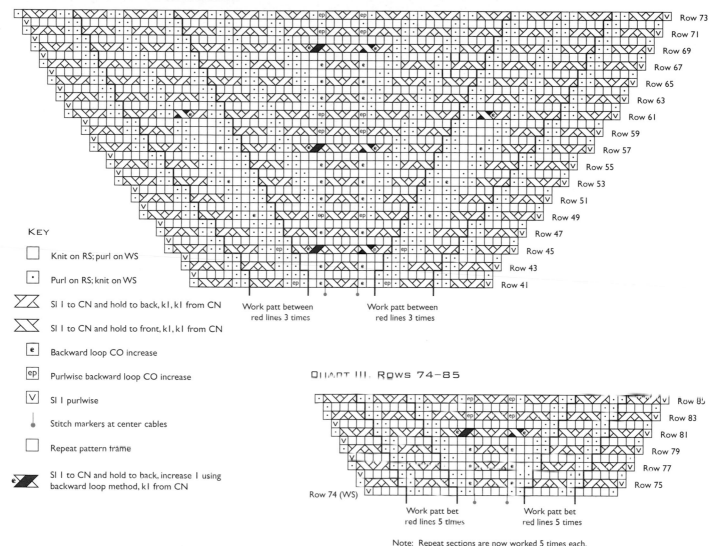

Row 73
Row 71
Row 69
Row 67
Row 65
Row 63
Row 61
Row 59
Row 57
Row 55
Row 53
Row 51
Row 49
Row 47
Row 45
Row 43
Row 41

KEY

☐ Knit on RS; purl on WS

· Purl on RS; knit on WS

⧄ SI 1 to CN and hold to back, k1, k1 from CN

⧅ SI 1 to CN and hold to front, k1, k1 from CN

e Backward loop CO increase

ep Purlwise backward loop CO increase

V SI 1 purlwise

↓ Stitch markers at center cables

☐ Repeat pattern frame

▰ SI 1 to CN and hold to back, increase 1 using backward loop method, k1 from CN

Work patt between red lines 3 times

Work patt between red lines 3 times

CHART III, ROWS 74–85

Row 85
Row 83
Row 81
Row 79
Row 77
Row 75

Row 74 (WS)

Work patt bet red lines 5 times

Work patt bet red lines 5 times

Note: Repeat sections are now worked 5 times each.
Medium size ends after working row 79; return to text to complete.

FOR SIZE LARGE ONLY:

ROWS 74–85: Repeat rows 2–13.

ROW 86: Remove markers in this row. Bind off 66 sts (this is the Right Front side), work sts as they appear to end.

ROW 87: Work in the established Honey Cable patt to the last 6 sts, wrap next st, turn work.

EVEN-NUMBERED ROWS FROM 88 TO 108: Work sts as they appear.

ODD-NUMBERED ROWS FROM 89 TO 107: Work in the established Honey Cable patt to the last 6 sts from the previous wrap (for example, in row 89 work to the last 12 sts, in row 91 work to the last 18 sts, and so on), wrap next st, turn work.

ROW 109 (SMOOTHING ROW): Note: Work wrap and purl st together as they occur. P1, * Honey Cable, p2; repeat from * to last 5 sts, Honey Cable, p1.

ROW 110: Bind off all sts (Raglan line).

KEY

☐ Knit on RS; purl on WS

· Purl on RS; knit on WS

⧄ SI 1 to CN and hold to back, k1, k1 from CN

⧅ SI 1 to CN and hold to front, k1, k1 from CN

e Backward loop CO increase

ep Purlwise backward loop CO increase

V SI 1 purlwise

↓ Stitch marker

☐ Repeat pattern frame

▰ SI 1 to CN and hold to back, increase 1 using backward loop method, k1 from CN

▱ SI 1 to CN and hold to front, increase 1 st using backward loop method, k1 from CN.

FLAMINGO CAPELET ■ 15

LEFT FRONT (AS WORN)

Work as for Right Front until row 73 (79, 85).

FOR SIZE SMALL ONLY:

ROW 74: Work sts as they appear.

ROW 75: Remove markers in this row. Bind off 60 sts (this is the Left Front side), work in the established Honey Cable patt to end.

ROW 76: Work sts as they appear to the last 6 sts, wrap next st, turn work.

ODD-NUMBERED ROWS FROM 77 TO 95: Work in the established Honey Cable patt to end.

EVEN-NUMBERED ROWS FROM 78 TO 94: Work sts as they appear to the last 6 sts from the previous wrap (for example in row 78 work to the last 12 sts, in row 80 work to the last 18 sts and so on), wrap next st, turn work.

ROW 96 (SMOOTHING ROW): Note: Work wrap and knit st together as they occur. K1, *p4, k2; repeat from * to last 5 sts, p4, k1.

ROW 97: Bind off all sts (Raglan line).

FOR SIZE MEDIUM ONLY:

ROW 80: Work sts as they appear.

ROW 81: Remove markers in this row. Bind off 63 sts (this is the Left Front side), work in the established Honey Cable patt to end.

ROW 82: Work sts as they appear to the last 9 sts, wrap next st, turn work.

ODD-NUMBERED ROWS FROM 83 TO 101: Work in the established Honey Cable patt to end.

EVEN-NUMBERED ROWS FROM 84 TO 100: Work sts as they appear to the last 6 sts from the previous wrap (for example in row 84 work to the last 15 sts, in row 86 work to the last 21 sts and so on), wrap next st, turn work.

ROW 102 (SMOOTHING ROW): Note: Work wrap and knit st together as they occur. K1, *p4, k2; repeat from * to last 8 sts, p7, k1.

ROW 103: Bind off all sts (Raglan line).

FOR SIZE LARGE ONLY:

ROW 86: Work sts as they appear.

ROW 87: Remove markers in this row. Bind off 66 sts (this is the Left Front side), work in the established Honey Cable patt to end.

ROW 88: Work sts as they appear to the last 6 sts, wrap next st, turn work.

ODD-NUMBERED ROWS FROM 89 TO 109: Work in the established Honey Cable patt to end.

EVEN-NUMBERED ROWS FROM 90 TO 108: Work sts as they appear to the last 6 sts from the previous wrap (for example in row 90 work to the last 12 sts, in row 92 work to the last 18 sts and so on), wrap next st, turn work.

ROW 110 (SMOOTHING ROW): Note: Work wrap and knit st together as they occur. K1, *p4, k2; repeat from * to last 5 sts, p4, k1.

ROW 111: Bind off all sts (Raglan line).

SLEEVE

Cast on 58 (64, 70) sts.

ROW 1 (RS): P1, work row 1 of Honey Cable patt to last st, p1.

ROW 2 AND ALL WS ROWS: Work sts as they appear (knit the knit sts, purl the purl sts).

ROW 3: P1, work row 3 of Honey Cable patt to last st, p1. Continue to work even in established patt for 10 (8, 6) rows total from CO.

NEXT RS ROW: Working in patt, increase 1 st at beg and end of row (work new sts into Honey Cable patt, when possible)—60 (66, 72) sts.

Rep these increases every 10 (8, 6)th row 11 (14, 17) times more—82 (94, 106) sts.

Continue working in patt as established until piece measures about 18½" (47cm), ending with WS row and at the same time row 4 of Honey Cable patt.

Cap Shaping

Bind off 7 sts at beginning of next 2 rows—68 (80, 92) sts.

ROW 3 (RS): P2, Honey Cable (row 3), p2tog, work in established Honey Cable patt to last 8 sts, p2tog, Honey Cable (row 3), p2—66 (78, 90) sts.

ROW 2 AND ALL WS ROWS UNTIL SPECIAL INSTRUCTIONS: Work sts as they appear.

ROW 5: P2, Honey Cable (row 1), k2tog, k1, sl 1 to CN and hold to front, k1, k1 from CN, continue in established patt to the last 9 sts, k1, ssk, Honey Cable (row 1), p2—64 (76, 88) sts.

ROW 7: P2, Honey Cable (row 3), ssk, sl 1 to CN and hold to back, k1, k1 from CN, continue in established patt to the last 8 sts, k2tog, Honey Cable (row 3), p2—62 (74, 86) sts.

ROW 9: P2, Honey Cable (row 1), k2tog, k1, continue in established patt to the last 9 sts, k1, ssk, Honey Cable (row 1), p2—60 (72, 84) sts.

ROW 11: P2, Honey Cable (row 3), ssk, continue in established patt to the last 8 sts, k2tog, Honey Cable (row 3), p2—58 (70, 82) sts.

ROW 13: P2, Honey Cable (row 1), p2tog, p1, continue in established patt to the last 9 sts, p1, p2tog, Honey Cable (row 1), p2—56 (68, 80) sts.

ROWS 15–26: Repeat rows 3 through 14—44 (56, 68) sts.

ROWS 27–37: Repeat rows 3 through 13—32 (44, 56) sts.

FOR SIZE SMALL ONLY:

ROW 38: Work sts as they appear.

ROWS 39–45: Repeat rows 3 through 9—24 sts.

FOR SIZE MEDIUM ONLY:

ROW 38 AND 40: Work sts as they appear.

ROW 39: Repeat row 3—42 sts.

ROW 41: Repeat row 5—40 sts.

ROW 42: K2, p4, p2tog, p2, *k2, p4; repeat from * to last 12 sts, k2, p2, p2tog, p4, k2—38 sts.

ROW 43: P2, Honey Cable (row 3), ssk, k1, continue in established patt to the last 9 sts, k1, k2tog, Honey Cable (row 3), p2—36 sts.

ROW 44: K2, p4, p2tog, *k2, p4; repeat from * to last 10 sts, k2, p2tog, p4, k2—34 sts.

ROW 45: Repeat row 13—32 sts.

ROW 46: K2, p4, k2tog, p4, *k2, p4; repeat from * to last 8 sts, k2tog, p4, k2—30 sts.

ROW 47: P2, Honey Cable (row 3), ssk, k1, sl 1 to CN and hold to back, k1, k1 from CN, continue in established patt to the last 9 sts, k1, k2tog, Honey Cable (row 3), p2—28 sts.

ROW 48: K2, p4, p2tog, p2, *k2, p4; repeat from * to last 12 sts, k2, p2, p2tog, p4, k2—26 sts.

ROW 49: Repeat row 9—24 sts.

FOR SIZE LARGE ONLY:

ROW 38: K2, p4, k2tog, p4, *k2, p4; repeat from * to last 8 sts, k2tog, p4, k2—54 sts.

ROW 39: P2, Honey Cable (row 3), ssk, k1, continue in established patt to the last 9 sts, k1, k2tog, Honey Cable (row 3), p2—52 sts.

ROW 40: K2, p4, p2tog, p2, *k2, p4; repeat from * to last 12 sts, k2, p2, p2tog, p4, k2—50 sts.

ROW 41: Repeat row 9—48 sts.

ROW 42: K2, p4, p2tog, *k2, p4; rep from * to last 10 sts, k2, p2tog, p4, k2—46 sts.

ROW 43: P2, Honey Cable (row 3), p2tog, p1, cont in established patt to the last 9 sts, p1, p2tog, Honey Cable (row 3), p2—44 sts.

ROW 44: K2, p4, k2tog, p4, *k2, p4; repeat from * to last

8 sts, k2tog, p4, k2—42 sts.

ROWS 45–53: Repeat rows 41–49 of size Medium—24 sts.

CONTINUE FOR ALL SIZES:

ROW 46 (50, 54): K2, p4, p2tog, k2, p4, k2, p2tog, p4, k2—22 sts.

ROW 47 (51, 55): P2, Honey Cable (row 3), p2tog, p1, Honey Cable (row 3), p1, p2tog, Honey Cable (row 3), p2—20 sts.

ROW 48 (52, 56): K2, p4, k2tog, p4, k2tog, p4, k2—18 sts.

ROW 49 (53, 57): P2, Honey Cable (row 1), k2tog, k2, ssk, Honey Cable (row 1), p2—16 sts.

ROW 50 (54, 58): K2, p4, p2tog, p2tog, p4, k2—14 sts.

ROW 51 (55, 59): P2, sl 1 to CN and hold to front, k1, k1 from CN, k2tog, k2, ssk, sl 1 to CN and hold to back, k1, k1 from CN, p2—12 sts.

ROW 52 (56, 60): K2, p1, p2tog, p2, p2tog, p1, k2—10 sts.

ROW 53 (57, 61): P2, k2tog, k2, ssk, p2—8 sts.

ROW 54 (58, 62): K2, p2tog, p2tog, k2—6 sts.

ROW 55 (59, 63): P1, p2tog, p2tog, p1—4 sts.

ROW 56 (60, 64): K2tog, k2tog—2 sts.

ROW 57 (61, 65): K2tog. Fasten off.

COLLAR

Sew Sleeves into the Back Armhole. Sew Sleeves into the Front Raglan line (central cable of the Front Side belongs to the Raglan line).

With RS facing, pick up and work in k1, pl rib 92 (98, 104) sts from upper Back plus 2 sts more from the first sl st of left side (to pick up 2 sts use the front and the back strand of the sl st)—94 (100, 106) sts.

NEXT ROW: Work in k1, pl rib and pick up 2 more sts at the end of the row from the first sl st of right side—96 (102, 108 sts).

NEXT ROW: Work in k1, pl rib and pick up 2 more sts at the end of the row from the next sl st of left side—98 (104, 110) sts.

Cont. working in this manner until there are 80 (82, 84) rows in the collar. Bind off tightly.

FINISHING

Sew Side and Sleeve seams. Weave in loose ends to WS.

RUFFLED CARDIGAN

MOHAIR LACE RUFFLES ADD A DRAMATIC FLOUR-
ISH TO THIS BASIC BLACK CARDIGAN. THIS PIECE
WILL HELP YOU LEARN TO CREATE PERFECTLY
LAID RUFFLES—IN THIS CASE, DOWN THE FRONT
AND AT THE SLEEVES. THE RESULT IS A GRACE-
FUL, FEMININE CARDIGAN THAT IS FUN TO WEAR
AND THAT REVEALS JUST A HINT OF ATTITUDE.

RUFFLED CARDIGAN

SIZES
To fit S (M, L). Directions are for the smallest size, with larger sizes in parentheses. If there is only one set of figures, it applies to all sizes.

KNITTED MEASUREMENTS
Bust: 32 (36, 40)" [81 (91.5, 101.5)cm]

Length with ruffle: 23 (23½, 24)" [58.5 (60, 61)cm]

Upper arm: 11 (12, 13)" [28 (30.5, 33)cm]

Arm length with ruffle: 24 (24½, 25)" [61 (62, 63.5)cm]

MATERIALS
7 (8, 9) balls Karabella Aurora 4 (100% extra fine merino wool; about 196 yds [180m] per 1¾ oz [50g] ball): color #1148, Black

2 balls Karabella Lace Mohair (61% super kid mohair, 8% wool, 31% polyester; about 540 yds [500m] per 1¾ oz [50g] ball): color #250, Black

Size 2 (2.75mm) needles, or size to obtain gauge

Size 7 (4.5mm) 24" [60cm] circular needle, or size to obtain gauge (to work ruffles)

GAUGE
30 sts and 40 rows = 4" (10cm) over St st, using size 2 needles and Aurora 4.

20 sts and 30 rows = 4" (10cm) over St st, using size 7 needle and Lace Mohair.

WIDE RUFFLE
(OVER 28 STS)
ROW 1 (RS): Knit to last 4 sts, wrap next st, turn work, leaving remaining sts unworked.

ROW 2 AND ALL WS ROWS UNTIL NEXT WS INSTRUCTIONS: Sl wrapped st, work sts as they appear to end of row.

ROW 3: Knit to last 7 sts, wrap next st, turn work.

ROW 5: Knit to last 10 sts, wrap next st, turn work.

ROW 7: Knit to last 13 sts, wrap next st, turn work.

ROW 9: Knit to last 16 sts, wrap next st, turn work.

ROW 11: Knit to last 19 sts, wrap next st, turn work.

ROW 13: Knit to last 22 sts, wrap next st, turn work.

ROW 15: Knit to last 25 sts, wrap next st, turn work.

ROW 17 (SMOOTHING ROW): K28 working wrap and knit st together when wrapped sts occur.

ROW 18: P28.

ROW 19: K3, wrap next st, turn work, leaving remaining 24 sts unworked.

ROW 20 AND ALL WS ROWS UNTIL NEXT WS INSTRUCTIONS: Sl wrapped st, work sts as they appear to end of row.

ROWS 21, 23, 25, 27, 29, 31, AND 33: Knit to 1 st before wrap, work next wrap and st together, k2, wrap next st, turn work.

ROW 35: Knit to 1 st before wrap, work next knit and wrap sts together, knit to end—28 sts.

ROW 36: P28.

NARROW RUFFLE
(OVER 18 STS)
ROW 1 (RS): Knit to last 3 sts, wrap next st, turn work, leaving remaining st unworked.

ROW 2 AND ALL WS ROWS UNTIL NEXT WS INSTRUCTIONS: Sl wrapped st, work sts as they appear to end of row.

ROW 3: Knit to last 6 sts, wrap next st, turn work.

ROW 5: Knit to last 9 sts, wrap next st, turn work.

ROW 7: Knit to last 12 sts, wrap next st, turn work.

ROW 9: Knit to last 15 sts, wrap next st, turn work.

ROW 11 (SMOOTHING ROW): K18 working wrap and knit st together when wrapped sts occurs.

ROW 12: P18.

ROW 13: K3, wrap next st, turn work.

ROW 14 AND ALL WS ROWS UNTIL NEXT WS INSTRUCTIONS: Sl wrapped st, work sts as they appear to end.

ROWS 15, 17, 19, AND 21: Knit to 1 st before wrap, work next knit and wrap st together, k2, wrap next st, turn work.

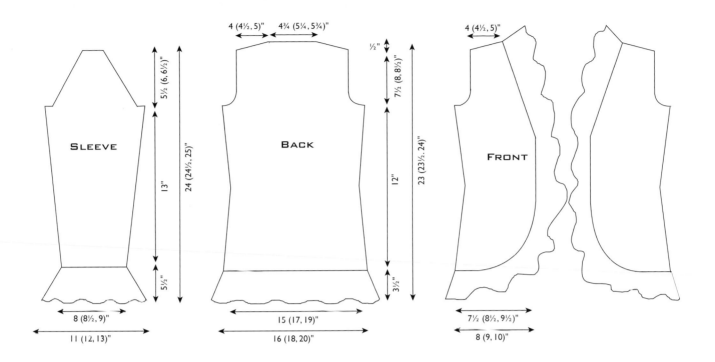

SLEEVE

5½ (6, 6½)"

13"

24 (24½, 25)"

5½"

8 (8½, 9)"

11 (12, 13)"

BACK

4 (4½, 5)"   4¾ (5¼, 5¾)"

½"

7½ (8, 8½)"

12"

23 (23½, 24)"

3½"

15 (17, 19)"

16 (18, 20)"

FRONT

4 (4½, 5)"

7½ (8½, 9½)"

8 (9, 10)"

ROW 23: Knit to 1 st before wrap, work next knit and wrap sts together, knit to end—18 sts.

ROW 24: P18.

BACK

Using size 2 needles and Aurora 4, cast on 120 (136, 152) sts. Beginning with knit row, work in St st (knit on RS, purl on WS) for 8 rows.

ROWS 9, 17, 25, 33, AND 41: K2, k2tog, knit to last 4 sts, ssk, k2—110 (126, 142) sts.

Work even in St st until piece measures 7" (18cm), ending with WS row.

NEXT RS ROW (INCREASES): K2, m1, knit to last 2 sts, m1, k2—112 (128, 144) sts.

Continue working in St st repeating increase row every 6th row 5 times more—122 (138, 154) sts.

When piece measures 12" (30.5cm), ending with WS row, start Armhole shaping.

ARMHOLE SHAPING

Bind off 4 (5, 6) sts at beginning of next 2 rows—114 (128, 142) sts.

NEXT RS ROW (DECREASE): K2, k2tog, knit to last 4 sts, ssk, k2—112 (126, 140) sts.

Continue working in St st repeating this decrease row every 4th row 8 (9, 10) times more—96 (108, 120) sts.

When Armhole measures 7½ (8, 8½)" [19 (20, 21.5)cm], shape Shoulders.

SHOULDER SHAPING

Bind off 10 (12, 13) sts in the next 2 rows— 76 (84, 94) sts.

Bind off 10 (11, 13) sts in the next 2 rows—56 (62, 68) sts.

Bind off 10 (11, 12) sts in the next 2 rows—36 (40, 44) sts.

Bind off remaining 36 (40, 44) sts for Back Neck.

RIGHT FRONT

Using size 2 needles and Aurora 4, cast on 20 (28, 36) sts.

ROW 1 (RS) AND ALL RS ROWS UNTIL NEW INSTRUCTIONS GIVEN: Knit.

ROWS 2, 4, 6 (WS): Purl to end, cast on 6 sts—38 (46, 54) sts after completing row 6.

ROWS 8, 10, 12, 14, 16, 18, 20, AND 22 (WS): Purl to end, CO 2 sts.

ROWS 9, 17, 25, 33, AND 41 (DECREASE): Knit to last 4 sts, ssk, k2.

ROWS 24, 28, 32, 36, 40, AND 44: Purl.

ROWS 26, 30, 34, 38, 42, AND 46: Purl to end, CO 1 st using backward loop method (e-wrap)—55 (63, 71) sts after completing row 46.

Continue in St st until piece measures 7" (18cm), ending with WS row.

NEXT RS ROW (INCREASE): Knit to last 2 sts, m1, k2—56 (64, 72) sts.

Continue working in St st repeating this increase row every 6th row 5 times more—61 (69, 77) sts.

AT THE SAME TIME, when piece measures 10" (25cm), begin decrease at Neck edge as follows:

NEXT RS ROW (DECREASE): K2, k2tog, knit to end (working increases at side edge when necessary).

Continue working in St st repeating this Neck edge decrease every 6th row 11 (9, 7) times more, and after that every 4th row 6 (10, 14) times more—43 (49, 55) sts.

AT THE SAME TIME, when piece measures about 12" (30.5cm), ending with a RS row, start Armhole shaping.

ARMHOLE SHAPING

NEXT WS ROW: Bind off 4 (5, 6) sts, work to end of row—39 (44, 49) sts.

NEXT RS ROW (DECREASE): Knit to last 4 sts, ssk, k2 (working Neck edge decreases when necessary).

Continue working in St st repeating this decrease every 4th row 8 (9, 10) times more. When Neck and Armhole shaping is finished, there are 30 (34, 38) sts remaining.

When Armhole measures 7½ (8, 8½)" [19 (20, 21.5)cm], ending with RS row, shape Shoulders as follows:

SHOULDER SHAPING

NEXT WS ROW: Bind off 10 (12, 13) sts at beginning of row—20 (22, 25) sts.

NEXT WS ROW: Bind off 10 (11, 13) sts at beginning of row—10 (11, 12) sts.

NEXT WS ROW: Bind off 10 (11, 12) sts.

LEFT FRONT

Using size 2 needles and Aurora 4, cast on 20 (28, 36) sts.

BALANCING ROW: Purl.

ROW 1 (RS): Knit to end, cast on 6 sts—26 (34, 42) sts.

ROW 2 AND ALL WS ROWS: Purl.

ROWS 3 AND 5: Knit to end, cast on 6 sts—38 (46, 54) sts.

ROWS 7, 11, 13, 15, 19, AND 21: Knit to end, cast on 2 sts.

ROWS 9 AND 17: K2, k2tog, knit to end, cast on 2 sts.

ROWS 23, 27, 31, 35, 39, AND 43: Knit.

ROWS 25, 33, AND 41: K2, k2tog, knit to end, cast on 1 st using the backward loop method (e-wrap).

ROWS 29, 37, AND 45: Knit to end, cast on 1 st using the backward loop method—55 (63, 71) sts after row 45 is finished.

Continue in St st until piece measures 7" (18cm), ending with WS row.

NEXT RS ROW (INCREASE): K2, m1, knit to end—56 (64, 72) sts.

Continue working in St st, repeating this increase row every 6th row 5 times more—61 (69, 77) sts.

AT THE SAME TIME, when piece measures 10" (25cm) start decreases at Neck edge as follows:

NEXT RS ROW (DECREASE): Knit to last 4 sts (working increases at side edge when necessary), ssk, k2.

Continue working in St st, repeating this Neck edge decrease every 6th row 11 (9, 7) times more, and after that every 4th row 6 (10, 14) times more.

AT THE SAME TIME, when piece measures about 12" (30.5cm), ending with WS row, start Armhole shaping.

ARMHOLE SHAPING

Bind off 4 (5, 6) sts at beginning of next RS row, continue as established, taking care of Neck edge decrease when necessary.

NEXT RS ROW (DECREASE): K2, k2tog, knit to end, working Neck edge decreases when necessary.

Continue working in St st, repeating this decrease every 4th row 8 (9, 10) times more. When Neck and Armhole shaping is finished, there are 30 (34, 38) sts remaining. When Armhole measures 7½ (8, 8½)" [19 (20, 21.5)cm], ending with WS row, shape Shoulders as follows:

SHOULDER SHAPING

NEXT RS ROW: Bind off 10 (12, 13) sts at beginning of row.

NEXT RS ROW: Bind off 10 (11, 13) sts at beginning of row.

NEXT RS ROW: Bind off 10 (11, 12) sts.

SLEEVES

Using size 2 needles and Aurora 4, cast on 60 (64, 68) sts. Work in St st (knit on RS, purl on WS) for 10 rows.

NEXT RS ROW (INCREASE): K2, m1, knit to last 2 sts, m1, k2—62 (66, 70) sts.

Continue working in St st, repeating this increase every 11 (10, 8) rows 10 (12, 14) times more—82 (90, 98) sts. Work even until piece measures 13" (33cm), begin Cap shaping.

CAP SHAPING

Bind off 5 sts at beginning of next 2 rows—72 (80, 88) sts.
NEXT RS ROW (DECREASE): K2, k2tog, knit to last 4 sts, ssk, k2—70 (78, 86) sts.
Continue working in St st repeating this decrease every RS row until there are 20 (22, 24) sts left.
Bind off remaining sts.

FINISHING

Sew Shoulder seams. Sew Sleeves into the Armholes. Sew side and Sleeve seams. Weave in loose ends to WS.

SLEEVE RUFFLE

Using size 7 needle and Lace Mohair, cast on 28 sts.
Work in St st for 6 (8, 6) rows.
NEXT 36 ROWS: work WIDE RUFFLE. Continue working in St st for 8 (8, 10) rows more × 4 times.
NEXT 36 ROWS: Work WIDE RUFFLE.
Continue working in St st for 6 (8, 6) rows or until unruffled edge of the piece measures 8 (8½, 9)" [20 (21.5, 23)cm]. Bind off.
Sew cast on and bind off rows of the ruffle together. Sew the unruffled edge of the ruffle to the bottom of the Sleeve.

BACK RUFFLE

Using size 7 needle and Lace Mohair, cast on 18 sts.
Work in St st for 8 rows.
NEXT 24 ROWS: Work NARROW RUFFLE. Continue working in St st for 10 rows more × 8 (9, 10) times.
NEXT 24 ROWS: Work NARROW RUFFLE.
Continue work in St st for 10 (8, 6) rows or until unruffled edge of the piece measures 16 (18, 20)" [40.5 (46, 51)cm]. Bind off.
Sew the unruffled edge of the Back Ruffle to the bottom of the back.

FRONT RUFFLE

Note: Measure the length of the edge where you will sew the Front Ruffle as follows: Starting from the side seam of the right side, going along the bottom of the right side, going up the middle opening of the right side, around the Neck, down the middle opening of the left side, along the bottom of the left side to the left side seam—about 54 (58, 63)" [137 (147, 160)cm]. If your measurements are different from above, you have to adjust the number of ruffles (24 rows of one NARROW RUFFLE plus 14 rows in St st, piece measures about 2½" [6cm] along the unruffled edge).
Using size 7 needle and Lace Mohair, cast on 18 sts.
Work in St st for 14 (12, 12) rows.
NEXT 24 ROWS: Work NARROW RUFFLE. Continue working in St st for 14 rows more x 21 (23, 25) times.
NEXT 24 ROWS: Work NARROW RUFFLE.
Continue working in St st until unruffled edge of the piece measures about 54 (58, 63)" [137, (147, 160)cm]. Bind off.
Sew the unruffled edge of the Front Ruffle to the work, starting from the side seam of the right side, going along the bottom of the right side, going up the middle opening of the right side, around the neck, down the middle opening of the left side, along the bottom of the left side to the left side seam.

VINTAGE SHAWL

The elegance of this mesh shawl lies in its simplicity. This rectangular-shaped piece knits up quickly, but its Art Deco stylishness is sure to turn heads during a night out on the town. Attach fringe at the bottom to give it that extra vintage flair.

VINTAGE SHAWL

SIZES
One size fits all.

KNITTED MEASUREMENTS
Length: 70½" (179cm), without fringe

Width: 22" (56cm), not stretched

MATERIALS
11 balls Karabella Aurora Bulky (100% extra fine merino wool; about 54 yds [50m] per 1¾ oz [50g] ball): color #9362, Natural

Size 10 (6mm) needles, or size to obtain gauge

Size J/10 (6mm) crochet hook for fringe

GAUGE
10 sts = 4" (10cm) over squared patt, using size 10 needles.

SHAWL
Cast on 68 sts.

ROWS 1 AND 3 (WS): Sl 1, p1, *k4, p1*; repeat from * to last st, k1.

ROWS 2 AND 4 (RS): Sl 1, k1, *p4, k1*; repeat from * to last st, k1.

ROW 5: Sl 1, yo, p1, *yo, (k1, yo, twice) 3 times, k1, yo, p1*; repeat from * to last st, yo, k1.

ROW 6: Work same as row 2 dropping *all* yo made in the previous row.

Repeat rows 1–6 thirty-five times—210 rows.

NEXT 4 ROWS: Repeat rows 1 and 2.

NEXT WS ROW: Work same as row 1.

NEXT ROW: Bind off 5 sts, *drop next knit st down to the cast-on row, pull the st onto the right-hand needle, making it about 1" (25cm) long, bind off 4 sts*; repeat from * to * to last 6 sts, bind off 6 sts.

FRINGE
For each group of fringe, cut five 14" (35.5cm) lengths of yarn.
Make 28 fringes (140 strands total).

FINISHING
Weave in loose ends to WS. Attach 14 pieces of fringe to each end of the shawl.

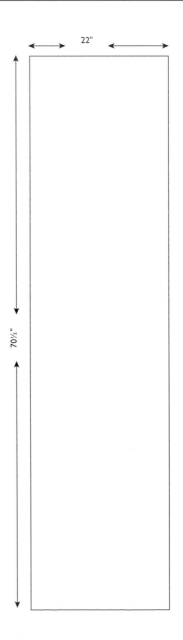

22"

70½"

HAMPTONS DRESS

Versatility is the key to this stylish khaki sundress. Wear it with a sunhat for a day at the beach or don it solo for a cocktail party. Inspired by a Barbara Walker stitch pattern, the lace has a unique dimensionality that only looks difficult to make. The shaping is achieved with just changing the needle size. Knit in my favorite Karabella Vintage cotton, the piece is breathable enough to beat the summer heat—just be sure to wear a slip underneath.

HAMPTONS DRESS

SIZES
To fit XS (S, M, L). Directions are for the smallest size, with larger sizes in parentheses. If there is only one set of figures, it applies to all sizes.

KNITTED MEASUREMENTS
Bust: 32 (35, 38, 41)" [81 (89, 96.5, 104)cm]

Length: 33½ (33½, 35, 35)" [85 (85, 89, 89)cm]

MATERIALS
10 (11, 12, 12) balls Karabella Vintage Cotton (100% mercerized cotton; about 140 yds [130m] per 1¾ oz [50g] ball): color #305, Khaki

Size 0 (2mm) needles

Size 0 (2mm) 16" [40cm] circular needle

Size 1 (2.5mm) needles, or size to obtain gauge

Size 2 (2.75mm) needles

Size 3 (3.25 mm) needles

Stitch holders

GAUGE
36 sts and 36 rows = 4" (10cm) in Sunspots patt, using size 1 needles.

SUNSPOTS PATTERN
(MULTIPLE OF 12 STS PLUS 3)
Notes: Double increase: Work the following double increase into the next st: Knit 1 through the back loop (k1tbl), then knit the same st in the front loop, then insert left-hand needle point behind the vertical strand that runs downward from between the 2 sts just made, and k1tbl into this strand to make the 3rd st of the group.

Increase 1 (lifted increase): Insert right needle downward into the back of the st (the purl nub) in the row below the first st on left-hand needle, and knit; then knit the st on needle.

ROW 1 (RS): K1, k2 tog, *yo, k2tog, yo, p5, yo, ssk, yo, sl 1-k2 tog-psso*; repeat from * to * to last 12 sts, yo, k2tog, yo, p5, yo, ssk, k1.

ROW 2: P5, *k5, p7*; repeat from * to * to last 10 sts, end row with k5, p5.

ROW 3: K1, *yo, k3tog, yo, p7, yo, ssk *; repeat from * to * to last 14 sts, yo, k3tog, yo, p7, yo, ssk, yo, k2tog.

ROWS 4, 6, AND 8: P4, *k7, p5*; repeat from * to * to last 11 sts, k7, p4.

ROW 5: Ssk, yo, *ssk, yo, p7, yo, sl 2-k1-p2sso, yo *; repeat from * to * to last 13 sts, ssk, yo, p7, yo, sl 2-k1-p2sso, yo, k1.

ROW 7: K1, *yo, sl 2-k1-p2sso, yo, p7, yo, k2tog*; repeat from * to * to last 14 sts, yo, sl 2-k1-p2sso, yo, p7, yo, k2tog, yo, k2tog.

ROW 9: K1, increase 1, *yo, ssk, yo, p2tog, p3tog, p2tog, yo, k2tog, yo, double increase*; repeat from * to * last 13 sts, yo, ssk, yo, p2tog, p3tog, p2tog, yo, k2tog, yo, increase 1, k1.

ROW 10 (DECREASE ROW): P6, *k3tog, p9*; repeat from * to * to last 9 sts, k3tog, p6.

ROW 11: K1, increase 1, *(yo, ssk) twice, p1, (k2tog, yo) twice, double increase*; repeat from * to * to last 11 sts, (yo, ssk) twice, p1, (k2tog, yo) twice, increase 1, k1.

ROW 12: P7, *k1, p11*; repeat from * to * to last 8 sts, end k1, p7.

ROW 13: K1, p3, *yo, ssk, yo, sl 1-k2tog-psso, yo, k2tog, yo, p5*; repeat from * to * to last 11 sts, yo, ssk, yo, sl 1-k2tog-psso, yo, k2tog, yo, p3, k1.

ROW 14: P1, k3, *p7, k5*; repeat from * to * to last 11 sts, end p7, k3, p1.

ROW 15: K1, p4, *yo, ssk, yo, k3tog, yo, p7*; repeat from * to * to last 10 sts, yo, ssk, yo, k3tog, yo, p4, k1.

ROWS 16, 18, AND 20: P1, k4, *p5, k7*; repeat from * to * to last 10 sts, p5, k4, p1.

ROW 17: K1, p4, *yo, sl 2-k1-p2sso, yo, ssk, yo, p7*; repeat from * to * to last 10 sts, yo, sl 2-k1-p2sso, yo, ssk, yo, p4, k1.

ROW 19: K1, p4, *yo, k2tog, yo, sl 2-k1-p2sso, yo, p7*; repeat from * to * to last 10 sts, yo, k2tog, yo, sl 2-k1-p2sso, yo, p4, k1.

ROW 21: K1, p2tog, *p2tog, yo, k2tog, yo, double increase, yo, ssk, yo, p2tog, p3tog*; repeat from * to * to last 12 sts,

Key

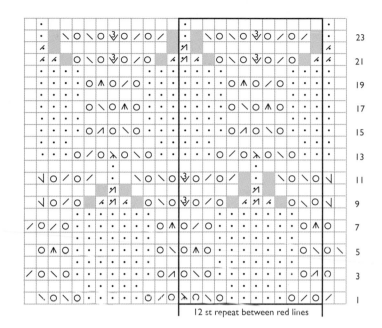

- ☐ Knit on RS; Purl on WS
- • Purl on RS; Knit on WS
- ╱ K2tog on RS
- ╲ Ssk on RS
- ◢ P2tog on RS; K2tog on WS
- ◿ K3tog on RS
- ⋉ P3tog on RS; K3tog on WS
- ⋏ Sl 2-k1-p2sso
- ⋋ Sl 1, k2tog, psso
- M Make 1 increase
- ⱱ Double increase, see special instructions at beginning of patt
- O Yarn over
- ⋁ Lifted increase, see special instructions listed under Increase 1
- ▨ No stitch
- ☐ Part repeat frame

12 st repeat between red lines

p2tog, yo, k2tog, yo, double increase, yo, ssk, yo, p2tog, p2tog, k1.

ROW 22 (DECREASE ROW): P1, k2tog, *p9, k3tog*; repeat from * to * last 12 sts, p9, k2tog, p1.

ROW 23: K1, p1, *(k2tog, yo) twice, double increase, (yo, ssk) twice, p1*; repeat from * to * last 11 sts, (k2tog, yo) twice, double increase, (yo, ssk) twice, p1, k1.

ROW 24: P1, k1, *p11, k1*; repeat from * to * last 13 sts, p11, k1, p1.

Rep rows 1–24 for Sunspots pattern.

BACK

Using size 3 needles, cast on 147 (159, 171, 183) sts.

Work 6 rows in garter st (knit every row).

Work 60 rows in Sunspots Patt.

Change to size 2 needles and continue in established Sunspots Patt for 48 rows more.

Change to size 1 needles and continue for 36 rows more.

Change to size 0 needles and continue for 72 rows more.

Change to size 1 needles and continue for 48 rows more.

ARMHOLE SHAPING

Change to size 0 needles.

ROW 1 (RS): Bind off 6 sts, p3, yo, ssk, yo, sl 1-k2tog-psso, repeat from * to * of Sunspots patt row 1 to last 12 sts,

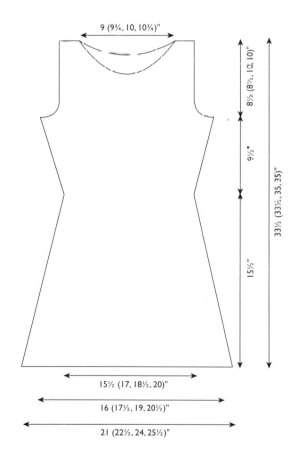

9 (9¾, 10, 10¾)"

8½ (8½, 10, 10)"

9½"

15½"

33½ (33½, 35, 35)"

15½ (17, 18½, 20)"

16 (17½, 19, 20½)"

21 (22½, 24, 25½)"

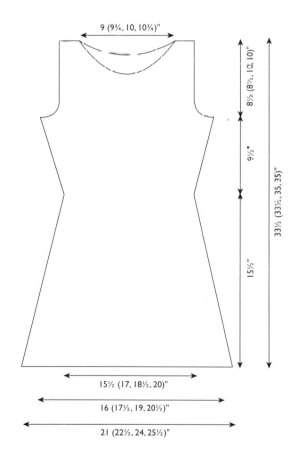

yo, k2tog, yo, p5, yo, ssk, yo, ssk, k1—141 (153, 165, 177) sts.

ROW 2: Bind off 5 sts, k4, p7, *k5, p7*; repeat from * to * to last 4 sts, k4—136 (148, 160, 172) sts.

ROW 3: Bind off 2 sts, p2, yo, ssk, repeat from * to * of Sunspots patt row 3 to last 9 sts, yo, k3tog, yo, p6—134 (146, 158, 170) sts.

ROW 4: Bind off 2 sts, k3, *p5, k7*; repeat from * to * to last 8 sts, p5, k3—132 (144, 156, 168) sts.

ROW 5: Bind off 2 sts, yo, sl 2-k1-p2sso, yo, repeat from * to * of Sunspots patt row 5 to last 6 sts, ssk, yo, p4—130 (142, 154, 166) sts.

ROW 6: Bind off 2 sts, k1, *p5, k7*; repeat from * to * to last 6 sts, p6—128 (140, 152, 164) sts.

ROW 7: Bind off 2 sts, repeat from * to * of Sunspots patt row 7 to last 5 sts, yo, sl 2-k1-p2sso, yo, p2—126 (138, 150, 162) sts.

ROW 8: Bind off 2 sts, p4, k7, *p5, k7*; repeat from * to * to last 4 sts, p4—124 (136, 148, 160) sts).

ROW 9: Bind off 1 st, k2, p2tog, p3tog, p2tog, yo, k2tog, yo, double increase, *yo, ssk, yo, p2tog, p3tog, p2tog, yo, k2tog, yo, double increase*; repeat from * to * last 14 sts, yo, ssk, yo, p2tog, p3tog, p2tog, yo, k2tog, yo, increase 1, k2—121 (133, 145, 157) sts.

ROW 10: Bind off 2 sts, p4, *k3tog, p9*; repeat from * to * to last 6 sts, k3tog, p3—114 (126, 138, 150) sts.

ROW 11: K1, yo, ssk, p1, (k2tog, yo) twice, double increase, repeat from * to * of Sunspots patt row 11 to last 10 sts, (yo, ssk) twice, p1, k5—117 (129, 141, 153) sts.

ROW 12: Bind off 2 sts, p2, k1, p11, *k1, p11*; repeat from * to * to last 3 sts, p3—114 (126, 138, 150) sts.

ROW 13: Bind off 1 st, yo, sl 1-k2tog-psso, yo, k2tog, yo, p5, repeat from * to * of Sunspots patt row 13 to last 7 sts, yo, ssk, yo, sl 1-k2tog-psso, yo, k1, yo, k1—115 (127, 139, 151) sts.

ROW 14: Bind off 2 sts, p5, *k5, p7*; repeat from * to * to last 11 sts, k5, p6—113 (125, 137, 149) sts.

ROW 15: Bind off 2 sts, ssk, yo, p7, repeat from * to * of Sunspots patt row 15 to last 5 sts, yo, ssk, yo, k2tog, k1—111 (123, 135, 147) sts.

ROW 16: Bind off 2 sts, p2, k7, *p5, k7*; repeat from * to * to last 3 sts, p3—109 (121, 133, 145) sts.

ROW 17: Bind off 2 sts, p7, repeat from * to * of Sunspots patt row 17 to last 3 sts, k3—107 (119, 131, 143) sts.

ROW 18: Bind off 2 sts, k7, *p5, k7*; repeat from * to * to last st, p1—105 (117, 129, 141) sts.

ROW 19: Bind off 1 st, p6, repeat from * to * of Sunspots patt row 19 to last st, k1—104 (116, 128, 140) sts.

ROW 20: Bind off 1 st, k6, *p5, k7*; repeat from * to end—103 (115, 127, 139) sts.

ROW 21: Bind off 1 st, k1, p2tog, repeat from * to * of Sunspots patt row 21 to last 3 sts, p3—102 (114, 126, 138) sts.

ROW 22: Bind off 1 st, *k3tog, p9*; repeat from * to * to last 4 sts, k3tog, k1—99 (111, 123, 135) sts.

ROW 23: K1, p1, repeat from * to * of Sunspots patt row 23 to last st, k1.

ROW 24: P1, *k1, p11*; repeat from * to * to last 2 sts, k1, p1.

Work next 48 (48, 60, 60) rows in Sunspots patt, ending with row (24, 24, 12, 12) of Sunspots patt.

Back Neck Shaping for Sizes X-Small/Small Only:

ROW 1 (RS): K1, k2tog, (yo, k2tog, yo, p5, yo, ssk, yo, sl 1-k2tog-psso) twice, yo, k2tog, yo, p5, yo, ssk, k1; join second ball of yarn and continue the other side as follows: bind off 25 (37) sts, k2tog, yo, (p5, yo, ssk, yo, sl 1-k2tog-psso, yo, k2tog, yo) twice, p5, (yo, ssk) twice, k1—37 sts each side.

ROW 2: (left side): P5, (k5, p7) twice, k5, p3; (right side): bind off 6 sts, k1, (p7, k5) twice, p5—31 sts.

ROW 3: (right side): K1, (yo, k3tog, yo, p7, yo, ssk) twice, yo, k3tog, yo, p3; (left side): bind off 6 sts, p2, yo, ssk, yo, k3tog, yo, p7) twice, yo, ssk, yo, k2tog—31 sts.

ROW 4: (left side): P4, (k7, p5) twice, k7, p3; (right side): bind off 6 sts, p1, k7, p5, k7, p4—25 sts.

ROW 5: (right side): (Ssk, yo) twice, p7, yo, sl 2-k1-p2sso, yo, ssk, yo, p7, k2; (left side): bind off 6 sts, k1, p7, yo, sl 2-k1-p2sso, yo, ssk, yo, p7, yo, sl 2-k1-p2sso, yo, k1—25 sts.

ROW 6: (left side): P4, k7, p5, k7, p2; (right side): bind off 3 sts, k5, p5, k7, p4—22 sts.

ROW 7: (right side): K1, yo, sl 2-k1-p2sso, yo, p7, yo, k2tog, yo, sl 2-k1-p2sso, yo, p6; (left side): bind off 4 sts, p4, yo, k2tog, yo, sl 2-k1-p2sso, yo, p7, (yo, k2tog) twice—21 sts.

ROW 8: (left side): P4, k7, p5, k5; (right side): bind off 3 sts, k2, p5, k7, p4—19 sts.

ROW 9: (right side): K1, increase 1, yo, ssk, yo, p2tog, p3tog, p2tog, yo, k2tog, yo, increase 1, yo, ssk, p3; (left side): bind off 3 sts, p1, k2tog, yo, increase 1, yo, ssk, yo, p2tog, p3tog, p2tog, yo, k2tog, yo, increase 1 st, k1—18 sts.

ROW 10: (left side): P6, k3tog, p9; (right side): bind off 2 sts, p7, k3tog, p6—15 sts.

ROW 11: (right side): K1, increase 1, (yo, ssk) twice, p1, (k2tog, yo) twice, increase 1, yo, ssk, p1; (left side): bind off 3 sts, increase 1, (yo, ssk) twice, p1, (k2tog, yo) twice, increase 1, k1—15 sts.

ROW 12: *(left side):* P7, k1, p7; *(right side):* bind off 2 sts, p6, k1, p7—15 sts.
Bind off 15 sts on each side.

BACK NECK SHAPING FOR SIZES MEDIUM/LARGE ONLY:

ROW 1 (RS): K1, p3, (yo, ssk, yo, sl 1-k2tog-psso, yo, k2tog, yo, p5) 3 times, yo, ssk, k2; join second ball of yarn and continue the other side as follows: bind off 35 (47) sts, k2, k2tog, yo, p5, (yo, ssk, yo, sl 1-k2tog-psso, yo, k2tog, yo, p5) twice, yo, ssk, yo, sl 1-k2tog-psso, yo, k2tog, yo, p3, k1—44 sts each side.

ROW 2: *(left side):* P1, k3, (p7, k5) 3 times, p4; *(right side):* bind off 5 sts, k3, (p7, k5) twice, p7, k3, p1—39 sts.

ROW 3: *(right side):* K1, p4, (yo, ssk, yo, k3tog, yo, p7) twice, yo, ssk, yo, k3tog, yo, p5; *(left side):* bind off 5 sts, p4, (yo, ssk, yo, k3tog, yo, p7) twice, yo, ssk, yo, k3tog, yo, p4, k1—39 sts.

ROW 4: *(left side):* P1, k4, (p5, k7) twice, p5, k5; *(right side):* bind off 5 sts, p4, k7, p5, k7, p5, k4, p1—34 sts.

ROW 5: *(right side):* K1, p4, (yo, sl 2-k1-p2sso, yo, ssk, yo, p7) twice, yo, sl 2-k1-p2sso, yo, k2; *(left side):* bind off 5 sts, k2, ssk, yo, (p7, yo, sl 2-k1-p2sso, yo, ssk, yo) twice, p4, k1—34 sts.

ROW 6: *(left side):* P1, k4, (p5, k7) twice, p5; *(right side):* bind off 5 sts, k6, p5, k7, p5, k4, p1—29 sts.

ROW 7: *(right side):* K1, p4, (yo, k2tog, yo, sl 2-k1-p2sso, yo, p7) twice; *(left side):* bind off 6 sts, p5, yo, k2tog, yo, sl 2-k1-p2sso, yo, p7, yo, k2tog, yo, sl 2-k1-p2sso, yo, p4, k1—28 sts.

ROW 8: *(left side):* P1, k4, p5, k7, p5, k6; *(right side):* bind off 3 sts, k3, p5, k7, p5, k4, p1—26 sts.

ROW 9: *(right side):* K1, p2tog, p2tog, yo, k2tog, yo, double increase, yo, ssk, yo, p2tog, p3tog, p2tog, yo, k2tog, yo, increase 1, yo, ssk, yo, p2tog, p2; *(left side):* bind off 4 sts, p1, k2tog, yo, increase 1, yo, ssk, yo, p2tog, p3tog, p2tog, yo, k2tog, yo, double increase, yo, ssk, yo, p2tog, p2tog, k1—24 sts.

ROW 10: *(left side):* P1, k2tog, p9, k3tog, p9; *(right side):* bind off 3 sts, p7, k3tog, p9, k2tog, p1—20 sts.

ROW 11: *(right side):* K1, p1, (k2tog, yo) twice, double increase, (yo, ssk) twice, p1, (k2tog, yo) twice, increase 1, yo, ssk, k1; *(left side):* bind off 3 sts, increase 1, (yo, ssk) twice, p1, (k2tog, yo) twice, double increase, (yo, ssk) twice, p1, k1—21 sts.

ROW 12: *(left side):* P1, k1, p11, k1, p7; *(right side):* bind off 2 sts, p6, k1, p11, k1, p1—21 sts.
Bind off 21 sts on each side.

FRONT

Work as for Back until row 24 of Armhole shaping is completed.
Work next 24 (24, 36, 36) rows in Sunspots patt, ending with row (24, 24, 12, 12) of Sunspots patt.

FRONT NECK SHAPING FOR SIZES X-SMALL/SMALL ONLY:

ROW 1 (RS): K1, k2tog, (yo, k2tog, yo, p5, yo, ssk, yo, sl 1-k2tog-psso) 3 times, yo, k2tog, yo, p3; join second ball of yarn and continue the other side as follows: bind off 11 (23) sts, p3, (yo, ssk, yo, sl 1-k2tog-psso, yo, k2tog, yo, p5) 3 times, (yo, ssk) twice, k1—44 sts each side.

ROW 2: *(right side of neck):* P5, (k5, p7) 3 times, k3; *(left side of neck):* bind off 3 sts, p6, k5, (p7, k5) 2 times, p5—41 sts.

ROW 3: *(left side):* K1, (yo, k3tog, yo, p7, yo, ssk) 3 times, yo, ssk, yo, k2tog, k2; *(right side):* bind off 3 sts, (yo, ssk, yo, k3tog, yo, p7) 3 times, yo, ssk, yo, k2tog—41 sts.

ROW 4: *(right side):* P4, (k7, p5) 3 times, p1; *(left side):* bind off 3 sts, p2, (k7, p5) twice, k7, p4—38 sts.

ROW 5: *(left side):* (Ssk, yo) twice, (p7, yo, sl 2-k1-p2sso, yo, ssk, yo) twice, p7, k3; *(right side):* bind off 3 sts, k2, (p7, yo, sl 2-k1-p2sso, yo, ssk, yo) twice, p7, yo, sl 2-k1-p2sso, yo, k1—38 sts.

ROW 6: *(right side):* P4, (k7, p5) twice, k7, p3; *(left side):* bind off 2 sts, (k7, p5) twice, k7, p4—36 sts.

ROW 7: *(left side):* K1, (yo, sl 2-k1-p2sso, yo, p7, yo, k2tog) twice, yo, sl 2-k1-p2sso, yo, p7, k1; *(right side):* bind off 2 sts, (p7, yo, k2tog, yo, sl 2-k1-p2sso, yo) twice, p7, (yo, k2tog) twice—36 sts.

ROW 8: *(right side):* P4, (k7, p5) twice, k7, p1; *(left side):* bind off 2 sts, k5, (p5, k7) twice, p4—34 sts.

ROW 9: *(left side):* K1, increase 1, yo, ssk, yo, p2tog, p3tog,

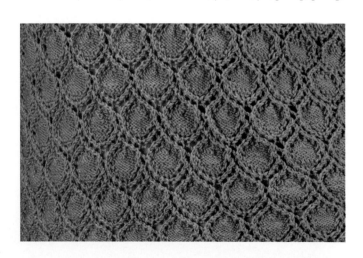

p2tog, yo, k2tog, yo, double increase, yo, ssk, yo, p2 tog, p3tog, p2tog, yo, k2tog, yo, increase 1, ssk, p6; *(right side):* bind off 2 sts, p5, k2tog, yo, increase 1, yo, ssk, yo, p2tog, p3tog, p2tog, yo, k2tog, yo, double increase, yo, ssk, yo, p2tog, p3tog, p2tog, yo, k2tog, yo, increase 1, k1—34 sts.

ROW 10: *(right side):* P6, k3tog, p9, k3tog, p8, k5; *(left side):* bind off 2 sts, k2, p8, k3tog, p9, k3tog, p6—28 sts.

ROW 11: *(left side):* K1, increase 1, (yo, ssk) twice, p1, (k2tog, yo) twice, double increase, (yo, ssk) twice, p1, (k2tog, yo) twice, increase 1, yo, ssk, k2, p2; *(right side):* bind off 2 sts, p1, k2, k2tog, yo, increase 1, (yo, ssk) twice, p1, (k2tog, yo) twice, double increase, (yo, ssk) twice, p1, (k2tog, yo) twice, increase 1, k1—32 sts.

ROW 12: *(right side):* P7, (k1, p11) twice, k2; *(left side):* bind off 2 sts, p9, k1, p11, k1, p7—30 sts.

ROW 13: *(left side):* K1, p3, (yo, ssk, yo, sl 1-k2tog-psso, yo, k2tog, yo, p5) twice, k2; *(right side):* bind off 2 sts, k1, (p5, yo, ssk, yo, sl 1-k2 tog-psso, yo, k2tog, yo) twice, p3, k1—30 sts.

ROW 14: *(right side):* P1, k3, (p7, k5) twice, p2; *(left side):* bind off 2 sts, k4, p7, k5, p7, k3, p1—28 sts.

ROW 15: *(left side):* K1, p4, yo, ssk, yo, k3 tog, yo, p7, yo, ssk, yo, k3tog, yo, p6; *(right side):* bind off 2 sts, p5, yo, ssk, yo, k3tog, yo, p7, yo, ssk, yo, k3tog, yo, p4, k1—28 sts.

ROW 16: *(right side):* P1, k4, p5, k7, p5, k6; *(left side):* bind off 2 sts, k3, p5, k7, p5, k4, p1—26 sts.

ROW 17: *(left side):* K1, p4, yo, sl 2-k1-p2sso, yo, ssk, yo, p7, yo, sl 2-k1-p2sso, yo, ssk, yo, p4; *(right side):* bind off 2 sts, p3, yo, sl 2-k1-p2sso, yo, ssk, yo, p7, yo, sl 2-k1-p2sso, yo, ssk, yo, p4, k1—26 sts.

ROW 18: *(right side):* P1, k4, p5, k7, p5, k4; *(left side):* bind off 2 sts, k1, p5, k7, p5, k4, p1—24 sts.

ROW 19: *(left side):* K1, p4, yo, k2tog, yo, sl 2-k1-p2sso, yo, p7, yo, k2tog, yo, sl 2-k1-p2sso, yo, p2; *(right side):* bind off 2 sts, p1, yo, k2tog, yo, sl 2-k1-p2sso, yo, p7, yo, k2tog, yo, sl 2-k1-p2sso, yo, p4, k1—24 sts.

ROW 20: *(right side):* P1, k4, p5, k7, p5, k2; *(left side):* bind off 1 st, p5, k7, p5, k4, p1—23 sts.

ROW 21: *(left side):* K1, p2tog, p2tog, yo, k2tog, yo, double increase, yo, ssk, yo, p2tog, p3tog, p2tog, yo, k2 tog, yo, increase 1, k2, p1; *(right side):* bind off 2 sts, k1, increase 1, yo, ssk, yo, p2tog, p3tog, p2tog, yo, k2tog, yo, double increase, yo, ssk, yo, p2tog, p2tog, k1—22 sts.

ROW 22: *(right side):* P1, k2tog, p9, k3tog, p7; *(left side):* bind off 1 st, p6, k3tog, p9, k2tog, p1—19 sts.

ROW 23: *(left side):* K1, p1, (k2tog, yo) twice, double increase, (yo, ssk) twice, p1, (k2tog, yo) twice, increase 1, k2; *(right side):* bind off 1 st, increase 1, (yo, ssk) twice, p1, (k2tog, yo) twice, double increase, (yo, ssk) twice, p1, k1—21 sts.

ROW 24: *(right side):* P1, k1, p11, k1, p7; *(left side):* bind off 2 sts, p6, k1, p11, k1, p1—21 sts.

ROW 25: *(left side):* K1, (k2tog, yo) twice, p5, yo, ssk, yo, sl 1-k2tog-psso, yo, k2tog, yo, p4; *(right side):* bind off 1 st, p2, yo, ssk, yo, sl 1-k2tog-psso, yo, k2tog, yo, p5, (yo, ssk) twice, k1—20 sts.

ROW 26: *(right side):* P5, k5, p7, k3; *(left side):* bind off 1 st, k2, p7, k5, p5—20 sts.

ROW 27: *(left side):* K1, yo, k3tog, yo, p7, yo, ssk, yo, k3tog, yo, p4; *(right side):* bind off 1 st, p2, yo, ssk, yo, k3tog, yo, p7, yo, ssk, yo, k2tog—19 sts.

ROW 28: *(right side):* P4, k7, p5, k3; *(left side):* bind off 1 st, k2, p5, k7, p4—19 sts.

ROW 29: *(left side):* (Ssk, yo) twice, p7, yo, sl 2-k1 p2sso, yo, ssk, yo, p3; *(right side):* bind off 1 st, p1, yo, sl 2-k1-p2sso, yo, ssk, yo, p7, yo, sl 2-k1-p2sso, yo, k1—18 sts.

ROW 30: *(right side):* P4, k7, p5, k2; *(left side):* bind off 1 st, k1, p5, k7, p4—18 sts.

ROW 31: *(left side):* K1, yo, sl 2 k1-p2sso, yo, p7, yo, k2tog, yo, sl 2-k1-p2sso, yo, p2; *(right side):* bind off 1 st, yo, k2tog, yo, sl 2-k1-p2sso, yo, p7, (yo, k2 tog) twice—17 sts.

ROW 32: *(right side):* P4, k7, p5, k1; *(left side):* bind off 1 st, p5, k7, p4—17 sts.

ROW 33: *(left side):* K1, increase 1, yo, ssk, yo, p2tog, p3tog, p2tog, yo, k2tog, yo, increase 1, k2, p1; *(right side):* bind off 1 sts, k1, increase 1, yo, ssk, yo, p2tog, p3tog, p2tog, yo, k2tog, yo, increase 1, k1—16 sts.

ROW 34: *(right side):* P6, k3tog, p7; *(left side):* bind off 1 st, p6, k3tog, p6—16 sts.

ROW 35: *(left side):* K1, increase 1, (yo, ssk) twice, p1, (k2tog, yo) twice, increase 1, k2; *(right side):* bind off 1 st, increase 1, (yo, ssk) twice, p1, (k2tog, yo) twice, increase 1, k1—15 sts.

ROW 36: *(right side):* P7, k1, p7; *(left side):* bind off 1 st, p6, k1, p7—15 sts.

Bind off 15 sts on each side.

Front Neck shaping for sizes Medium/Large only:

ROW 1 (RS): K1, p3, (yo, ssk, yo, sl 1-k2tog-psso, yo, k2tog, yo, p5) 3 times, yo, ssk, yo, sl 1-k2tog-psso, yo, k2tog, yo, p3; join second ball of yarn and continue the other side as follows: bind off 23 (35) sts, p3, (yo, ssk, yo, sl 1-k2tog-psso, yo, k2tog, yo, p5) 3 times, twice, yo, ssk, yo, sl 1-k2tog-psso, yo, k2tog, yo, p3, k1—50 sts each side.

ROW 2: *(right side):* P1, k3, (p7, k5) 3 times, p7, k3; *(left side):* bind off 3 sts, p6, k5, (p7, k5) twice, p7, k3, p1— 47 sts.

ROW 3: *(left side):* K1, p4, (yo, ssk, yo, k3tog, yo, p7) 3 times, yo, ssk, yo, k2tog, k2; *(right side):* bind off 3 sts, (yo, ssk, yo, k3tog, yo, p7) 3 times, yo, ssk, yo, k3tog, yo, p4, k1— 47 sts.

ROW 4: *(right side):* P1, k4, (p5, k7) 3 times, p6; *(left side):* bind off 3 sts, p2, (k7, p5) 3 times, k4, p1—44 sts.

ROW 5: *(left side):* K1, p4, (yo, sl 2-k1-p2sso, yo, ssk, yo, p7) 3 times, k3; *(right side):* bind off 3 sts, k2, (p7, yo, sl 2-k1-p2sso, yo, ssk, yo,) 3 times, p4, k1—44 sts.

ROW 6: *(right side):* P1, k4, (p5, k7) 3 times, k3; *(left side):* bind off 3 sts, k6, p5, (k7, p5) twice, k4, p1—41 sts.

ROW 7: *(left side):* K1, p4, (yo, k2tog, yo, sl 2-k1-p2sso, yo, p7) 3 times; *(right side):* bind off 3 sts, p6, yo, k2tog, yo, sl 2-k1-p2sso, yo, (p7, yo, k2tog, yo, sl 2-k1-p2sso, yo) twice, p4, k1—41 sts.

ROW 8: *(right side):* P1, k4, (p5, k7) 3 times; *(left side):* bind off 2 sts, k4, (p5, k7) twice, p5, k4, p1—39 sts.

ROW 9: *(left side):* K1, p2tog, p2tog, (yo, k2tog, yo, double increase, yo, ssk, yo, p2tog, p3tog, p2tog) twice, yo, k2tog, yo, increase 1, k3, p4; *(right side):* bind off 2 sts, p3, k3, increase 1, yo, ssk, yo, (p2tog, p3tog, p2tog, yo, k2tog, yo, double increase, yo, ssk, yo) twice, p2tog, p2tog, k1—39 sts.

ROW 10: *(right side):* P1, k2tog, (p9, k3tog) twice, p9, k3; *(left side):* bind off 2 sts, (p9, k3tog) twice, p9, k2tog, p1— 32 sts.

ROW 11: *(left side):* K1, (p1, (k2tog, yo) twice, double increase, (yo, ssk) twice) twice, p1, (k2tog, yo) twice, increase 1, k5; *(right side):* bind off 2 sts, k4, increase 1, (yo, ssk) twice, [(p1, (k2 tog, yo) twice, double increase, (yo, ssk) twice] twice, p1, k1—37 sts.

ROW 12: *(right side):* P1, (k1, p11) 3 times; *(left side):* bind off 2 sts, p8, (k1, p11) twice, k1, p1—35 sts.

ROW 13: *(left side):* K1, k2tog, (yo, k2tog, yo, p5, yo, ssk, yo, sl 1-k2 tog-psso) twice, yo, k2tog, yo, p6; *(right side):* bind off 2 sts, p5, (yo, ssk, yo, sl 1-k2tog-psso, yo, k2tog, yo, p5) twice, (yo, ssk) twice, k1—35 sts.

ROW 14: *(right side):* P5, (k5, p7) twice, k5, p1; *(left side):* bind off 2 sts, k3, (p7, k5) twice, p5—33 sts.

ROW 15: *(left side):* K1, (yo, k3tog, yo, p7, yo, ssk) twice, yo, k3tog, yo, p5; *(right side):* bind off 2 sts, p4, (yo, ssk, yo, k3tog, yo, p7) twice, yo, ssk, yo, k2tog—33 sts.

ROW 16: *(right side):* P4, (k7, p5) twice, k5; *(left side):* bind off 2 sts, k2, (p5, k7) twice, p4—31 sts.

ROW 17: *(left side):* (Ssk, yo) twice, (p7, yo, sl 2-k1-p2sso, yo, ssk, yo) twice, p3; *(right side):* bind off 2 sts, p2, (yo, sl 2-k1-p2sso, yo, ssk, yo, p7) twice, yo, sl 2-k1-p2sso, yo, k1—31 sts.

ROW 18: *(right side):* P4, (k7, p5) twice, k3; *(left side):* bind off 1 st, k1, (p5, k7) twice, p4—30 sts.

ROW 19: *(left side):* K1, (yo, sl 2-k1-p2sso, yo, p7, yo, k2tog) twice, yo, sl 2-k1-p2sso, yo, p2; *(right side):* bind off 2 sts, (yo, k2tog, yo, sl 2-k1-p2sso, yo, p7) twice, (yo, k2tog) twice—29 sts.

ROW 20: *(right side):* P4, (k7, p5) twice, k1; *(left side):* bind off 1 st, (p5, k7) twice, p4—29 sts.

ROW 21: *(left side):* K1, increase 1, yo, ssk, yo, p2tog, p3tog, p2tog, yo, k2tog, yo, double increase, yo, ssk, yo, p2 tog, p3tog, p2tog, yo, k2tog, yo, increase 1, k2, p1; *(right side):* bind off 1 st, k1, increase 1, yo, ssk, yo, p2tog, p3 tog, p2tog, yo, k2tog, yo, double increase, yo, ssk, yo, p2tog, p3tog, p2tog, yo, k2tog, yo, increase 1, k1—28 sts.

ROW 22: *(right side):* P6, k3tog, p9, k3tog, p7; *(left side):* bind off 1 st, p6, k3tog, p9, k3tog, p6—24 sts.

ROW 23: *(left side):* K1, increase 1, (yo, ssk) twice, p1, (k2tog, yo) twice, double increase, (yo, ssk) twice, p1, (k2tog, yo) twice, increase 1, k2; *(right side):* bind off 1 st, increase 1, (yo, ssk) twice, p1, (k2tog, yo) twice, double increase, (yo, ssk) twice, p1, (k2tog, yo) twice, increase 1, k1—27 sts.

ROW 24: *(right side):* P7, k1, p11, k7; *(left side):* bind off 1 st, p6, k1, p11, k1, p7—27 sts.

ROW 25: *(left side):* K1, p3, yo, ssk, yo, sl 1-k2 tog-psso, yo, k2tog, yo, p5, yo, ssk, yo, sl 1-k2tog-psso, yo, k2tog, yo, p4; *(right side):* bind off 1 st, p2, yo, ssk, yo, sl 1-k2tog-psso, yo, k2tog, yo, p5, yo, ssk, yo, sl 1-k2 tog-psso, yo, k2tog, yo, p3, k1—26 sts.

ROW 26: *(right side):* P1, k3, p7, k5, p7, k3; *(left side):* bind off 1 st, k2, p7, k5, p7, k3, p1—26 sts.

ROW 27: *(left side):* K1, p4, yo, ssk, yo, k3tog, yo, p7, yo, ssk, yo, k3tog, yo, p4; *(right side):* bind off 1 st, p2, yo, ssk, yo, k3tog, yo, p7, yo, ssk, yo, k3tog, yo, p4, k1—25 sts.

ROW 28: *(right side):* P1, k4, p5, k7, p5, k3; *(left side):* bind off 1 st, k2, p5, k7, p5, k4, p1—25 sts.

ROW 29: *(left side):* K1, p4, yo, sl 2-k1-p2sso, yo, ssk, yo, p7, yo, sl 2-k1-p2sso, yo, ssk, yo, p3; *(right side):* bind off 1 st, p1, yo, sl 2-k1-p2sso, yo, ssk, yo, p7, yo, sl 2-k1-p2sso, yo, ssk, yo, p4, k1—24 sts.

ROW 30: *(right side):* P1, k4, p5, k7, p5, k2; *(left side):* bind off 1 st, k1, p5, k7, p5, k4, p1—24 sts.

ROW 31: *(left side):* K1, p4, yo, k2tog, yo, sl 2-k1-p2sso, yo, p7, yo, k2tog, yo, sl 2-k1-p2sso, yo, p2; *(right side):* bind off 1 st, yo, k2tog, yo, sl 2-k1-p2sso, yo, p7, yo, k2tog, yo, sl 2-k1-p2sso, yo, p4, k1—23 sts.

ROW 32: *(right side):* P1, k4, p5, k7, p5, k1; *(left side):* bind off 1 sts, p5, k7, p5, k4, p1—23 sts.

ROW 33: *(left side):* K1, p2tog, p2tog, yo, k2tog, yo, double increase, yo, ssk, yo, p2tog, p3tog, p2tog, yo, k2tog, yo, increase 1, k2, p1; *(right side):* bind off 1 st, k1, increase 1, yo, ssk, yo, p2tog, p3tog, p2tog, yo, k2tog, yo, double increase, yo, ssk, yo, p2tog, p2tog, k1—22 sts.

ROW 34: *(right side):* P1, k2tog, p9, k3tog, p7; *(left side):* bind off 1 sts, p6, k3tog, p9, k2tog, p1 — 22 sts.

ROW 35: *(left side):* K1, p1, (k2tog, yo) twice, double increase, (yo, ssk) twice, p1, (k2tog, yo) twice, increase 1, k2; *(right side):* bind off 1 st, increase 1, (yo, ssk) twice, p1, (k2tog, yo) twice, double increase, (yo, ssk) twice, p1, k1—21 sts.

ROW 36: *(right side):* P1, k1, p11, k1, p7; *(left side):* bind off 1 st, p6, k1, p11, k1, p1—21 sts.

Bind off 21 sts on each side.

FINISHING

Sew side and Shoulder seams.

NECKBAND

Join yarn. With size 0 circular needle and RS facing, starting from Back, pick up and knit sts evenly around the Neck (about 7 sts per inch [2.5cm]). Join sts in round, place marker at beginning of round and work 6 rounds in garter st (purl on odd rounds, knit on even rounds). K3tog at the Shoulder seams in every knit round (this will help contour the Neckband and create a better fit). Bind off tightly.

ARMHOLE FINISHING

Work same as neckband, starting from Underarm, pick up and knit about 7 sts per inch (2.5cm) spaced evenly around each Armhole, join sts in round, place marker at beginning of round and work 6 rounds in garter st, (purl on odd rounds, knit on even rounds) working k3tog at Underarm in every knit round. Bind off tightly.

SEA-FOAM TOP

This summery top may be simple to knit, but it's the little extras that make it special. The ruffled V-neck and cap sleeves give it a delicate, playful appeal, but the eyelet lace pattern and hem will dress you up. Mercerized cotton yarn adds durability and helps the beautiful sea-foam color retain its brilliance.

SEA-FOAM TOP

SIZES

To fit S (M, L, XL). Directions are for the smallest size, with larger sizes in parentheses. If there is only one figure, it applies to all sizes.

KNITTED MEASUREMENTS

Bust: 32 (35, 38, 41)" [81 (89, 96.5, 104)cm]

Length: 22½ (22¾, 23¼, 23½)" [57 (58, 59, 60)cm]

MATERIALS

6 (7, 7, 8) balls Karabella Zodiac (100% mercerized cotton; about 98 yds [90m] per 1¾ oz (50g) ball): color #405, Sea Foam

Size 5 (3.75mm) 24" [6ocm] circular needles, or size to obtain gauge

Size 4 (3.5mm) needles

GAUGE

20 sts and 30 rows = 4" (10cm) over easy eyelet lace pattern, using size 5 needles, or size to obtain gauge.

EASY EYELET LACE PATTERN (MULTIPLE OF 8 STS)

ROW 1 (RS): Knit.

ROW 2 AND ALL OTHER WS ROWS: Purl.

ROW 3: *K6, yo, k2tog; repeat from *.

ROW 5: Knit.

ROW 7: K2, *yo, k2tog, k6; repeat from * to last 6 sts, end last repeat as yo, k2tog, k4.

ROW 8: Purl.

Repeat rows 1–8 for patt.

BACK

With size 4 needles, cast on 80 (88, 96, 104) sts.

EYELET HEM

ROW 1: Knit.

ROW 2: Purl.

ROW 3 (EYELET ROW): K1, *k2tog, yo; repeat from * to * to last st, k1.

Continue with main body.

MAIN BODY

Change to size 5 needles.

ROW 4 AND ALL OTHER WS ROWS: Purl.

ROW 5: Knit.

ROW 7 (ROW 3 OF EASY EYELET LACE PATT): *K6, yo, k2tog; repeat from * to end of row.

ROW 9: (row 5 of easy eyelet lace patt) Knit.

ROW 11 (ROW 7 OF EASY EYELET LACE PATT): K2, *yo, k2tog, k6; repeat from * to last 6 sts, end last repeat as yo, k2tog, k4.

ROW 13 (ROW 1 OF EASY EYELET LACE PATT): Knit.

ROW 14 (ROW 2 OF EASY EYELET LACE PATT): Purl.

Work even in easy eyelet lace patt until work measures 2" (5cm) from eyelet hem row 3, ending with WS row.

NEXT RS ROW: Decrease 1 st at beginning and end of next row (work decreases after the first and before the last st)—78 (86, 94, 102) sts.

Repeat this decrease row every 1½" (4cm) twice more—74 (82, 90, 98) sts.

Work even in established patt for 2" (5cm) ending with WS row.

Increase 1 st at beginning and end of next row (work increases after the first and before the last st)—76 (84, 92, 100) sts.

Repeat this increase every 3" (7.5cm) twice more—80 (88, 96, 104) sts.

Work even in established patt until piece measures 14½" (37cm) from eyelet hem row 3, ending with WS row.

ARMHOLE SHAPING

Bind off 5 (6, 7, 8) sts at beginning of next 2 rows—70 (76, 82, 88) sts.

NEXT ROW: Sl 1, k1, k2tog, work in patt to last 4 sts, ssk, k2—68 (74, 80, 86) sts.

NEXT ROW: Sl 1, purl to the end.

Repeat these 2 rows 4 (5, 6, 7) times more—60 (64, 68, 72) sts.

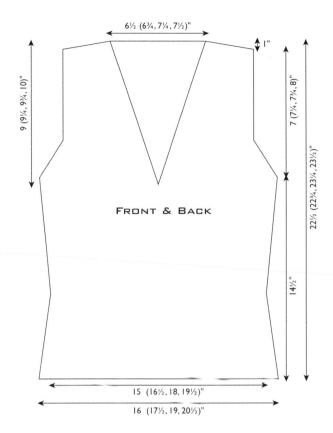

Continue in established pattern until armhole measures 7 (7¼, 7¾, 8)" [18 (18.5, 19.5, 20)cm].

SHOULDER SHAPING

Bind off 5 (5, 5, 6) sts at beginning of next 2 rows —50 (54, 58, 60) sts.

Bind off 5 (5, 5, 6) sts at beginning of next 2 rows—40 (44, 48, 48) sts.

Bind off 4 (5, 6, 5) sts at beginning of next 2 rows—32 (34, 36, 38) sts.

Bind off 32 (34, 36, 38) sts for Back Neck.

FRONT

Work as for Back until piece measures 13½" (34cm) from eyelet hem row 3, ending with WS row. Divide front into 2 parts, place marker in the center for V-neck.

NEXT ROW (DECREASES): Work in patt to last 4 sts before marker, k2tog, k2, join second ball of yarn sl 1, k1, ssk, work in pattern to end—39 (43, 47, 51) sts on each side of neck.

Note: Sl first st at beginning of each row on right and left side of the garment for neat edge.

NEXT ROW: Purl.

Working both sides at the same time, repeat the decrease row 15 (16, 17, 18) times more every 4 rows—68 (70, 72, 76) rows total, 24 (27, 30, 33) sts on each side of Neck. At the same time when piece measures 14½" (37cm), begin shaping Armholes as for Back.

When Armhole measures 7 (7¼, 7¾, 8)" [18 (18.5, 19.5, 20)cm], shape Shoulders as for Back.

NECK RUFFLE

Sew Shoulder seams. With WS facing, starting at left Shoulder seam pick up and knit 2 sts (from the back and front of each st) of bind-off row across the Back Neck, 2 sts of each edge st down the Right Front, and up the Left Front, count the sts to make sure you have an even number, join in the round.

Rnd 1: *K2tog, yo; repeat from * to end of rnd.
Rnd 2: Knit.
Repeat last 2 rows 7 times more.
Bind off.

SLEEVE RUFFLE

With RS facing, place 2 markers 3½ (4, 4½, 5)" [9 (10, 11, 12.5)cm] down on both sides from Shoulder seam. Pick up and knit 2 sts from each edge st between markers. Make sure you have an even number.

ROW 1 (WS): *P2, m1; repeat from * to end of picked up sts, turn.

ROW 2 (RS): *K2tog, yo; repeat from * to end of row then pick up and knit 2 additional sts from Sleeve edge, turn.

ROW 3: Purl to end of row, pick up and purl 2 additional sts from Sleeve edge, turn.

Repeat last 2 rows 4 (4, 5, 5) times more.
Bind off.

FINISHING

Sew side seams. Fold the hem at the lower edge to WS at eyelet hem row and sew in place, carefully matching knitting tension. Don't allow the sewing sts to become tighter than the knitting.

SEASHELL SHRUG

The body of this merino wool shrug is worked in one piece, but the real magic lies in the shaping. Figuring out how to put on the piece for the first time may be a bit of a puzzler, but once you slip into its cozy contours, you'll love the snug, slimming fit.

SEASHELL SHRUG

SIZES

To fit S/M, L/XL. Directions given are for the smaller size, with the larger size in parentheses. If there is only one figure, it applies to all sizes.

KNITTED MEASUREMENTS

Width (folded in half): 22 (24½)" [56 (62)cm]

Length: 21 (21½)" [53 (54.5)cm]

Upper arm: 13 (13½)" [33 (34)cm]

MATERIALS

19 (21) balls Karabella Aurora 8 (100% extra fine merino wool; about 98 yds [90m] per 1¾ oz [50g] ball): color #35, Pale Gray

Size 7 (4.5mm) needles

Size 7 (4.5mm) 40" [101.5cm] circular needle

Stitch markers

GAUGE

26 sts and 28 rows = 4" (10cm) over k2, p2 rib, slightly stretched, using size 7 needles.

FIRST SLEEVE

With size 7 needle, cast on 78 (82) sts.

ROW 1 (RS): *K2, p2; repeat from * to last 2 sts, k2.

ROW 2 (WS): *P2, k2; repeat from * to last 2 sts, p2.

Repeat these 2 rows until work measures 18½" (47cm) from CO.

FRONT SHAPING

Place marker to indicate beginning of RS row.

Continue in established patt.

FOR SIZE SMALL/MEDIUM ONLY:

Decrease 1 st at the beginning of each RS row (after the first st) and at the end of each WS row (before the last st) for 52 rows. Omit decrease in rows 2, 6, 10, 14, 18, 22, 26, 30, 34, 38, 42, and 50—38 sts.

FOR SIZE LARGE/X-LARGE ONLY:

Decrease 1 st at beginning of each RS row (after the first st) and end of each WS row (before the last st) for 60 rows. Omit decrease in rows 2, 4, 8, 10, 14, 16, 20, 22, 26, 28, 32, 36, 38, 40, 44, 48, 52, 54, 58, and 60—42 sts.

Work even for 4½ (5½)" [11 (14)cm] from last decrease row. Continue in established patt.

FOR SIZE SMALL/MEDIUM ONLY:

Increase 1 st at beginning of each RS row (after the first st) and at the end of each WS row (before the last st) for 52 rows. Omit increase in rows 2, 6, 10, 14, 18, 22, 26, 30, 34, 38, 42, and 50—78 sts.

FOR SIZE LARGE/X-LARGE ONLY:

Increase 1 st at beginning of each RS row (after the first st) and the end of each WS row (before the last st) for 60 rows. Omit increase in rows 2, 4, 8, 10, 14, 16, 20, 22, 26, 28, 32, 36, 38, 40, 44, 48, 52, 54, 58, and 60—82 sts.

SECOND SLEEVE

Work even in patt for 18½" (47cm) . Bind off.

Sew Sleeve seams together.

BODY

Note: Worked in the round as one piece. Please be sure to place markers exactly as indicated below to guarantee that the finished garment has a symmetrical look.

With WS of the shrug facing, place 8 markers around the opening as follows:

Beginning across as follows:

1ST MARKER: in the middle of Back Neck, between the 2 Sleeves,

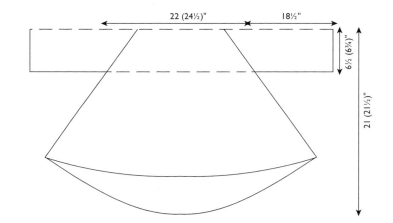

2ND MARKER: in the middle of Right Front Raglan line,

3RD MARKER: in the middle of Left Front Raglan line,

4TH MARKER: at the end of seam of Right Sleeve (beginning of Right Front Raglan),

5TH MARKER: at the end of seam of Left Sleeve (beginning of Left Front Raglan),

6TH MARKER: in the middle of Lower Back,

7TH MARKER: in the middle of 4th and 6th marker,

8TH MARKER: in the middle of 5th and 6th marker.

With RS facing, starting at 4th marker, pick up and knit 32 (36) sts between each marker—256 (288) sts. Join in the round, place round marker on the needle to indicate the beginning of rnd.

RND 1: Place marker, k2, place marker, m1, (k2, p2) repeat 6 (7) times more, k2, [m1, place marker, p2, place marker, m1, (k2, p2) repeat 6 (7) times more, k2] 3 times, [m1, place marker, k2, place marker, m1, (k2, p2) repeat 6 (7) times more, k2] 4 times, m1—272 (304) sts.

RNDS 2–4: Work sts as they appear, purl all added sts. Note: Don't forget to sl all markers with each row.

RND 5: Sl marker, k2, sl marker, m1, p1, (k2, p2) repeat 6 (7) times more, k2, [p1, m1, sl marker, p2, sl marker, m1, p1, (k2, p2) repeat 6 (7) times more, k2] 3 times, [p1, m1, sl marker, k2, sl marker, m1, p1, (k2, p2) repeat 6 (7) times more, k2], 4 times, p1, m1—288 (320) sts.

RNDS 6–8: Repeat rnds 2–4.

RND 9: Sl marker, k2, sl marker, m1, p2, (k2, p2) repeat 6 (7) times more, k2, [p2, m1, sl marker, p2, sl marker, m1, p2, (k2, p2) repeat 6 (7) times more, k2] 3 times, [p2, m1, sl marker, k2, sl marker, m1, p2, (k2, p2) repeat 6 (7) times more, k2] 4 times, p2, m1—304 (336) sts.

RNDS 10–12: Work sts as they appear, knit all added sts.

RND 13: Sl marker, k2, sl marker, m1, k1, p2, (k2, p2) repeat 6 (7) times more, k2, [p2, k1, m1, sl marker, p2, sl marker, m1, k1, p2, (k2, p2) repeat 6 (7) times more, k2] 3 times, [p2, k1, m1, sl marker, k2, sl marker, m1, k1, p2, (k2, p2) repeat 6 (7) times more, k2] 4 times, p2, k1, m1—320 (352) sts.

RNDS 14–16: Repeat rnds 10–12.

Continue in established pattern, repeat rows 1–16 five times—640 (672) sts. Bind off loosely.

Weave in loose ends to wrong side.

CHAPTER 2: PLAYFUL

INGÉNUE HAT & SCARF SET

Sweeten up your winter wardrobe with this matching cable-knit hat and scarf. The lovely lace-cable pattern looks more complicated to knit than it really is. The pristine white of the yarn adds a glimmer of sweetly innocent romance on those cold days when you just have to bundle up.

INGÉNUE HAT & SCARF SET

SIZES
One size fits all.

KNITTED MEASUREMENTS
Scarf:

Length: 88" (224cm)

Width: 8" (20cm)

Hat:

To fit 20 (22)" [51 (56)cm] head

MATERIALS
Scarf:

10 balls Karabella Aurora bulky (100% extra fine merino wool; about 54 yds [50m] per

1¾ oz [50g] ball): color #3, White

Hat:

2 balls Karabella Aurora bulky (100% extra fine merino wool; about 56 yds [52m] per 1¾ oz [50g] ball): color #3, White

Size 10½ (6.5mm) needles, or size to obtain gauge

Size 10½ (6.5mm) double-pointed needles.

Cable needles

GAUGE
19 sts and 20 rows = 4" (10cm) over lace cable patt, using size 10½ needles.

SCARF
Cast on 38 sts.

ROWS 1, 5, AND 9 (RS): Sl 1, p1, k1, p1,*k2tog, yo, p2, k3, k2tog, yo, k3, p2*; repeat from * to * once more, k2tog, yo, p1, k1, p1, k1.

ROW 2 AND ALL WS ROWS: Sl 1, work sts as they appear (knit the knit sts, purl the purl sts, and purl all yo's).

ROWS 3, 7, AND 11: Sl 1, p1, k1, p1, *yo, ssk, p2, k3, yo, ssk, k3, p2*; repeat from * to * once more, yo, ssk, p1, k1, p1, k1.

ROW 13: Sl 1, p1, k1, p1, *k2tog, yo, p2, k8, p2*; repeat from * to * once more, k2tog, yo, p1, k1, p1, k1.

ROW 15: Sl 1, p1, k1, p1, *yo, ssk, p2, sl 4 sts to CN and hold to front, k4, k4 from CN, p2*; repeat from * to * once more, yo, ssk, p1, k1, p1, k1.

ROWS 17–28: Repeat rows 1–12.

Repeat these 28 rows 14 times more or to desired length. Bind off. Weave in loose ends.

If making a longer scarf, you will need more yarn.

HAT
Cast on 30 sts.

ROWS 1, 5, AND 9 (RS): Sl 1, k3, k2tog, yo, k3, p2, k2tog, yo, p2, k3, k2tog, yo, k3, p2, k2tog, yo, p1, k2.

ROW 2 AND ALL WS ROWS: Sl 1, work sts as they appear (knit the knit sts, purl the purl sts, and purl all yo's).

ROWS 3, 7, AND 11: Sl 1, k3, yo, ssk, k3, p2, yo, ssk, p2, k3, ssk, yo, k3, p2, yo, ssk, p1, k2.

ROW 13: Sl 1, k8, p2, k2tog, yo, p2, k8, p2, k2tog, yo, p1, k2.

ROW 15: Sl 1, Sl 4 sts to CN and hold to front, k4, k4 from CN, p2, yo, ssk, p2, sl 4 sts to CN and hold to front, k4, k4 from CN, p2, yo, ssk, p1, k2.

ROWS 17–28: Repeat rows 1–12.

Repeat these 28 rows 2 times more.

Bind off.

Sew cast-on edge to bind-off edge.

CROWN

With RS facing, pick up 66 sts evenly along top edge (the beginning of the RS row) using size 10½ dpn. Place marker at beginning of rnd.

Rnd 1: *K2tog, k9*; repeat from * to * to end of rnd—(60 sts).
Rnd 2: *K2tog, k8*; repeat from * to * to end of rnd—(54 sts).
Rnd 3: *K2tog, k7*; repeat from * to * to end of rnd—(48 sts).
Rnd 4: *K2tog, k6*; repeat from * to * to end of rnd—(42 sts).
Rnd 5: *K2tog, k5*; repeat from * to * to end of rnd—(36 sts).
Rnd 6: *K2tog, k4*; repeat from * to * to end of rnd—(30 sts).
Rnd 7: *K2tog, k3*; repeat from * to * to end of rnd—(24 sts).
Rnd 8: *K2tog, k2*; repeat from * to * to end of rnd—(18 sts).
Rnd 9: *K2tog, k1*; repeat from * to * to end of rnd—(12 sts).
Rnd 10: *K2tog; repeat from * to end of rnd—(6 sts remain).
Cut yarn leaving 4" (10cm) tail. Draw yarn through remaining 6 sts and pull them together to close top of hat. Weave in loose ends to WS.

SPRINGTIME IN PARIS

Beat those winter-weekend blahs with this jaunty shrug. The bright green color brings out the details of the brioche stitch, but the eye-catching wide lapels are the real highlight. Careful construction and shaping are essential in creating this wool/cashmere piece.

SPRINGTIME IN PARIS

SIZES
To fit S (M, L, XL). Directions given are for the smallest size, with larger sizes in parentheses. If there is only one figure, it applies to all sizes.

KNITTED MEASUREMENTS
Bust: 34 (36, 38, 40)" [86 (91.5, 96.5, 101.5)cm]

Length: 18 (18½, 19, 19½)" [46 (47, 48, 49.5)cm]

Upper arm: 11 (12, 13, 14)" [28 (30.5, 33, 35.5)cm]

MATERIALS
9 (9, 10, 11) balls Karabella Margrite (80% extra fine merino wool, 20% cashmere; about 154 yds [140m] per 1¾ oz [50g] ball): color #9096, Spring Green

Size 11 (8mm) needles

Size 5 (3.75mm) needles

GAUGE
24 sts and 30 rows = 4" (10cm) over St st, using size 5 needles with single strand of Margrite.

12 sts and 14 rows = 4" (10cm) over brioche st, using size 11 needles with 2 strands of yarn held together.

BRIOCHE STITCH (EVEN NUMBER OF STITCHES)
ROW 1 (PREPARATION ROW): Sl 1, *yo, sl 1, k1*; repeat from * to *, end k1.
ROW 2: Sl 1, *yo, sl 1, k2tog (use sl-stitch and yo of previous row)*; repeat from * to *, end k1.
Repeat Row 2 for patt.

BODY
With two strands of yarn held together, using size 11 needle, cast on 46 sts.
ROW 1: Sl 1, *yo, sl 1, k1*; repeat from * to * to last stitch, k1.
ROW 2: Sl 1, *yo, sl 1, k2tog (use sl stitch and yo of previous row)*; repeat from * to * to last stitch, k1.
Repeat row 2 until piece measures 44 (46, 48, 50)" [112 (117, 122, 127)cm]. Bind off.
Fold the piece in half, place marker at fold to denote Center Back. Place two additional markers on both sides of center marker as follows:
9 (9½, 10, 10½)" [23 (24, 25, 26.5)cm] from Center Back to mark each side.
With RS facing, starting from right marker, with size 5 needle and single strand of yarn pick up 108 (114, 120, 126) sts evenly spaced between the markers and ending at left marker.

BACK SHAPING
ROW 1 (RS): K1, k2tog, knit to last 3 sts, ssk, k1—106 (112, 118, 124) sts.

ROW 2 AND ALL (WS) ROWS: Purl.

FOR SIZE SMALL ONLY:
Repeat these 2 rows until 66 sts remain (42 rows). Bind off.

FOR SIZE MEDIUM ONLY:
Repeat these 2 rows until 72 sts are left, omitting decreases in rows 9 and 29 (46 rows). Bind off.

FOR SIZE LARGE ONLY:
Repeat these 2 rows until 78 sts are left, omitting decreases in rows 9, 19, 29, and 39 (50 rows). Bind off.

FOR SIZE X-LARGE ONLY:
Repeat these 2 rows until 84 sts are left (52 rows, plus 2 more), omitting decreases in rows 9, 19, 29, 39, and 49. Bind off.

SLEEVES
With single strand of yarn, using size 5 needles, cast on 46 (48, 50, 52) sts.
Work in k1, p1 rib for 4 rows.
ROW 5 (RS): Knit.
ROW 6 AND ALL WS ROWS: Purl.
Continue working in St st for 10 rows more.
ROW 17: K1, m1, knit to last st, m1, k1—48 (50, 52, 54) sts.
Repeat this increase row every 12 (10, 9, 8) rows 9 (11, 13, 15) times more—66 (72, 78, 84) sts.
Work even until piece measures 17½" (44.5cm) from cast-on.

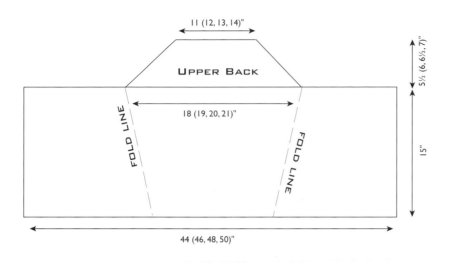

11 (12, 13, 14)"

UPPER BACK

FOLD LINE

18 (19, 20, 21)"

FOLD LINE

5½ (6, 6½, 7)"

15"

44 (46, 48, 50)"

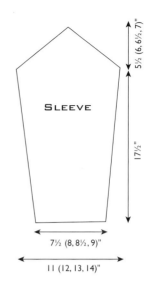

SLEEVE

5½ (6, 6½, 7)"

17½"

7½ (8, 8½, 9)"

11 (12, 13, 14)"

ARMHOLE SHAPING

ROW 1 (RS): K1, k2tog, knit to last 3 sts, ssk, k1—64 (70, 76, 82) sts.

ROW 2 (WS): P1, ssp, purl to last 3 sts, p2tog, p1—62 (68, 74, 80) sts.

Continue these decreases every row until 2 sts remain—42 (46, 50, 54) rows, omitting decreases in rows 4, 8, 12, 16, 20, 24, 28, 32, 36, and 40 for all sizes. Additionally, omit decreases in row 44 for sizes Medium, Large, and X-Large, and in row 48 for Large and X-Large, and row 52 for X-Large only. Work last 2 sts as ssk on RS row. Fasten off remaining st.

FINISHING

Sew back of the Sleeves to the Upper Back (knitted with finer yarn). Match the two ends (CO and BO edges) of bulky body with the center of Upper Back. Starting from center of Upper Back, sew half of the bulky body to Upper Back, then continue sewing down the fronts of the Sleeves. Return to center of Upper Back, and, working in opposite direction of first half, sew second half of bulky body to Upper Back and fronts of Sleeves, same as first half. Starting from the center Upper Back, sew 2½" (6cm) of the bulky body together along the CO and BO edges to form a collar. Weave in loose ends to WS.

THE LITTLE BLACK DRESS

This cotton dress is refined enough to meet the parents for dinner but fetching enough to wear to a cocktail party. Knit in stockinette stitch, it sports Starlight Lace embellishments on the sleeves and hemline that add both softness and chic allure to its vintage look.

THE LITTLE BLACK DRESS

SIZES

To fit S (M, L). Directions are for the smallest size, with larger sizes in parentheses. If there is only one figure, it applies to all sizes.

KNITTED MEASUREMENTS

Bust: 32 (35, 38)" [81 (89, 96.5)cm]

Length: 34½ (35, 35½)" [87.5 (89, 90)cm]

Upper arm: 11 (12, 13)" [28 (30.5, 33)cm]

MATERIALS

10 (11, 12) balls Karabella Vintage Cotton (100% mercerized cotton; about 140 yds [130m] per 1¾ oz [50g] ball): color # 310, Black

Size 3 (3.25mm) needles, or size to obtain gauge

Size 3 (3.25mm) 16" [40cm] circular needle or size to obtain gauge

Stitch holders

Stitch markers

GAUGE

26 sts and 33 rows = 4" (10cm) over St st, using size 3 needles.

PORCUPINE STITCH
(12 STS + 4)

ROW 1: K2, *yo, k2tog*; repeat from * to * to last 2 sts, k2.

ROWS 2 AND 4: K2, purl to last 2 sts, k2.

ROW 3: Knit.

ROWS 5 AND 8: K2, *sl 1-k2tog-psso, k4, yo, k1, yo, k4*; repeat from * to * to last 2 sts, k2.

ROWS 6, 7, AND 9: K2, *p3tog, p4, yo, p1, yo, p4*; repeat from * to * to last 2 sts, k2.

Repeat rows 1–9 for patt.

STARLIGHT LACE
(6 STS + 7)

ROW 1 (WS) AND ALL WS ROWS: Purl.

ROW 2 (RS): K3, *yo, ssk, k1, yo, ssk, k1tbl*; repeat from * to * to last 4 sts, yo, ssk, k2.

ROW 4: K4, *k2tog, yo, k1tbl, yo, ssk, k1tbl*; repeat from * to * to last 3sts, k3.

ROW 6: K3, k2tog, *yo, sl 2-k1-p2sso, yo, sl 1-k2tog-psso*; repeat from * to * to last 8 sts, yo, sl 2-k1-p2sso, yo, ssk, k3.

ROW 8: K4, *k1tbl, yo, k1, yo, k1tbl, k1*; repeat from * to * to last 3sts, k3.

ROW 10: K3, *yo, ssk, k1tbl, yo, ssk, k1* repeat from * to * to last 4 sts, yo, ssk, k2.

ROW 12: K1, *K2tog, yo, k1tbl, yo, ssk, k1tbl*; repeat from * to * to last 6 sts, k2tog, yo, k1tbl, yo, ssk, k1.

ROW 14: K2, *yo, sl 2-k1-p2sso, yo, sl 1-k2tog-psso*;

repeat from * to * to last 5 sts, yo, sl 2-k1-p2sso, yo, k2.

ROW 16: K2, k1tbl, *k1, yo, k1tbl, k1, k1tbl, yo*; repeat from * to * to last 4 sts, k1, k1tbl, k2.

Repeat rows 1–16 for patt.

BACK

Cast on 136 (148, 160) sts. Work 40 rows in porcupine stitch pattern (piece will measure about 5½" [14cm] from CO). Change to St st (knit on RS, purl on WS) and work 18 (12, 6) rows in St st, ending with WS row.

Next row: NEXT RS ROW (DECREASE): K1, ssk, knit to last 3 sts, k2tog, k1.

Continue in St st repeating the decrease row every 6 rows 17 (18, 19) times more. AT THE SAME TIME, when piece measures about 12" (30.5cm) from beginning of St st, with 14 (15, 16) decrease rows completed, ending with WS row [108 (118, 128) sts remaining], prepare work for dart shaping. Place markers for shaping darts on next RS row as follows: K32 (k36, k40), place marker, k3, place marker, k38 (k40, k42), place marker, k3, place marker, k32 (k36, k40). Sl markers in every row. Purl, slipping markers in place.

Knit to 2 sts before the marker, k2tog, sl marker, k3, sl marker, ssk; repeat from * to * once more, knit to end of row. Continue in St st repeating side decreases as established, and working decrease row in the middle of the back every 6th row 2 times more; then work side decreases only until there are 88 (98, 108) sts remaining.

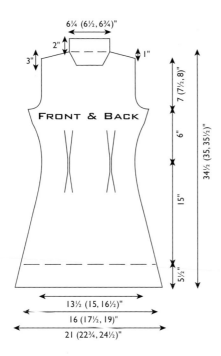

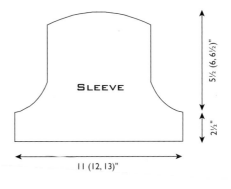

Work even in St st without further decreases until the stock inette portion of the piece measures 15" (38cm), ending with WS row.

NEXT RS ROW (INCREASES IN THE MIDDLE)
Knit to marker, m1, sl marker, k3, sl marker, m1; repeat from * to * once more, knit to end of row—90 (100, 110) sts. Repeat increases in the middle of the back every 6 rows 3 times more (remove markers in the last increase row). AT THE SAME TIME, when the stockinette portion of the piece measures 16½" (42cm), ending with WS row, begin increases on each side edge as follows: K1, m1, knit to last st, m1, k1. Repeat this increase row every 8 rows 3 times more—104 (114, 124) sts.
Work even in St st until the stockinette portion of the piece measures 21½" (54.5cm), ending with WS row.

ARMHOLE SHAPING
Bind off 6 (7, 8) sts at the beginning of next two rows—92 (100, 108) sts.
NEXT RS (ARMHOLE DECREASE): K1, ssk, knit to last 3 sts, k2tog, k1—90 (98, 106) sts.
Repeat this Armhole decrease row every RS row 3 (5, 7) times more—84 (88, 92) sts.
Continue even in St st until Armhole measures 7 (7½, 8)" [18 (19, 20)cm], ending with WS row.

SHOULDER SHAPING
Bind off 8 sts at the beginning of next two rows—68 (72, 76) sts.

Bind off 7 (8, 8) sts at the beginning of next two rows—54 (56, 60) sts.
Bind off 7 (7, 8) sts at the beginning of next two rows—40 (42, 44) sts.
Place remaining 40 (42, 44) sts on stitch holder for Back Neck.

FRONT
Work as for back until Armhole measures 5 (5½, 6)" [12.5 (14, 15)cm], ending with WS row—84 (88, 92) sts.

NECK AND SHOULDER SHAPING
NEXT ROW (RS): K27 (k28, k29), k2tog, k1, place next 24 (26, 28) sts on stitch holder, join second ball of yarn, continue other side as follows: k1, ssk, k27 (k28, k29)—29 (30, 31) sts each side.
Working both sides at once, repeat this decrease row each side of Neck every other row 7 times more—22 (23, 24) sts each side. Work even until Armhole measures 7 (7½, 8)" [18 (19, 20)cm]. Shape Shoulders as for Back.

MOCK TURTLENECK
Sew Shoulder seams. With RS facing and circular needle, work across 40 (42, 44) sts from Back Neck holder, pick up 20 sts from right side of Neck, work across 24 (26, 28) sts from Front Neck holder, pick up 20 sts from left side of Neck—104 (108, 112) sts. Join rnd and work in St st for 2" (5cm).

NEXT ROUND (EYELET ROUND): *K2tog, yo*; repeat from * to * to end of round. Work 8 more rounds (about 1" [2.5cm]) in St st. Bind off loosely. Fold the edge to WS at eyelet row and sew in place, carefully matching knitting tension. Don't allow the sewing sts to become tighter than the knitting.

SLEEVES

Cast on 50 (56, 62) sts.

Work 2 rows in St st.

NEXT RS ROW (EYELET ROUND): *K2tog, yo*; repeat from * to * to end of row. Work in St st for 2 rows more.

ROW 6 (WS): P1, p2tog (to balance sts for the Starlight Lace patt), purl to end. This row is the first row of the Starlight Lace patt—49 (55, 61) sts.

FOR SIZE SMALL ONLY:

ROW 7 (RS): Work 49 sts in Starlight Lace patt (row 2 of Starlight Lace patt).

ROW 8 AND ALL WS ROWS: Purl.

ROW 9: Work 49 sts in Starlight Lace patt (row 4 of Starlight Lace patt).

Continue working 49 sts in Starlight Lace patt ending with row 22 (row 1 of starlight lace patt).

Cap Shaping

ROW 23 (RS): Bind off 3 sts, k2, yo, ssk, k1tbl, *yo, ssk, k1, yo, ssk, k1tbl*; repeat from * to * to last 4 sts, yo, ssk, k2—46 sts.

ROW 24 (WS): Bind off 3 sts, purl to end—43 sts.

ROW 25: Bind off 1 st, k1, k1tbl, yo, ssk, k1tbl, *k2tog, yo, k1tbl, yo, ssk, k1tbl*; repeat from * to * to last 6 sts, work last repeat as k2tog, yo, k1tbl, k3—42 sts.

ROWS 26, 28, AND 30: Bind off 1 st, purl to end— (37 sts remain after row 30 is completed).

ROW 27: Bind off 1 st, k2, sl 1-k2tog-psso, *yo, sl 2-k1-p2sso, yo, sl 1-k2tog-psso*; repeat from * to * to last 4 sts, k4—(28 sts).

ROW 29: Bind off 1 st, yo, k1tbl, k1, *k1tbl, yo, k1, yo, k1tbl, k1*; repeat from * to * to last 4 sts, k1tbl, yo, k3—38 sts.

ROW 31: Work 37 sts in Starlight Lace patt (row 10 of starlight lace patt).

ROW 32 AND ALL WS ROWS: Purl.

ROW 33: Work 37 sts in Starlight Lace patt (row 12 of starlight lace patt).

Continue working 37 sts in Starlight Lace patt, ending with row 65 (row 12 of starlight lace patt).

ROW 66 AND 68 (WS): Bind off 6 sts, purl to end—(13 sts remain after row 68 is completed).

ROW 67 (RS): Bind off 6 sts, k1, *yo, sl 2-k1-p2sso, yo, sl 1-k2tog-psso*; repeat from * to * to last 5 sts, yo, sl 2-k1-p2sso, yo, k2.

ROW 69: Bind off 6 sts, knit to end—7 sts.

ROW 70: Bind off remaining 7 sts.

FOR SIZES MEDIUM/LARGE ONLY:

ROW 7 (RS): K6 (k9), *yo, ssk, k1, yo, ssk, k1tbl*; repeat from * to * to last 7 (10) sts, yo, ssk, k5 (k8).

ROW 8 AND ALL WS ROWS: Purl.

ROW 9: K7 (10), *k2tog, yo, k1tbl, yo, ssk, k1tbl*; repeat from * to * to last 6 (9) sts, k6 (k9).

ROW 11: K6 (k9), k2tog, *yo, sl 2-k1-p2sso, yo, sl 1-k2tog-psso*; repeat from * to * to last 11 (14) sts, yo, sl 2-k1-p2sso, yo, ssk, k6 (k9)—41 (47) sts.

ROW 13: K7 (k10), *k1tbl, yo, k1, yo, k1tbl, k1*; repeat from * to * to last 6 (9) sts, k6 (k9)—55 (61) sts.

ROW 15: K6 (k9), *yo, ssk, k1tbl, yo, ssk, k1*; repeat from * to * to last 7 (10) sts, yo, ssk, k5 (k8).

ROW 17: K4 (k7), *K2tog, yo, k1tbl, yo, ssk, k1tbl*; repeat from * to * to last 9 (12) sts, k2tog, yo, k1tbl, yo, ssk, k4 (k7).

ROW 19: K5 (k8), *yo, sl 2-k1-p2sso, yo, sl 1-k2tog-psso* repeat from * to * to last 8 (11) sts, yo, sl 2-k1-p2sso, yo, k5 (k8)—41 (47) sts.

ROW 21: K5 (k8), k1tbl, *k1, yo, k1tbl, k1, k1tbl, yo*; repeat from * to * to last 7 (10) sts, k1, k1tbl, k5 (k8)—55 (61) sts.

FOR SIZE MEDIUM ONLY:

ROW 23 (RS): Bind off 4 sts, k1, *yo, ssk, k1, yo, ssk, k1tbl*; repeat from * to * to last 7 sts, yo, ssk, k5—51 sts

ROW 24 (WS): Bind off 4 sts, purl to end—47 sts.

ROW 25: Bind off 1 st, k1, *k2tog, yo, k1tbl, yo, ssk, k1tbl*; repeat from * to * to last 2sts, k2—46 sts.

ROWS 26, 28, 30, 32 AND 34: Bind off 1 st, purl to end—(37 sts after row 34 is completed).

ROW 27: Bind off 1 st, k1, *yo, sl 2-k1-p2sso, yo, sl 1-k2tog-psso*; repeat from * to * to last 6 sts, yo, sl 2-k1-p2sso, yo, k3—32 sts.

ROW 29: Bind off 1 st, k2, yo, k1tbl, k1, *k1tbl, yo, k1, yo, k1tbl, k1*; repeat from * to * to last 5 sts, k1tbl, yo, k4—42 sts.

ROW 31: Bind off 1 st, k3, *yo, ssk, k1tbl, yo, ssk, k1*; repeat from * to * to last 6 sts, yo, ssk, k4—40 sts.

ROW 33: Bind off 1 st, *k2tog, yo, k1tbl, yo, ssk, k1tbl*; repeat from * to * to last 7 sts, k2tog, yo, k1tbl, yo, ssk, k2—38 sts.

ROW 35: Work 37 sts in Starlight Lace patt (row 14 of Starlight Lace patt).

ROW 36 AND ALL WS ROWS: Purl.

ROW 37: Work 37 sts in Starlight Lace patt (row 16 of Starlight Lace patt).

Continue working 37 sts in Straight Lace patt, ending with row 67 (row 14 of Starlight Lace patt)—27 sts.

ROW 68 (WS): Bind off 6 sts, purl to end—21 sts.

ROW 69 (RS): Bind off 6 sts, yo, *k1, yo, k1tbl, k1, k1tbl, yo*; repeat from * to * to last 2 sts, k2—22 sts.

ROW 70 (WS): Bind off 7 sts, purl to end—15 sts.

ROW 71: Bind off 7 sts, knit to end—8 sts.

ROW 72: Bind off remaining 8 sts.

FOR SIZE LARGE ONLY:

ROW 23 (RS): Bind off 5 sts, yo, ssk, k1tbl, *yo, ssk, k1, yo, ssk, k1tbl*; repeat from * to * to last 10 sts, yo, ssk, k8—56 sts.

ROW 24 (WS): Bind off 5 sts, purl to end—51 sts.

ROW 25: Bind off 1 st, yo, ssk, k1tbl, *k2tog, yo, k1tbl, yo, ssk, k1tbl*; repeat from * to * to last 4sts, k2tog, yo, k2—50 sts.

ROWS 26, 28, 30, 32, 34, 36, AND 38: Bind off 1 st, purl to end—(37 sts after row 38 is completed).

ROW 27: Bind off 1 st, k1, k2tog, *yo, sl2-k1-p2sso, yo, sl 1-k2tog-psso*; repeat from * to * to last 8 sts, yo, sl 2-k1-p2sso, yo, ssk, k3—34 sts.

ROW 29: Bind off 1 st, k1, *k1tbl, yo, k1, yo, k1tbl, k1*; repeat from * to * to last 2 sts, k2—46 sts.

ROW 31: Bind off 1 st, k1, k1tbl, yo, ssk, k1, *yo, ssk, k1tbl, yo, ssk, k1*; repeat from * to * to last 2 sts, k2—44 sts.

ROW 33: Bind off 1 st, k1, k1tbl, *k2tog, yo, k1tbl, yo, ssk, k1tbl*; repeat from * to * to last 3 sts, k3—42 sts.

ROW 35: Bind off 1 st, k2tog, *yo, sl 2-k1-p2sso, yo, sl 1-k2tog-psso*; repeat from * to * to last 7 sts, yo, sl 2-k1-p2sso, yo, ssk, k2—28 sts.

ROW 37: Bind off 1 st, k1, yo, *k1, yo, k1tbl, k1, k1tbl, yo*; repeat from * to * to last 4sts, k1, yo, k3—38 sts.

ROW 39: Work 37 sts in Starlight Lace patt (row 2 of Starlight Lace patt).

ROW 40 AND ALL WS ROWS: Purl.

ROW 41: Work 37 sts in Starlight Lace patt (row 4 of Starlight Lace patt).

Continue working 37 sts in Starlight Lace patt, ending with row 69 (row 16 of Starlight Lace patt).

ROWS 70 AND 72 (WS): Bind off 7 sts, purl to end—(16 sts after row 72 is completed).

ROW 71 (RS): Bind off 7 sts, k1tbl, *yo, ssk, k1, yo, ssk, k1tbl*; repeat from * to * to last 3 sts, yo, ssk, k1—23 sts.

ROW 73: Bind off 7 sts, knit to end—9 sts.

ROW 74: Bind off remaining 9 sts.

FINISHING

Fold the edge of the sleeves to WS at eyelet row and sew in place. (Follow the same sewing instructions as for Neck.) Sew Sleeves into Armholes. Sew side and Sleeve seams. Weave in loose ends to WS.

DIAMOND TOP

This top's moss diamond pattern, combined with cap sleeves, flatters most figures. It works like an optical illusion, with the dimensionality emerging when it's viewed from certain angles. The epitome of simple, urban sophistication, this subtly slimming mock turtleneck looks best over a pair of black jeans.

DIAMOND TOP

SIZES
To fit S (M, L, XL). Directions are for the smallest size, with larger sizes in parentheses. If there is only one figure, it applies to all sizes.

KNITTED MEASUREMENTS
Bust: 32 (35, 38, 41)" [81 (89, 96.5, 104)cm]

Length: 21 (21½, 22, 22½)" [53 (54.5, 56, 57)cm]

MATERIALS
7 (8, 9, 10) balls Karabella Zodiac (100% mercerized cotton; about 98 yds [90m] per 1 ¾ [50g] ball): color #451, Blue/Green

Size 5 (3.75mm) needles

Size 3 (3.25mm) needles

Size 3 (3.25mm) 16" [40cm] circular needle

Stitch holders

GAUGE
21 sts and 32 rows = 4" (10cm) over Moss Diamonds patt, using size 5 needles.

MOSS DIAMONDS PATTERN (16 STS OVER 16 ROWS)
ROWS 1 AND 9 (RS): K4, p1, k7, p1, k3.

ROWS 2 AND 8 (WS): P10, k1, p1, k1, p3.

ROWS 3 AND 7: K2, (p1, k1) twice, p1, k5, p1, k3.

ROWS 4 AND 6: P2, k1, p1, k1, p3, (k1, p1) 3 times, k1, p1.

ROW 5 AND 13: (P1, k1) 8 times.

ROWS 10 AND 16: P2, k1, p1, k1, p11.

ROWS 11 AND 15: K4, p1, k5, (p1, k1) twice, p1, k1.

ROWS 12 AND 14: (K1, p1) 3 times, k1, p3, k1, p1, k1, p3.

BACK
With size 3 needles, cast on 83 (91, 99,107) sts and work in k1, p1 rib as follows:

ROW 1 (RS): *K1, p1*; repeat from * to * to last st, k1.

ROW 2 (WS): P1, *k1, p1*; repeat from * to * to end of row.

Repeat these 2 rows for rib patt. Continue in rib until work measures 3" (7.5cm) from CO, ending with WS row. Change to size 5 needles and continue as follows:

FOR SIZE SMALL ONLY:
ROWS 1 AND 9 (RS): K1, p1, k7, p1, k3, work 64 sts in Moss Diamonds patt (rows 1 and 9), k4, p1, k1.

ROWS 2 AND 8 (WS): P2, k1, p3, work 64 sts in Moss Diamonds patt (rows 2 and 8), p10, k1, p2.

ROWS 3 AND 7: K1, p1, k1, p1, k5, p1, k3, work 64 sts in Moss Diamonds patt (rows 3 and 7), k2, p1, k1, p1, k1.

ROWS 4 AND 6: P2, (k1, p1) twice, work 64 sts in Moss Diamonds patt (rows 4 and 6), p2, k1, p1, k1, p3, (k1, p1) twice, p1.

ROWS 5 AND 13: K1, (p1, k1) 6 times, work 64 sts in Moss Diamonds patt (rows 5 and 13), (p1, k1) 3 times.

ROWS 10 AND 16: P6, work 64 sts in Moss Diamonds patt (rows 10 and 16), p2, k1, p1, k1, p8.

ROWS 11 AND 15: K1, p1, k5, (p1, k1) twice, p1, k1, work 64 sts in Moss Diamonds patt (rows 11 and 15), k4, p1, k1.

ROWS 12 AND 14: P2, k1, p3, work 64 sts in Moss Diamonds patt (rows 12 and 14), (k1, p1) 3 times, k1, p3, k1, p2.

FOR SIZE MEDIUM ONLY:
ROWS 1 AND 9 (RS): K1, work 80 sts in Moss Diamonds patt (rows 1 and 9), k4, p1, k5.

ROWS 2 AND 8 (WS): P4, k1, p1, k1, p3, work 80 sts in Moss Diamonds patt (rows 2 and 8), p1.

ROWS 3 AND 7: K1, work 80 sts in Moss Diamonds patt (rows 3 and 7), k2, (p1, k1) 3 times, k2.

ROWS 4 AND 6: P2, (k1, p1) 4 times, work 80 sts in Moss Diamonds patt (rows 4 and 6), p1.

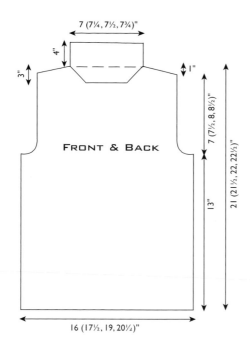

7 (7¼, 7½, 7¾)"

4"

3"

1"

FRONT & BACK

7 (7½, 8, 8½)"

13"

21 (21½, 22, 22½)"

16 (17½, 19, 20¼)"

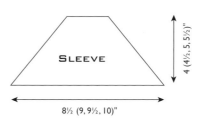

SLEEVE

4 (4½, 5, 5½)"

8½ (9, 9½, 10)"

ROWS 5 AND 13: K1, work 80 sts in Moss Diamonds patt (rows 5 and 13), (p1, k1) 5 times.

ROWS 10 AND 16: P10, work 80 sts in Moss Diamonds patt (rows 10 and 16), p1.

ROWS 11 AND 15: K1, work 80 sts in Moss Diamonds patt (rows 11 and 15), k4, p1, k5.

ROWS 12 AND 14: P4, k1, p1, k1, p3, work 80 sts in Moss Diamonds patt (rows 12 and 14), p1.

FOR SIZE LARGE ONLY:

ROWS 1 AND 9 (RS): K1, p1, k3, work 80 sts in Moss Diamonds patt (rows 1 and 9), k4, p1, k7, p1, k1.

ROWS 2 AND 8 (WS): P8, k1, p1, k1, p3, work 80 sts in Moss Diamonds patt (rows 2 and 8), p5.

ROWS 3 AND 7: K1, p1, k3, work 80 sts in Moss Diamonds patt (rows 3 and 7), k2, (p1, k1) 3 times, k4, p1, k1.

ROWS 4 AND 6: P2, k1, p3, (k1, p1) four, work 80 sts in Moss Diamonds patt (rows 4 and 6), p2, k1, p2.

ROWS 5 AND 13: K1, (p1, k1) twice, work 80 sts in Moss Diamonds patt (rows 5 and 13), (p1, k1) 7 times.

ROWS 10 AND 16: P2, k1, p11, work 80 sts in Moss Diamonds patt (rows 10 and 16), p2, k1, p2.

ROWS 11 AND 15: K1, (p1, k1) twice, work 80 sts in Moss Diamonds patt (rows 11 and 15), k4, p1, k5, (p1, k1) twice.

ROWS 12 AND 14: P2, k1, p1, k1, p3, k1, p1, k1, p3, work 80 sts in Moss Diamonds patt (rows 12 and 14), (k1, p1) twice, p1.

FOR SIZE X-LARGE ONLY:

ROWS 1 AND 9 (RS): K5, p1, k3, work 96 sts in Moss Diamonds patt (rows 1 and 9), k2.

ROWS 2 AND 8 (WS): P2, work 96 sts in Moss Diamonds patt (rows 2 and 8), p9.

ROWS 3 AND 7: K5, p1, k3, work 96 sts in Moss Diamonds patt (rows 3 and 7), k2.

ROWS 4 AND 6: P2, work 96 sts in Moss Diamonds patt (rows 4 and 6), p2, k1, p1, k1, p4.

ROWS 5 AND 13: K1, (p1, k1) 4 times, work 96 sts in Moss Diamonds patt (rows 5 and 13), p1, k1.

ROWS 10 AND 16: P2, work 96 sts in Moss Diamonds patt (rows 10 and 16), p2, k1, p1, k1, p4.

ROWS 11 AND 15: K3, (p1, k1) 3 times, work 96 sts in Moss Diamonds patt (rows 11 and 15), k2.

ROWS 12 AND 14: P2, 96 sts in Moss Diamonds patt (rows 12 and 14), (k1, p1) 4 times, p1.

CONTINUE FOR ALL SIZES:

Repeat rows 1–16 four times more (80 rows), piece measures about 13" (33cm) from CO.

ARMHOLE SHAPING

Note: Sl first st at beginning of each row for neat Armhole edge line.

Continuing working in established patt, and at the same time work Armhole shaping as follows:

Bind off 3 (5, 6, 7) sts at beginning of next 2 rows—77 (81, 87, 93) sts.

Bind off 2 (2, 3, 3) sts at beginning of next 2 rows—73 (77, 81, 87) sts.

Bind off 2 (2, 2, 3) sts at beginning of next 2 rows—69 (73, 77, 81) sts.

Bind off 1 st at beginning of next 2 rows—67 (71, 75, 79) sts. Work even in established patt until armhole measures 7 (7½, 8, 8½)" [18 (19, 20, 21.5) cm], ending with WS row.

SHOULDER SHAPING

Continue working in established patt, and at the same time work Shoulder shaping as follows:

Bind off 6 (7, 7, 7) sts at beginning of next 2 rows—55 (57, 61, 65) sts.

Bind off 6 (6, 7, 7) sts at beginning of next 2 rows—43 (45, 47, 51) sts.

Bind off 6 (6, 6, 7) sts at beginning of next 2 rows—31 (33, 35, 37) sts.

Place remaining 31 (33, 35, 37) sts on stitch holder for Back Neck.

FRONT

Work as for Back until Armhole measures 5 (5½, 6, 6½)" [12.5 (14, 15, 16.5)cm], ending with WS row—67 (71, 75, 79) sts.

NECK SHAPING

NEXT ROW (RS): Work in established patt for 23 (24, 25, 26) sts, k2tog, k1; place next 15 (17, 19, 21) sts on stitch holder for Front Neck, join the second ball of yarn and continue as follows: k1, ssk, work in established patt to the end of row—25 (26, 27, 28) sts each side of neck.

NEXT ROW (WS): Work even in patt.

NEXT ROW (RS): (left side): Work in established patt for 22 (23, 24, 25) sts, k2tog, k1; (right side): k1, ssk, work in established patt to end of row—24 (25, 26, 27) sts each side of neck.

NEXT ROW (WS): Work even in patt.

Working both sides at once repeat above 2 rows (working 1 st fewer on each side of neck) and making decreases at neck edge in every RS row 6 times more—18 (19, 20, 21) sts each side.

When Armhole measures 7 (7½, 8, 8½)" [18 (19, 20, 21.5)cm] shape Shoulders as for Back.

SLEEVES

With size 3 needles, cast on 45 (47, 49, 51) sts.

ROW 1 (RS): *K1, p1; repeat from * to last st, k1.

ROW 2 (WS): P1, *k1, p1; repeat from * to end of row.

NEXT RS ROW (DECREASE): k1, k2tog, work as established to last 3 sts, ssk, k1.

Repeat this decrease in every RS row until 15 sts remain. Bind off 15 sts.

MOCK TURTLENECK

Sew Shoulder seams. With RS facing and circular needle, join yarn and work in k1,p1 rib beginning with the 31 (33, 35, 37) sts from Back Neck holder (ending with k1), then pick up 20 sts from Right Neck edge, maintaining the rib patt, then work the 15 (17, 19, 21) sts from Front Neck holder in rib patt (ending with p1), pick up 20 sts from Left Neck side, maintaining rib patt—86 (90, 94, 98) sts. Join in rnd and continue around in established rib patt until mock turtleneck measures 4" (10cm). Bind off tightly.

FINISHING

Sew side seams. Sew Sleeves into Armholes, beginning from Shoulder seam down. Weave in loose ends to WS.

LEAF-PANELED SWEATER

The mercerized cotton yarn used in this design will keep you cool, while the mock turtleneck and leaf motif add sleekness and a beautiful line. The key to creating that line is to run the leaf motif along the body shaping finished at the neck.

LEAF-PANELED SWEATER

SIZES
To fit XS (S, M, L). Directions are for the smallest size, with larger sizes in parentheses. If there is only one figure, it applies to all sizes.

KNITTED MEASUREMENTS
Bust: 31 (33, 35, 38)" [79 (84, 89, 96.5)cm]

Length: 22 (22½, 22½, 22½)" [56 (57, 57, 57)cm]

MATERIALS
6 (6, 7, 7) balls Karabella Zodiac (100% mercerized cotton; about 98 yds [90m] per 1¾ oz [50g] ball): color #234, Mint Green

Size 6 (4mm) needles, or size to obtain gauge

Size 6 (4mm) 16" [40] circular needle

Stitch holders

Stitch marker

GAUGE
20 sts and 24 rows = 4" (10cm) over St stitch.

RIGHT LEAF PANEL (10 STS)
ROW 1 (WS) AND ALL OTHER WS ROWS: P10.
ROW 2: K6, ssk, return the resulting stitch to left-hand needle and with point of right-hand needle pass the next stitch on the left needle over the returned st and off the needle; then sl the returned stitch back to the right-hand needle (this is "ssk and pass"); yo, k1, yo.
ROW 4: K4, ssk and pass, k1, (yo, k1) twice.
ROW 6: K2, ssk and pass, k2, yo, k1, yo, k2.
ROW 8: Ssk and pass, k3, yo, k1, yo, k3.
Repeat rows 1–8 for patt.

LEFT LEAF PANEL (10 STS)
ROW 1 (WS) AND ALL OTHER WS ROWS: P10.
ROW 2: Yo, k1, yo, SK2P, k6.
ROW 4: K1, (yo, k1) twice, SK2P, k4.
ROW 6: K2, yo, k1, yo, k2, SK2P, k2.
ROW 8: K3, yo, k1, yo, k3, SK2P.
Repeat rows 1–8 for patt.

BACK
With size 6 needles, cast on 86 (90, 94, 100) sts.
ROW 1 (WS): K2, work Left Leaf Panel, k20 (22, 24, 27), work Right Leaf Panel, k2, work Left Leaf Panel, k20 (22, 24, 27), work Right Leaf Panel, k2.

ROW 2 (RS): P2, work Left Leaf Panel, p20 (22, 24, 27), work Right Leaf Panel, p2, work Left Leaf Panel, p20 (22, 24, 27), work Right Leaf Panel, p2.
Repeat these two rows 14 times more.
NEXT ROW (WS): K2, work Left Leaf Panel, place marker, k2tog, k18 (20, 22, 25), work Right Leaf Panel, k2, work Left Leaf Panel, k18 (20, 22, 25), ssk, place marker, work Right Leaf Panel, k2—84 (88, 92, 98) sts.
Work 11 rows even in patt, slipping markers. Repeat decrease row (decreasing after first marker and before last marker)—82 (86, 90, 96) sts. Work 11 rows even.
NEXT ROW (WS): M1 after first marker, work in patt between markers, M1 before last marker—84 (88, 92, 98) sts. Repeat this increase row every 16th row twice more—88 (92, 96, 102) sts.
Work even until piece measures 14" (35.5cm) from cast-on.

Armhole Shaping
Note: Sl first st of every row for a neat edge (RS rows as if to purl, WS rows as if to knit).

FOR SIZES X-SMALL/SMALL:
Keeping continuity of Leaf Panels, decrease as follows:
ROW 1 (WS): Sl 1, k1, work Left Leaf Panel, sl marker, k2tog, work in patt across row to 2 sts before next marker, ssk, sl marker, work Right Leaf Panel, k2—86 (90) sts.
ROW 2: Sl 1, work even in patt.
ROW 3: Work decreases as in Row 1—84 (88) sts.
ROW 4: Work even in patt.

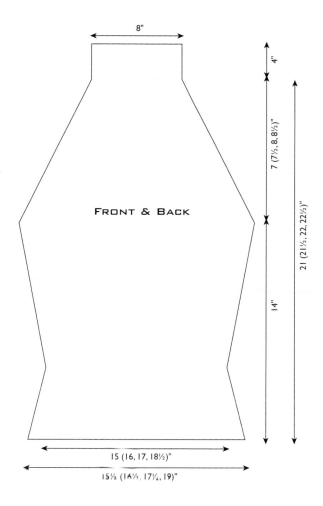

8"

Front & Back

4"

7 (7½, 8, 8½)"

21 (21½, 22, 22½)"

14"

15 (16, 17, 18½)"

15½ (16¼, 17¼, 19)"

ROW 5: Work even in patt.
Repeat these 5 rows until 2 sts remain before, after, and between each of the Leaf Panels. Place remaining 50 sts on a holder for Neck.

FOR SIZES MEDIUM/LARGE:
ROW 1 (WS): Sl 1, k1, work Left Leaf Panel, sl marker, k2tog, work in patt across row to 2 sts before next marker, ssk, sl marker, work Right Leaf Panel, k2—(94, 100) sts.
ROW 2: Sl 1 purlwise, work even in patt.
Repeat these 2 rows until 2 sts remain before, after, and between each of the leaf panels.

FOR SIZE MEDIUM ONLY:
Work even in patt for 6 rows more.

FOR SIZES MEDIUM AND LARGE:
Place remaining 50 sts on a holder for Neck.

FRONT
Work same as for Back.

MOCK TURTLENECK
Note: Neck is worked in round; when working the leaf panels, the purl sts listed on odd-numbered rows are now worked as knit sts. That is, Right Leaf Panel, Row 1: P10, will now be worked as Round 1: K10 and so forth.
Place 50 sts from front and 50 sts from back onto 16" (40cm) circular needle. With RS facing, rejoin yarn and keeping continuity of leaf panels, *p2tog, work Left Leaf Panel, p2, work Right Leaf Panel, p2, work Left Leaf Panel, p2, work Right Leaf Panel, p2tog*; repeat from * to * once more. Join sts in round and work even in patt without further decreases for 4" (10cm). Bind off.

FINISHING
Sew side seams. Weave in ends to WS.

MARBLED TOP

Knock pleats flat on their backs with this feathered turtleneck, which features rows of horizontal pleats on the front, around the armholes, and around the upper yoke. Create the pleats from rows of eyelets, and use circular needles to help with alignment. Made from an alpaca-wool blend, this supersoft sweater is sure to be one of your favorites.

MARBLED TOP

SIZES
To fit S (M, L, XL). Directions are for the smallest size, with larger sizes in parentheses. If there is only one figure, it applies to all sizes.

KNITTED MEASUREMENTS
Bust: 33 (36, 39, 42)" [84 (91, 99, 106)cm]

Length: 23½, (24, 24½, 25)" [60 (61, 62, 63.5)cm]

Upper arm: 11 (12, 13, 14)" [28 (30.5, 33, 35.5)cm]

MATERIALS
8 (9, 9, 10) balls Karabella Marble (55% wool, 45% superfine alpaca; about 95 yds [87m] per 1¾ oz [50g] ball): color #35353, Pink

Size 9 (5.5mm) 24" [60cm] circular needle, or size to obtain gauge

Size 8 (5mm) 16" [40cm] circular needle

Size 1 (2.25mm) circular or any smaller-size needles to use as holding needles

Note: Although the body pieces are worked flat (except for the turtleneck), circular needles are used to make it easier to align and work both sets of sts when making the horizontal pleats.

GAUGE
18 sts and 22 rows = 4" (10cm) over St st, using size 9 needles.

HORIZONTAL PLEAT
ROWS 1 AND 5 (RS): Knit.

ROWS 2, 4, AND 6: Purl.

ROW 3 (EYELET ROW): K1, *k2tog, yo*; repeat from * to * to last st, k1.

Using small needle (holding needle) and WS of work facing, pick up the same number of sts as on main needle from 3rd row *below* eyelet row. (This will be CO edge in the beginning hem, and 3 rows below the eyelet row when making the horizontal pleats.)

ROW 7: Holding both needles together in parallel position, knit together 1 st from main needle and 1 st from holding needle.

BACK
With size 9 needles, cast on 70 (78, 86, 94) sts.

ROWS 1 AND 5 (RS): Knit.

ROWS 2, 4, AND 6 (WS): Purl.

ROW 3 (EYELET ROW): K1, *k2tog, yo*; repeat from * to * to last st, k1.

Using small-size needle (holding needle) and WS of work facing, pick up 70 (78, 86, 94) sts from cast-on edge.

ROW 7 (RS): With both needles held together in the parallel position, knit together 1 st from main needle and 1 st from holding needle.

Continue working in St st for 9 rows more.

NEXT RS ROW (DECREASES): K2, k2tog, knit to last 4 sts, ssk, k2—68 (76, 84, 92) sts.

Repeat this decrease row every 10 rows 2 times more—64 (72, 80, 88) sts. Work even in St st for 9 rows more.

NEXT RS ROW (INCREASES): K2, m1, knit to last 2 sts, m1, k2—66 (74, 82, 90) sts. Repeat this increase row every 10 rows 3 times more—72 (80, 88, 96) sts. Work even until piece measures 15" (38cm) from CO, ending with WS row.

ARMHOLE SHAPING
Bind off 4 (4, 5, 5) sts at beginning of next 2 rows—64 (72, 78, 86) sts.

NEXT RS ROW (DECREASES): K2, k2tog, knit to last 4 sts, ssk, k2—62 (70, 76, 84) sts.

Repeat this decrease row every other row 2 (3, 3, 4) times more—58 (64, 70, 76) sts. Work even until armhole measures 7½ (8, 8½, 9)" [19 (20, 21.5, 23)cm].

SHOULDERS AND NECK SHAPING
Bind off 6 (6, 7, 8) sts at beginning of next 2 rows—46 (52, 56, 60) sts.

Bind off 5 (6, 7, 7) sts at beginning of next 2 rows—36 (40, 42, 46) sts.

Bind off 5 (6, 6, 7) sts at beginning of next 2 rows. Place remaining 26 (28, 30, 32) sts on a stitch holder for Back Neck.

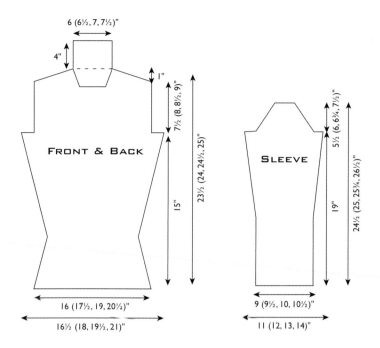

6 (6½, 7, 7½)"

4"

FRONT & BACK

1"

7½ (8, 8½, 9)"

15"

23½ (24, 24½, 25)"

16 (17½, 19, 20¼)"

16½ (18, 19½, 21)"

SLEEVE

5½ (6, 6¾, 7½)"

19"

24½ (25, 25¾, 26½)"

9 (9½, 10, 10½)"

11 (12, 13, 14)"

FRONT

Work as for Back until Armhole decreases are finished and there are 58 (64, 70, 76) sts on the needle, ending with WS row.

NEXT 7 ROWS: Work 1 horizontal pleat (centering the eyelet row by picking up sts 3 rows below the eyelet row). Continue even in St st for 11 rows more, ending with WS row. Next 7 rows: Work 1 horizontal pleat. Work even until armhole measures 5 (5½, 6, 6½)" [12.5 (14, 15, 16.5)cm] from beginning of Armhole, ending with WS row.

NECK AND SHOULDERS SHAPING

NEXT RS ROW (DECREASES): K18 (20, 22, 24), k2tog, k1, place next 16 (18, 20, 22) sts on stitch holder, join second ball of yarn, continue other side as follows: k1, ssk, k18 (20, 22, 24)—20 (22, 24, 26) sts on each side of Neck. Working both sides at once, repeat this decrease row every other row 4 times more—16 (18, 20, 22) sts each Shoulder. Continue even until Armhole measures 7½ (8, 8½, 9)" [19 (20, 21.5, 23)cm]. Shape Shoulders as for Back.

TURTLENECK

Sew shoulders seams.

With RS facing and 16" (40.5cm) circular needle, work across 26 (28, 30, 32) sts from Back Neck holder, pick up 10 sts along right side edge of Neck, work across 16 (18, 20, 22) sts

from Front Neck holder, pick up 10 sts from left side edge of neck— 62 (66, 70, 74) sts. Join sts into rnd and work in circular St st (knit every rnd) for 4" (10cm).

NEXT RND (EYELET RND): *K2tog, yo*; repeat from * to * to end of rnd. Work 3 rnds more in St st. Bind off loosely. Fold the turtleneck edge to WS at eyelet row and sew in place, carefully matching knitting tension.

SLEEVES

With size 9 needles, cast on 40 (42, 44, 46) sts.

ROWS 1 AND 5 (RS): Knit.

ROWS 2, 4, AND 6 (WS): Purl.

ROW 3 (EYELET ROW): K1, *k2tog, yo*; repeat from * to * to last st, k1.

Using small size needle (holding needle) and WS facing, pick up 40 (42, 44, 46) sts from cast on row.

ROW 7 (RS): With both needles held together in the parallel position, knit together 1 st from main needle and 1 st from holding needle. Continue working in St st for 17 rows more, ending with WS row.

NEXT 7 ROWS: Work horizontal pleat. Form horizontal pleat every 17 rows 2 times more. Work even in St st for 7 rows more.

NEXT RS ROW (INCREASES): K2, m1, knit to last 2 sts, m1, k2 —42 (44, 45, 48) sts.

Repeat this increase row every 8 (6, 6, 4) rows 4 (5, 6, 7) times more—50 (54, 58, 62) sts. Work even until piece measures 19" (48cm), ending with WS row.

CAP SHAPING

Bind off 4 (4, 5, 5) sts at beginning of next 2 rows—40 (46, 48, 52) sts.

NEXT ROW: K2, ssk, knit to last 4 sts, k2tog, k2—38 (44, 46, 50) sts.

Repeat this decrease row every other row until 10 sts remain. Bind off remaining sts.

FINISHING

Sew sleeves into Armholes. Sew side and Sleeve seams. Weave in loose ends to WS.

CHAPTER 3: DEMURE

ULTRAVIOLET V-NECK

You'll love the slimming effects of this sweater's four-stitch cable pattern, not to mention the wonderful Karabella Magritte wool/cashmere-blend yarn. The V-neck and darts at the bust and neckline enhance your feminine shapeliness without being too revealing.

ULTRAVIOLET V-NECK

SIZES
To fit XS (S, M, L). Directions are for the smallest size, with larger sizes in parentheses.

If there is only one set of figures, it applies to all sizes.

KNITTED MEASUREMENTS
Bust: 32 (35, 38, 41)" [81 (89, 96.5, 104)cm]

Length: 23 (23¾, 24½, 25¼)" [58.5 (60, 62, 64)cm]

Upper arm: 10 (11, 12, 13)" [25 (28, 30.5, 33)cm]

MATERIALS
9 (10, 11, 12) Karabella Margrite (80% extra fine merino wool, 20% cashmere; about 154 yds [140m] per 1¾ oz [50g] ball): color #8604, Lilac

Size 6 (4mm) needles, or size to obtain gauge for sizes XS and M

Size 5 (3.75mm) needles, or size to obtain gauge for sizes S and L

Cable needles

Stitch markers

Stitch holders

GAUGE
28 sts and 28 rows = 4" (10cm) in Cable patt, using size 6 needles.

32 sts and 32 rows = 4" (10cm) in Cable patt, using size 5 needles.

4-STITCH RIGHT CABLE (RC)
ROW 1: K4.
ROWS 2 AND 4: P4.
ROW 3: Sl 2 to CN and hold to back, k2, k2 from CN.
Repeat these 4 rows for patt.

BACK

FOR SIZES X-SMALL/MEDIUM ONLY:
Using size 6 needles, cast on 110 (134) sts.

FOR SIZES SMALL/LARGE ONLY:
Using size 5 needles, cast on 134 (158) sts.

FOR ALL SIZES:
NEXT ROW (RS): P2, *work 4 sts as for RC, p2*; repeat from * to * to end of row. Total of 18 (22, 22, 26) cables established.
NEXT AND ALL WS ROWS: Work the sts as they appear.
Repeat these 2 rows until piece measures 4" (10cm) from CO row, ending with WS row.
NEXT RS ROW (INCREASE ROW): P1, m1, p1, work in established patt to last 2 sts, p1, m1, p1—112 (136, 136, 160) sts.

Note: Knit all new sts on WS, and purl on RS.
Continue in established patt, repeating this increase row every 4" (10cm) 2 times more—116 (140, 140, 164) sts. Work even until piece measures about 15" (38cm) from beginning, ending with WS row (4th row of cable patt).

RAGLAN AND NECK SHAPING
Bind off 4 sts at beginning of next 2 rows—108 (132, 132, 156) sts.
Note: For the rest of Raglan shaping as the number of sts declines, work in cable patt when possible, knit the sts when there are not enough to complete the cable.
RS DECREASE ROW: P1, RC, p2tog, work in established patt to last 7 sts, p2tog, RC, p1—106 (130, 130, 154) sts.
WS DECREASE ROW: K1, RC, k2tog, work as sts appear to last 7 sts, k2tog, RC, k1—104 (128, 128, 152) sts.
Work RS decrease row every RS row.
Work WS decrease row in rows 2, 4, and 6 only. For the remaining WS rows work sts as they appear without decreasing.
Continue working decreases until 48 (60, 60, 72) sts remain, ending with WS row.
Bind off remaining sts very tightly.

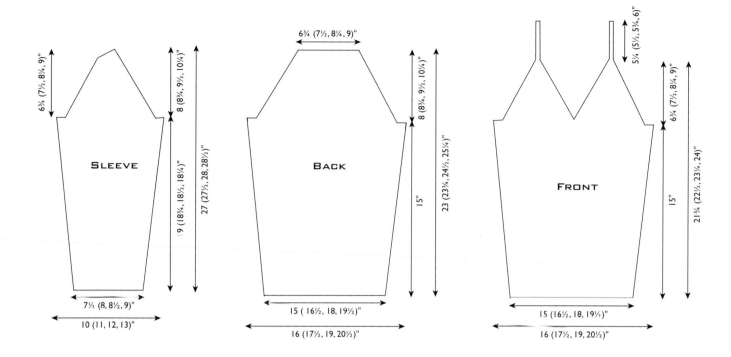

FRONT

Work as for Back until Raglan and Neck shaping.

RAGLAN AND NECK SHAPING

Bind off 4 sts at beginning of next 2 rows and at same time place markers before and after cables 5 (6, 6, 7) and 14 (17, 17, 20) and sl the markers every row with your knitting—108 (132, 132, 156) sts.

ROW 1 (RS): P1, *RC, p2*; repeat from * to * 2 (3, 3, 4) times more, RC, p2tog, RC, p2tog, RC, *p2, RC*; repeat from * to * 2 (3, 3, 4) times more, k1; join the second ball of yarn (for the right side of neck), k1, *RC, p2*; repeat from * to * 2 (3, 3, 4) times more, RC, p2tog, RC, p2tog, RC, *p2, RC*; repeat from * to * 2 (3, 3, 4) times more, p1—52 (64, 64, 76) sts on each side of neck.

Note: Sl first st at neck edges for tighter fit (for left side, in WS row; for right side, in RS row).

Right side mirrors left side.

Work both sides at once as follows:

ROW 2 AND ALL WS ROWS: Work sts as they appear.

ROW 3: Left side: Work in patt to last 5 sts before the marker, k3, p2tog, RC, p2tog, k3, work in established patt—50 (62, 62, 74) sts each side.

ROW 5: Left side: Work in patt to last 4 sts before the marker, k2, p2tog, RC, p2tog, k2, work in established patt—48 (60, 60, 72) sts.

ROW 7: Left side: —Work in patt to last 3 sts before the marker, k1, p2tog, RC, p2tog, k1, work in established patt—46 (58, 58, 70) sts.

ROW 9: Left side: —Work in patt to last 2 sts before the marker, p2tog, RC, p2tog, work in established patt—44 (56, 56, 68) sts.

ROW 11: Left side: —Work in patt to last 3 sts before the marker, p1, p2tog, RC, p2tog, p1, work in established patt—42 (54, 54, 66) sts.

Continue working decreases in the same manner (p2tog before and after marked cable) until 8 sts remain.

NEXT RS ROW: Left side: —K2tog, RC, k2tog—6 sts. Place remaining 6 sts of each neck side on stitch holders.

SLEEVES

FOR SIZES X-SMALL/MEDIUM ONLY:

Using size 6 needles, cast on 54 (60) sts.

NEXT ROW (RS): K2, p2, *work 4 sts as for RC, p2*; repeat from * to * to last 2 sts, k2.

FOR SIZES SMALL AND LARGE ONLY:

Using size 5 needles, cast on 66 (72) sts.

NEXT ROW (RS): P1, *work 4 sts as for RC, p2*; repeat from * to * to last 5 sts, RC, p1.

FOR ALL SIZES:

NEXT AND ALL WS ROWS: Work the sts as they appear.

Continue in patt, increase 1 st each side (working increased sts into patt when possible) every 16 (14, 8, 8) rows 7 (10, 13, 16) times—68 (86, 86, 104) sts.

Work even in established patt until piece measures about 19 (18¾, 18½, 18¼)" [19 (47.5, 47, 46)cm], ending with WS row (4th row of cable patt).

Raglan Shaping

Bind off 4 sts at beginning of next 2 rows—60 (78, 78, 96) sts.

Note: For the rest of Raglan shaping as number of sts declines, work in cable patt when possible, knit the sts when there are not enough to complete the cable.

FOR SIZE X-SMALL ONLY:

ROW 1 (RS): P1, RC, p2tog, work in patt to last 7 sts, p2tog, RC, p1—58 sts.

ROW 2 AND ALL WS ROWS: Work sts as they appear. Repeat these 2 rows until 12 sts remain, ending with RS row for right sleeve and WS row for left sleeve.

FOR SIZES SMALL/MEDIUM/LARGE ONLY:

RS DECREASE ROW: P1, RC, p2tog, work in patt to last 7 sts, p2tog, RC, p1—(76, 76, 94) sts.

WS DECREASE ROW: K1, RC, k2tog, work as sts appear to last 7 sts, k2tog, RC, k1—(74, 74, 92) sts.

Work RS decrease row in every RS row.

Work WS decrease row in rows 2, 4, and 6 for sizes Small and Medium. Work WS decrease row in rows 2, 4, 6, 8, 10 and 12 for size Large. For the remaining WS rows work sts as they appear, continue working decreases until 12 sts remain, ending with RS row for Right Sleeve and WS row for Left Sleeve.

RIGHT SLEEVE

NEXT WS ROW: Work 9 sts as appear, wrap the last st, turn work.

NEXT RS ROW: Work in patt to end.

NEXT WS ROW: Work 6 sts as appear, wrap the last st, turn.

NEXT RS ROW: Work in patt to end.

NEXT WS ROW: Work 3 sts as appear, wrap the last st, turn.

NEXT RS ROW: Work in patt to end.

NEXT WS ROW: Work all 12 sts as appear.

NEXT RS ROW: Bind off 12 sts.

LEFT SLEEVE

NEXT RS ROW: Work 9 sts in patt, wrap the last st, turn.

NEXT WS ROW: Work sts as they appear to end.

NEXT RS ROW: Work 6 sts in patt, wrap the last st, turn.

NEXT WS ROW: Work sts as they appear to end.

NEXT RS ROW: Work 3 sts in patt, wrap the last st, turn.

NEXT WS ROW: Work sts as they appear to end.

NEXT RS ROW: Work all 12 sts in patt.

NEXT WS ROW: Bind off 12 sts.

FINISHING

Sew Raglan seams. Sew side and Sleeve seams.

Neckband Shaping

Pick up 6 sts for Left Neckband from left side stitch holder.

NEXT RS ROW: Sl 1, RC as established, k1. Next WS row: Sl 1, p4, k1. Repeat last 2 rows until piece fits along the Sleeve top and half of the Back Neck. Bind off. Repeat for the Right Neckband. Sew Neckband to the Neck edge. Sew Neckband ends together. Weave in all loose ends to WS of work.

CABLED CARDIGAN

It's the cable shaping that lends this piece its distinctive flair and gives experienced knitters a chance to show off their technical savvy. With its clean, fluid look, this cardigan easily smartens up any work ensemble or casual outfit.

CABLED CARDIGAN

SIZES
To fit S (M, L). Directions are for the smallest size, with larger sizes in parentheses. When only one set of instructions appears, it applies for all sizes.

KNITTED MEASUREMENTS
Bust: 32 (36, 40)" [81 (91.5, 101.5)cm]

Length: 25¼ (27, 28¾)" [64 (68.5, 73)cm]

Upper arm: 12 (13, 14)" [30.5 (33, 35.5)cm]

MATERIALS
10 (11, 12) balls Karabella Super Yak (50% yak, 50% merino wool; about 125 yds [115m] per 1¾ oz [50g] ball): color #10151, Oxford Grey

Size 10½ (6.5mm) needles

Stitch holders

Stitch markers

GAUGE
20 sts and 20 rows = 4" (10cm) over cable patt, using size 10½ needles.

4-STITCH RIGHT CABLE (4RC)
ROW 1: K4.

ROWS 2 AND 4: P4.

ROW 3 (RCC: RIGHT CABLE CROSSING ROW): Sl 2 to CN and hold to back, k2, k2 from CN.

Repeat these 4 rows for patt.

4-STITCH LEFT CABLE (4LC)
ROW 1: K4.

ROWS 2 AND 4: P4.

ROW 3 (LCC: LEFT CABLE CROSSING ROW): Sl 2 to CN and hold to front, k2, k2 from CN.

Repeat these 4 rows for patt.

BACK
Cast on 72 (84, 96) sts.

ROW 1 (RS): P1, k4, *p2, k4*; repeat from * to * to last st, p1.

ROW 2 AND ALL WS ROWS: Work sts as they appear (knit the knit sts, purl the purl sts).

ROW 3: P1, LCC, *p2, LCC*; repeat from * to * to last st, p1.
Work even in 4LC patt for a total 26 rows total from CO.

NEXT RS ROW: Working row 3 of 4LC patt, increase 1 st at beginning and end of row (work new sts as knit st on WS rows and as purl st on RS rows)—74 (86, 98) sts.

Repeat these increases every 26th row 2 times more—78 (90, 102) sts.

Continue working in patt as established until piece measures about 16¼ (17½, 18¾)" [41 (44.5, 47.5)cm], ending with WS row and row 2 of 4LC patt.

Armhole Shaping
Bind off 4 sts at beginning of next 2 rows—70 (82, 94) sts.

NEXT RS ROW (ROW 1 OF 4LC): P1, ssk, k1, *p2, k4*; repeat from * to * to last 6 sts, p2, k1, k2tog, p1—68 (80, 92) sts.

NEXT RS ROW (ROW 3 OF 4LC): P1, ssk, *p2, LCC*; repeat from * to * to last 5 sts, p2, k2tog, p1—66 (78, 90) sts.

NEXT RS ROW (ROW 1 OF 4 LC): P1, ssk, p1, *k4, p2*; repeat from * to * to last 8 sts, k4, p1, k2tog, p1—64 (76, 88) sts.

NEXT RS ROW (ROW 3 OF LC): P1, ssk, *LCC, p2*; repeat from * to * to last 7 sts, LCC, k2tog, p1—62 (74, 86) sts.

Work even in patt without further decreases until Armhole measures 8 (8½, 9)" [20 (21.5, 23)cm].

Shoulder Shaping
Bind off 7 (9, 11) at beginning of next 4 rows—34 (38, 42) sts.

Bind off 6 (8, 10) at beginning of next 2 rows—22 sts.

Bind off remaining 22 sts for Back Neck.

LEFT FRONT (AS WORN)
Cast on 54 (60, 66) sts. Begin working short rows as follows:

ROW 1 (WS): Sl 1, *p4, k2*; repeat from * to * to last 11 sts, p4, wrap next st, turn work

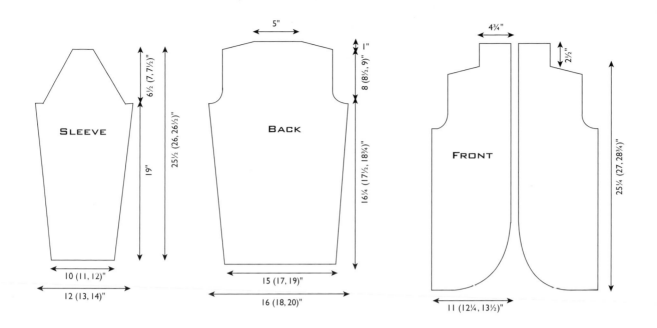

Diagram labels:

SLEEVE
6½ (7, 7½)"
19"
25½ (26, 26½)"
10 (11, 12)"
12 (13, 14)"

BACK
5"
8 (8½, 9)"
1"
16¼ (17½, 18¾)"
15 (17, 19)"
16 (18, 20)"

FRONT
4¾"
2½"
25¼ (27, 28¾)"
11 (12¼, 13½)"

ROW 2 (RS): Sl wrapped st, *RCC, p2*; repeat from * to * to last 5 sts, RCC, k1.

ROW 3: Sl 1, work sts as they appear to last 13 sts, wrap next st, turn work.

ROW 4 AND ALL RS ROWS: Sl wrapped st, work in established 4RC patt to last st, k1.

ROW 5: Sl 1, work sts as they appear to last 19 sts, wrap next st, turn work.

ROW 7: Sl 1, work sts as they appear to last 25 sts, wrap next st, turn work.

ROW 9: Sl 1, work sts as they appear to last 31 sts, wrap next st, turn work.

ROW 11: Sl 1, work sts as they appear to last 37 sts, wrap next st, turn work.

ROW 13: Sl 1, work sts as they appear to last 43 sts, wrap next st, turn work.

ROW 15: Sl 1, work sts as they appear to last 49 sts, wrap next st, turn work.

FOR SIZES MEDIUM/LARGE ONLY:

ROW 17: Sl 1, work sts as they appear to last 55 sts, wrap next st, turn work.

ROW 18: Work same as RS rows.

FOR SIZE LARGE ONLY:

ROW 19: Sl 1, work sts as they appear to last 61 sts, wrap next st, turn work.

ROW 20: Work same as RS rows.

FOR ALL SIZES, CONTINUE AS FOLLOWS:

ROW 17 (19, 21) (SMOOTHING ROW): Note. Work wrap and knit st together as they occur. Sl 1, *p4, k2*; repeat from * to * to last 5 sts, p3, wrap next st, turn work.

ROW 18 (20, 22): Sl wrapped st, k3, p2, *k4, p2, RCC, p2*; repeat from * to * to last 11 (5, 11) sts, k4 (0, 4), p2 (0, 2), RCC, (k5, RCC), k1 (0, 1).

ROW 19 (21, 23): Work same as row 1.

ROW 20 (22, 24): Sl wrapped st, *RCC, p2, k4, p2*; repeat from * to * to last 11 (5, 11) sts, RCC, p2 (0, 2), k5 (1, 5).

ROW 21 (23, 25): Work same as row 3.

ROW 22 (24, 26): Sl wrapped st, *RCC, p2, k4, p2*; repeat from * to * to last 5 (11, 5) sts, RCC, p0 (2, 0), k1 (5, 1).

ROW 23 (25, 27): Work same as row 5.

ROW 24 (26, 28): Work same as row 20 (22, 24).

ROW 25 (27, 29): Work same as row 7.

ROW 26 (28, 30): Work same as row 22 (24, 26).

ROW 27 (29, 31): Work same as row 9.

ROW 28 (30, 32): Work same as row 20 (22, 24).

ROW 29 (31, 33): Work same as row 11.

ROW 30 (32, 34): Sl wrapped st, *RCC, p2, k4, p2*; repeat from * 0 (0, 1) time, RCC, p0 (2, 0), k1 (5, 1).

ROW 31 (33, 35): Work same as row 13.

ROW 32 (34, 36): Sl wrapped st, RCC, p2, k5 (4, 4), p0 (2, 2), k0, (RCC, RCC), p0 (0, 2), k0 (1, 5).

ROW 33 (35, 37): Work same as row 15.

ROW 34 (36, 38): Sl wrapped st, RCC, p0 (2, 2), k1 (5, 4), p0 (0, 2), p0 (p0, RCC), k0 (0, 1).

FOR SIZES MEDIUM/LARGE ONLY:

ROW (37, 39): Work same as row 17.

Row (38, 40): Sl wrapped st, RCC, p0 (2), k1 (5).

FOR SIZE LARGE ONLY:

ROW (41): Work same as row 19.

ROW (42): Sl wrapped st, RCC, k1.

FOR ALL SIZES, CONTINUE AS FOLLOWS:

ROW 35 (39, 43) (SMOOTHING ROW): Note: Work wrap and knit st together as they occur. Sl 1, *p4, k2*; repeat from * to * to last 5 sts, p2, wrap next st, turn work.

ROW 36 (40, 44): Sl wrapped st, k2, *p2, k4*; repeat from * to * to last st, k1.

FOR SIZE SMALL ONLY:

Repeat rows 1–16.

FOR SIZE MEDIUM ONLY:

Repeat rows 1–18.

FOR SIZE LARGE ONLY:

Repeat rows 1–20.

FOR ALL SIZES, CONTINUE AS FOLLOWS:

ROW 53 (59, 65) (SMOOTHING ROW): Note: Work wrap and knit st together as they occur. Sl 1, *p4, k2*; repeat from * to last 5 sts, p1, wrap next st, turn work.

ROW 54 (60, 66): Sl wrapped st, k1, p2, *k4, p2, RCC, p2*; repeat from * to * to last 11 (5, 11) sts, k4 (0, 4), p2 (0, 2), RCC (k5, RCC), k1 (0, 1).

FOR SIZE SMALL ONLY:

Next 16 rows, repeat rows 19–34.

FOR SIZE MEDIUM ONLY:

Next 18 rows, repeat rows 21–38.

FOR SIZE LARGE ONLY:

Next 20 rows, repeat rows 23–42.

FOR ALL SIZES, CONTINUE AS FOLLOWS:

ROW 71 (79, 87) (SMOOTHING ROW): Note: Work wrap and knit st together as they occur. Sl 1, *p4, k2*; repeat from * to * to last 5 sts, p4, k1 (end of short rows).

NEXT 10 ROWS: Beginning with next RS row, work even in established cable patt, ending with a completed WS row.

NEXT RS ROW: Increase 1 st at beginning of row (work new st as knit st on WS rows and as purl st on RS rows), work in patt to end of row. Repeat this increase row every 10th row 2 times more, on the last increase row place marker before last 23 sts, sl marker in place each row—57 (63, 69) sts.

Work even in patt until piece measures about 14¾ (16, 17¼)" [37.5 (40.5, 44)cm], or 1½" (4cm) before the beginning of Armhole shaping, ending with WS row (row 2 of 4RC patt), then work as follows:

ROW 1 (RS): Work as established to last 2 sts before marker, p2tog, work as established to end of row—56 (62, 68) sts.

ROWS 2–8: Work in established patt.

BEGIN ARMHOLE SHAPING:

ROW 9 (RS): Bind off 4 sts, work as established to last 5 sts before marker, sl 2 to CN and hold to back, k2tog, k2 from CN, p1, work as established to end of row—51 (57, 63) sts.

ROW 10 AND ALL WS ROWS: Work in established patt.

ROW 11: P1, ssk, k1, work as established to end of row—50 (56, 62) sts.

ROW 13: P1, ssk, work as established to last 4 sts before marker, sl 2 to CN and hold to back, k1, k2 from CN, p1, work as established to end of row—49 (55, 61) sts.

ROW 15: P1, ssk, p1, work as established to end of row—48 (54, 60) sts.

ROW 17: P1, ssk, work as established to last 4 sts before marker, sl 2 to CN and hold to back, k1, ssk from CN, p1, work as established to end of row—46 (52, 58) sts.

ROW 19: Work as established.

ROW 21: Work as established to last 3 sts before marker, sl 1 to CN and hold to back, k1, k1 from CN, p1, work as established to end of row.

ROW 23: Work as established.

ROW 25: Work as established to last 3 sts before marker, k2tog, p1, work as established to end of row—45 (51, 57) sts.

ROWS 27, 29, AND 31: Work as established to last 2 sts before marker, k1, p1, work as established to end of row.

ROW 33: Work as established to last 3 sts before marker, p2tog, p1, work as established to end of row—44 (50, 56) sts.

ROWS 35, 37, AND 39: Work as established to last 3 sts before marker, p3, work as established to end of row.

ROW 41: Work as established to last 3 sts before marker, p2tog, p1, work as established to end of row—43 (49, 55) sts. Work even in patt until Armhole measures 8 (8½, 9)" [20 (21.5, 23)cm], ending with WS row.

Shoulder Shaping

NEXT RS ROW: Bind off 7 (9, 11), work as established to end of row—36 (40, 44) sts.

NEXT RS ROW: Bind off 7 (9, 11), work as established to end of row—29 (31, 33) sts.

NEXT RS ROW: Bind off 6 (8, 10), work as established to end of row—23 sts.

Work even in patt on remaining 23 sts for 2½" (6cm) more for the Left Collar. Bind off all sts.

RIGHT FRONT (AS WORN)

Cast on 54 (60, 66) sts. Begin short rows.

ROW 1 (RS): Sl 1, k4, *p2, k4*; repeat from * to * last 7 sts, wrap next st, turn work.

ROW 2 AND ALL WS ROWS: Sl wrapped st, work sts as they appear to last st, k1.

ROW 3: Sl 1, LCC, *p2, LCC*; repeat from * to * to last 13 sts, wrap next st, turn work.

ROW 5: Sl 1, k4, *p2, k4*; repeat from * to * to last 19 sts, wrap next st, turn work.

ROW 7: Sl 1, LCC, *p2, LCC*; repeat from * to * to last 25 sts, wrap next st, turn work.

ROW 9: Sl 1, k4, *p2, k4*; repeat from * to * to last 31 sts, wrap next st, turn work.

ROW 11: Sl 1, LCC, *p2, LCC*; repeat from * to * to last 37 sts, wrap next st, turn work.

ROW 13: Sl 1, k4, *p2, k4*; repeat from * to * to last 43 sts, wrap next st, turn work.

ROW 15: Sl 1, LCC, *p0 (2, 2), k0 (LCC, LCC)*; repeat from * to * to last 49 sts, wrap next st, turn work.

ROW 16: Work same as row 2.

FOR SIZES MEDIUM/LARGE ONLY:

ROW 17: Work sts as they appear to last 55 sts, wrap next st, turn work.

ROW 18: Work same as row 2.

FOR SIZE LARGE ONLY:

ROW 19: Sl 1, LCC, wrap next st, turn work, 61 sts remain.

ROW 20: Work same as row 2.

FOR ALL SIZES, CONTINUE AS FOLLOWS:

ROW 17 (19, 21) (SMOOTHING ROW):
Note: Work wrap and purl st together as they occur.
Sl 1, k0 (0, 4), p0 (0, 2), k0 (LCC, LCC), p0 (2, 2), *k4, p2, LCC, p2*; repeat from * to * to last 17 sts, k4, p2, LCC, p2, k3, wrap next st, turn work (1 st remains on needle).

ROW 19 (21, 23): Sl 1, k0 (0, LCC), p0 (0, 2), k0 (4, 4), p0 (2, 2), LCC, p2, k4, *p2, LCC, p2, k4*; repeat from * to * to last 7 sts, wrap next st, turn work.

ROW 21 (23, 25): Sl 1, k0 (0, 4), p0 (0, 2), k0 (LCC, LCC), p0 (2, 2), k4, *p2, LCC, p2, k4*; repeat from * to * to last 13 sts, wrap next st, turn work.

ROW 23 (25, 27): Sl 1, k0 (0, LCC), p0 (0, 2), k0 (4, 4), p0 (2, 2), LCC, p2, k4, *p2, LCC, p2, k4*; repeat from * to * to last 19 sts, wrap next st, turn work.

ROW 25 (27, 29): Sl 1, k0 (0, 4), p0 (0, 2), k0 (LCC, LCC), p0 (2, 2), k4, *p2, LCC, p2, k4*; repeat from * to * to last 25 sts, wrap next st, turn work.

ROW 27 (29, 31): Sl 1, k0 (0, LCC), p0 (0, 2), k0 (4, 4), p0 (2, 2), LCC, p2, k4, p2, LCC, p2, k4, wrap next st, turn work.

ROW 29 (31, 33): Sl 1, k0 (0, 4), p0 (0, 2), k0 (LCC, LCC), p0 (2, 2), k4, p2, LCC, p2, k4, wrap next st, turn work.

ROW 31 (33, 35): Sl 1, k0 (0, LCC), p0 (0, 2), k0 (4, 4), p0 (2, 2), LCC, p2, k4, wrap next st, turn work.

ROW 33 (35, 37): Sl 1, k0 (0, 4), p0 (0, 2), k0 (LCC, LCC), p0 (2, 2), k4, wrap next st, turn work.

FOR SIZES MEDIUM/LARGE ONLY:

ROW (37, 39): Sl 1, k0 (LCC), p0 (2), k4, wrap next st, turn work.

ROW (38, 40): Work same as row 2.

FOR SIZE LARGE ONLY:

ROW 41: Sl 1, k4, wrap next st, turn work.

ROW 42: Work same as row 2.

FOR ALL SIZES, CONTINUE AS FOLLOWS:

ROW 35 (39, 43) (SMOOTHING ROW):
Note: Work wrap and purl st together as they occur.
Sl 1, k0 (0, LCC), p0 (0, 2), k0 (LCC, LCC), p0 (2, 2), *LCC, p2*; repeat from * to * to last 11 sts, LCC, p2, k2, wrap next st, turn work.

ROW 36 (40, 44): Same as row 2.

FOR SIZE SMALL ONLY:
Repeat rows 1–16.

FOR SIZE MEDIUM ONLY:
Repeat rows 1–18.

FOR SIZE LARGE ONLY:
Repeat rows 1–20.

FOR ALL SIZES, CONTINUE AS FOLLOWS:

ROW 53 (59, 65) (SMOOTHING ROW):
Note: Work wrap and purl st together as they occur.
Sl 1, k0 (0, 4), p0 (0, 2), k0 (LCC, LCC), p0 (2, 2), *k4, p2, LCC, p2*; repeat from * to * to last 17 sts, k4, p2, LCC, p2, k1, wrap next st, turn work.

ROWS 54 (60, 66): Same as row 2.

FOR SIZE SMALL ONLY:
Repeat rows 19–34.

FOR SIZE MEDIUM ONLY:
Repeat rows 21–38.

FOR SIZE LARGE ONLY:
Repeat rows 23–42.

FOR ALL SIZES, CONTINUE AS FOLLOWS:

ROW 71 (79, 87) (SMOOTHING ROW):
Note: Work wrap and purl st together as they occur.
Sl 1, *LCC, p2*; repeat from * to * to last 5 sts, LCC, k1.
Continue working established patt for 9 rows.

NEXT RS ROW: Working in established patt, increase 1 st at the end of the row (work new st as knit st on WS side and as purl st on RS side).
Repeat this increase row every 10th row 2 times more, on the last RS increase row place marker after first 23 sts, slip marker in place each row—57 (63, 69) sts.

When piece measures about 14¾ (16, 17¼)" [37.5 (40.5, 44)cm], or 1½" (4cm) to the beginning of Armhole ending with WS row which is also row 2 of 4LC patt, work as follows:

ROW 1 (RS): Work as established to marker, sl marker, p2tog, work as established to end of row—56 (62, 68) sts.

ROWS 2–8: Work even in patt.

ROW 9: Work as established to marker, sl marker, p1, sl 2 to CN and hold to front, k2tog, k2 from CN, work as established to end of row—55 (61, 67) sts.

ROW 10 (BEGIN ARMHOLE SHAPING): Bind off 4 sts, work as established to end of row—51 (57, 63) sts.

ROW 11: Work as established to last 4 sts, k1, k2tog, p1—50 (56, 62) sts.

ROW 13: Work as established to the marker, sl marker, p1, sl 2 to CN and hold to front, k1, k2 from CN, work as established to last 3 sts, k2tog, p1—49 (55, 61) sts.

ROW 15: Work as established to last 4 sts, p1, k2tog, p1—48 (54, 60) sts.

ROW 17: Work as established to the marker, sl marker, p1, sl 2 to CN and hold to front, k1, ssk from CN, work as established to last 3 sts, k2tog, p1—46 (52, 58) sts.

ROW 19: Work as established.

ROW 21: Work as established to marker, sl marker, p1, sl 1 to CN and hold to front, k1, k1 from CN, work as established to end of row.

ROW 23: Work as established.

ROW 25: Work as established to marker, sl marker, p1, ssk, work as established to end of row—45 (51, 57) sts.

ROWS 27, 29, AND 31: Work as established to marker, sl marker, p1, k1, work as established to end of row.

ROW 33: Work as established to marker, sl marker, p1, p2tog, p1, work as established to end of row—44 (50, 56) sts.

ROWS 35, 37, 39: Work as established to marker, sl marker, p3, work as established to end of row.

ROW 41: Work as established to the marker, sl marker, p1, p2tog, work as established to end of row—43 (49, 55) sts.

Work even as established until Armhole measures 8 (8½, 9)" [20 (21.5, 23)cm], ending with RS row.

SHOULDER SHAPING
NEXT WS ROW: Bind off 7 (9, 11), work as established to end of row—36 (40, 44) sts.
Work RS rows as established.

NEXT WS ROW: Bind off 7 (9, 11), work as established to end of row—29 (31, 33) sts.

NEXT WS ROW: Bind off 6 (8, 10), work as established to end of row—23 sts.

Continue working remaining 23 sts as established for 2½" (6cm) more for the Right Collar. Bind off all sts.

SLEEVES

LEFT SLEEVE

Cast on 48 (54, 60) sts.

ROW 1 (RS): P1, k4, *p2, k4*; repeat from * to * to last st, p1.

ROW 2 AND ALL WS ROWS: Work sts as they appear (knit the knit sts, purl the purl sts).

ROW 3: P1, RCC, *p2, RCC*; repeat from * to * to last st, p1.

Work even in 4RC patt for a total of 14 rows.

NEXT RS ROW: Working row 3 of 4RC patt, increase 1 st at beginning and end of row— 50 (56, 62) sts.

Repeat this increase row every 14th row 4 times more, working new sts into the cable patt when possible—58 (64, 70) sts. Work even as established in 4RC patt until piece measures 19" (48cm), ending with WS row (row 4 of 4RC patt).

CAP SHAPING

Note: When there are not enough stitches to complete the RCC because of cap shaping, work those stitches as knits and continue the rest of row in patt.

Bind off 4 sts at beginning of next 2 rows, work in established patt to end of row—50 (56, 62) sts.

ROW 5 (RS): K1, k4, p2tog, *k4, p2*; repeat from * to * to last 11 sts, k4, p2tog, k4, k1.

ROW 7 (RS): K1, RCC, p2tog, k3, p2, *RCC, p2*; repeat from * to * to last 10 sts, k3, p2tog, RCC, k1.

ROW 9 (RS): K1, k4, p2tog, k2, p2, *k4, p2*; repeat from * to * to last 9 sts, k2, p2tog, k4, k1.

ROW 11 (RS): K1, RCC, p2tog, k1, p2, *RCC, p2*; repeat from * to * to last 8 sts, k1, p2tog, RCC, k1.

ROW 13 (RS): K1, k4, p2tog, p2, *k4, p2*; repeat from * to * to last 7 sts, p2tog, k4, k1.

ROW 15 (RS): K1, RCC, p2tog, p1, *RCC, p2*; repeat from * to * to last 12 sts, RCC, p1, p2tog, RCC, k1.

ROWS 17–28: Repeat rows 5–16.

ROWS 29–34: Repeat rows 5–10.

FOR SIZE SMALL ONLY:
Bind off remaining sts.

FOR SIZES MEDIUM AND LARGE ONLY:
ROW 35: Repeat row 11.
ROW 36: Work sts as they appear.

FOR SIZE MEDIUM ONLY:
Bind off remaining sts.

FOR SIZE LARGE ONLY:
ROW 37: Repeat row 13.
ROW 38: Work sts as they appear.
Bind off remaining sts.

RIGHT SLEEVE

Work same as Left Sleeve using 4LC pattern instead of 4RC.

FINISHING

Sew sides, Shoulders, Sleeve, and Collar seams. Weave in loose ends to WS.

PLEATS, PLEASE

This darling grey wool skirt will help you do your part to promote pleats. Much easier to create than you may think, this skirt will teach you the basics of how to fold a pleat—and look wonderful with nearly every top in your winter wardrobe. Pair it with the Cravat-Necked Sweater on page 106 and some tall boots for an update on a classic look.

PLEATS, PLEASE

SIZES
To fit XS (S, M, L). Directions are for the smallest size, with larger sizes in parentheses. If there is only one set of figures, it applies to all sizes.

KNITTED MEASUREMENTS
Length: 19" (48cm)

Width at the skirt top: 15 (16, 17, 18)" [38 (40.5, 43, 46)cm]

Width at the skirt bottom: 19 (20, 21, 22)" [48 (51, 53, 56)cm]

MATERIALS
6 (6, 7, 7) balls Karabella Aurora 4 (100% extra fine merino wool; 196 yds [180m] per 1¾ oz [50g] ball): color # 22, Grey

Size 2 (2.75mm) 24" (60cm) circular needles, or size to obtain gauge

Size 1 (2.25mm) double-pointed 8" (20cm) needles

Note: Skirt is worked flat, not circular. Use circular needles to accommodate the large number of sts.

GAUGE
30 sts and 40 rows = 4" (10cm) over St st, using size 2 needles.

PLEATS
(18 STS PER PLEAT + 2)
FRONT

With size 2 needles, cast on 362 (380, 398, 416) sts.

ROW 1 (RS): Sl 1, k5, p1, k6, sl 1, *k10, p1, k6, sl 1*; repeat from * to * to last 6 sts, k6.

ROW 2 (WS): Sl 1, p13, k1, *p17, k1*; repeat from * to * to last 6 sts, p6.

Repeat these 2 rows until piece measures 4½" (11cm), ending with WS row.

NEXT RS ROW: Sl 1, *sl next 6 sts onto double-pointed needle, sl following 6 sts onto 2nd double-pointed needle, turn 2nd double-pointed needle so that the WS of these 6 sts are facing the WS of sts on LH needle, and right side of the 6 sts on 2nd double-pointed needle are facing the right-hand side of the 6 sts on the first double-pointed needle, and the two double-pointed needles are behind the LH needle with all sts on the same level (forming the pleat), [knit together the first st on LH needle with the first st on each of the double-pointed needles] 6 times (pleat completed)*; repeat from * to * last st, k1.

NEXT ROW: Bind off all sts.

BACK
Work as for Front.

BODY
FRONT

With RS facing, pick up and knit 142 (149, 156, 163) sts evenly along the bind off row of the pleats (about 7 sts per pleat + 2 selvage sts).

NEXT 5 ROWS: Work in St st, beginning with WS row.

ROW 7: Decrease 1 st at beginning and end of row—140 (147, 154, 161) sts.

Continue working in St st repeating the decrease row every 8th row 14 times until there are 112 (119, 126, 133) sts.

Work in St st until piece measures 14½" (37cm) from pick-up sts row, ending with WS row.

NEXT RS ROW (FOLDING ROW): Purl.

NEXT WS ROW: Purl.

Continue in St st for 1" (2.5cm) after the folding row. Bind off tightly.

BACK
Work same as Front.

FINISHING
Sew side seams of the Body and the pleats. Fold the top of the skirt to WS at folding row, and sew the top to the Body of the skirt. Weave in ends to WS.

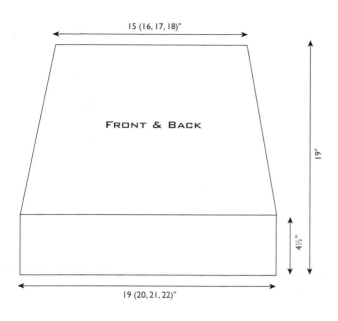

15 (16, 17, 18)"

FRONT & BACK

19"

4½"

19 (20, 21, 22)"

COSMOPOLITAN CARDIGAN

KNIT IN SEED STITCH, THIS CHIC WOOL CARDIGAN IS ALL ABOUT TEXTURE AND ATTITUDE. THE MUSTARD-COLORED YARN SHOWS OFF THE FINISH AND OFFERS A STUNNING CONTRAST TO THE BROWN FUR COLLAR AND TRIM AT THE SPLIT CUFFS. ADD HOOK-AND-EYE FASTENERS AT THE TOP FOR AN EXTRA MODISH FIT AND A FLATTERING REVERSE V-LINE.

COSMOPOLITAN CARDIGAN

SIZES
To fit S (M, L, XL). Directions are for the smallest size, with larger sizes in parentheses. If there is only one figure, it applies to all sizes.

KNITTED MEASUREMENTS
Bust: 35 (37, 39, 41)" [89 (94, 99, 104)cm]

Length: 18½ (19, 19½, 20)" [47 (48, 49.5, 51)cm]

Upper arm: 11½ (12, 13, 13¾)" [29 (30.5, 33, 35)cm]

MATERIALS
13 (14, 15, 16) balls Karabella Aurora Bulky (100% extra fine merino wool, about 54 yds [49m] per 1¾ oz [50g] ball): color #27, Gold

1 ball Karabella Aurora Bulky (100% extra fine merino wool, about 54 yds [49m] per 1¾ oz [50g] ball): color #25, Dark Brown

21 (21, 22, 22) yds Karabella Fur (100% fur): color #4, Dark Brown

Size 10 (6mm) needles, or size to obtain gauge

Size G/6 (4mm) crochet hook

Stitch holders

3 hook-and-eye fasteners

GAUGE
14 sts and 24 rows = 4" (10cm) over seed st using size 10 needles.

SEED STITCH (OVER EVEN NUMBER OF STS):
ROW 1: *K1, p1*; repeat from * to *.
ROW 2: *P1, k1*; repeat from * to *.
Repeat rows 1 and 2.

BACK
Cast on 52 (56, 60, 64) sts.

Work in seed st for 70 rows, increasing 1 st after first st and before last st on rows 11, 31, and 51, working new sts into seed st patt—58 (62, 66, 70) sts. Piece measures 11½" (29cm) from beginning.

ARMHOLE SHAPING
Bind off 3 (3, 4, 5) sts at beginning of next 2 rows—52 (56, 58, 60) sts. Decrease 1 st at the beginning and end of every RS row 3 (4, 4, 4) times—46 (48, 50, 52) sts. Work even until Armhole measures 7 (7½, 8, 8½)" [18 (19, 20, 21.5)cm].

SHOULDER SHAPING
Bind off 4 (4, 4, 5) sts at beginning of next 2 rows—38 (40, 42, 42) sts.

Bind off 4 (5, 5, 5) sts at beginning of next 2 rows—30 (30, 32, 32) sts.

Bind off 5 sts at beginning of next 2 rows—20 (20, 22, 22) sts. Place remaining 20 (20, 22, 22) sts on stitch holder for Back Neck.

RIGHT FRONT (AS WORN)
Cast on 10 (12, 14, 16) sts.

ROW 1 (WS): *K1, p1*; repeat from * to * to last 2 sts, m1, p1, k1.

Note: Sl first st at beginning of every RS row for neat edge.

ROW 2 (RS): Sl 1, k1, m1, *k1, p1*; repeat from * to * to last st, k1.

ROWS 3, 5, 7, 9, AND 11: Repeat row 1.

Note: On rows 11, 31 and 51, increase 1 st at beginning of WS row for side shaping.

ROWS 4, 6, 8, 10, AND 12: Repeat row 2—23 (25, 27, 29) sts.

Continue in seed st repeating front increases as in row 1 on rows 13, 21, 29, 37, 45, 53, 61, and 70—33 (35, 37, 39) sts. Continue in seed st until piece is same length as Back to Armhole.

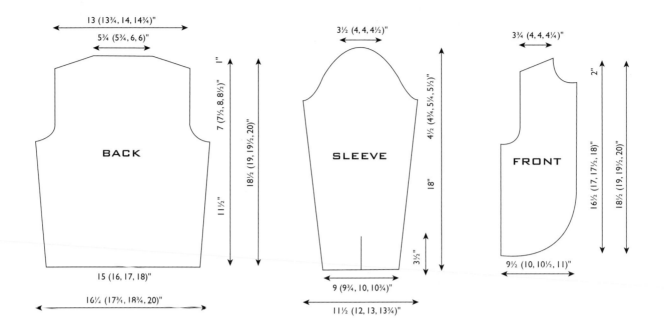

ARMHOLE AND NECK SHAPING

Bind off 3 (3, 4, 4) sts at beginning of next WS row, continue as established.

Decrease 1 st at the beginning of every WS row 3 (4, 4, 4) times—27 (28, 29, 31) sts.

Work in pattern until Armhole measures 5 (5½, 6, 6½)" [12.5 (14, 15, 16.5)cm], ending with WS.

NEXT ROW (RS): Work 8 (8, 9, 10) sts in pattern and place them on stitch holder for neck, k1, ssk, work in pattern to end of row.

Repeat this decrease row at Neckline every RS row 5 times more.

AT THE SAME TIME, when Armhole measures 7 (7½, 8, 8½)" [18 (19, 20, 21.5)cm], shape Shoulders at beginning of WS rows, same as Back.

LEFT FRONT

Work as for Right Front, reversing all shaping.

SLEEVES

Note: Sleeve has 3½" (9cm) slit in the center on the bottom edge. Cast on 16 (17, 18, 19) sts.

Work in seed st for 20 rows. Place on stitch holder. Make 2nd piece and leave on the needle.

ROW 21 (RS): Work in pattern connecting two pieces together.

Note: For sizes Medium and X-Large, work 2 sts together at connecting point to keep in pattern and increase 1 st at the end of row for balance—32 (34, 36, 38) sts.

Continue in established pattern, increase 1 st at the beginning and end of RS rows.

Every 20 rows 4 (4, 5, 5) times—40 (42, 46, 48) sts.

Work even until piece measures 18" (46cm), ending with RS row.

CAP SHAPING

Bind off 3 (3, 4, 4) sts at beginning of next 2 rows—34 (36, 38, 40) sts.

ROW 3 (RS): K1, decrease 1 st in patt, work until last 3 sts, decrease 1 st in patt, k1.

ROWS 4, 5, AND 6: Work in pattern.

Repeat last 4 rows 4 (5, 6, 6) times—24 (24, 24, 26) sts.

Decrease 1 st at beginning and end of every row 6 (5, 5, 5) times starting with rows 21 (24, 28, 29)—12 (14, 14, 16) sts. Bind off.

FUR COLLAR

Sew Shoulder seams.

With dark brown yarn and RS facing, pick up and knit 8 (8, 9, 10) sts from Right Front stitch holder, 8 (9, 10, 10) sts from side of Right Front Neck, 20 (20, 22, 22) sts from Back stitch holder, 8 (9, 10, 10) sts from side of Left Front, 8 (8, 9, 10) sts from Left Front stitch holder—52 (54, 60, 62) sts.

Join fur.

NEXT ROW (WS): *K1 with fur, k1 with yarn, carrying strands not in use along the Back*; repeat from * to * to end.

NEXT ROW (RS): *P1 with fur, p1 with yarn, carrying strands not in use along the Front*; repeat from * to * to end.

Repeat last 2 rows 5 times more.

Bind off with yarn.

FINISHING

Sew Sleeves into Armholes. Sew side and Sleeve seams. Starting at Sleeve seams and using crochet hook and fur, sc evenly spaced along bottom edge of the Sleeve, up and down around the slits, and along second bottom edge of the Sleeve. Sew 2 hook-and-eye fasteners on fur collar edges and 1 hook-and-eye fastener down the front (if desired).

CRAVAT-NECKED SWEATER

You may look all business, but you will feel seriously warm and fuzzy in this sweater's Karabella Boise cashmere/merino-blend yarn. The neck is knit as a V, and, later, the scarf is sewn along the edge. Wear it with the charcoal skirt on page 96 for a little pleated charm.

CRAVAT-NECKED SWEATER

SIZES
To fit S (M, L, XL). Directions given are for the smallest size, with larger sizes in parentheses. If there is only one figure, it applies to all sizes.

KNITTED MEASUREMENTS
Bust: 32 (35, 38, 41)" [81 (89, 96.5, 104) cm]

Length: 21½ (22, 22½, 23)" [54.5 (56, 57, 58.5) cm]

Upper arm: 11 (12, 13, 14)" [28 (30.5, 33, 35.5) cm]

MATERIALS
6 (7, 7, 8) balls Karabella Boise (50% cashmere, 50% merino wool; about 163 yds [150m] per 1¾ oz [50g] ball): color #58, Black

Size 5 (3.75mm) needles

Size 4 (3.5mm) needles

GAUGE
22 sts and 28 rows = 4" (10cm) over St st using size 5 needles.

BACK
With smaller needles, cast on 90 (98, 106, 114) sts.

ROW 1 (RS): *K2, p2*; repeat from * to * to last 2 sts, k2.

ROW 2 (WS): *P2, k2*; repeat from * to * to last 2 sts, p2.

Repeat these 2 rows for 6" (15cm) ending with WS row. Change to larger needles and continue in St st (knit on RS rows, purl on WS rows) until piece measures 13½" (34cm) from beginning, ending with WS row.

ARMHOLE SHAPING
Bind off 4 (5, 6, 7) sts at beginning of next 2 rows—82 (88, 94, 100) sts.

NEXT ROW (RS): K2, ssk, knit to last 4 sts, k2tog, k2—80 (86, 92, 98) sts.

Repeat decrease row every RS row 4 (5, 6, 7) times more—72 (76, 80, 84) sts.

Work even until Armhole measures 7 (7½, 8, 8½)" [18 (19, 20, 21.5)cm], ending with WS row.

SHOULDER SHAPING
Bind off 6 (6, 7, 7) sts at beginning of next 2 rows—60 (64, 66, 70) sts.

Bind off 6 (7, 7, 7) sts at beginning of next 2 rows—48 (50, 52, 56) sts.

Bind off 7 (7, 7, 8) sts at beginning of next 2 rows—34 (36, 38, 40) sts.

Bind off remaining 34 (36, 38, 40) sts for Back Neck.

FRONT
Work as for back until Armhole measures 2¼ (2½, 2¾, 3)" [5.5 (6, 7, 7.5)cm], ending with WS row—72 (76, 80, 84) sts.

NECK SHAPING
NEXT ROW (RS): K32 (34, 36, 38), k2tog, k2, join second ball of yarn, k2, ssk, knit to end—70 (74, 78, 82) sts.

Next row and all WS rows: Purl.

Working both sides at same time decrease at Neck edge every RS row 16 (17, 18, 19) times more. AT THE SAME TIME, when Armhole measures 7 (7½, 8, 8½)" [18 (19, 20, 21.5)cm], shape Shoulders as for Back.

SLEEVES
With smaller needles, cast on 52 (56, 60, 64) sts.

NEXT ROW (RS): *K2, p2*; repeat from * to * across row.

NEXT ROW (WS): *P2, k2*; repeat from * to * across row.

Repeat these 2 rows for 8" (20cm), ending with WS row. Change to larger needle and St st, increasing 1 st at the beginning and end of row (after the first st and before the last st) every 16 (12, 12, 10) rows 4 (5, 6, 7) times—60 (66, 72, 78) sts.

Continue until piece measures 18½" (47cm) from beginning, ending with WS row.

CAP SHAPING
Bind off 4 (5, 6, 7) sts at beginning of next 2 rows—52 (56, 60, 64) sts.

ROW 3 (RS): K2, ssk, knit to the last 4 sts, k2tog, k2—50 (54, 58, 62) sts.

ROW 4 AND 6: Purl.

ROW 5 (RS): Knit.

Repeat rows 3–5 (total 4 rows) 6 (7, 7, 7) times more—38 (40, 44, 48) sts.

Decrease 1 st at the beginning and end of every row 6 (6, 7, 7)

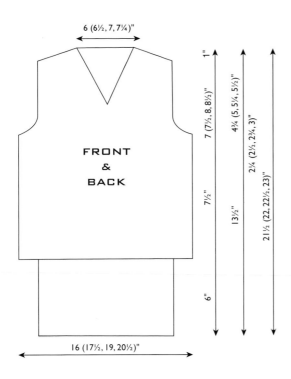

6 (6½, 7, 7¼)"

FRONT
&
BACK

1"

7 (7½, 8, 8½)"

4¾ (5, 5¼, 5½)"

2¼ (2½, 2¾, 3)"

7½"

13½"

21½ (22, 22½, 23)"

6"

16 (17½, 19, 20½)"

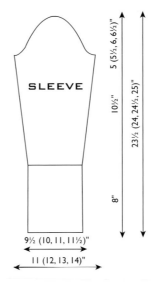

SLEEVE

5 (5½, 6, 6½)"

10½"

23½ (24, 24½, 25)"

8"

9½ (10, 11, 11½)"

11 (12, 13, 14)"

times starting with rows 29 (32, 33, 35)   26 (28, 30, 34) sts.
Bind off.

NECK SCARF

With larger needles, cast on 44 sts.

ROW 1 (RS): Sl 1, p1, *k4, p2*; repeat from * to * to last
6 sts, k4, p1, k1.

ROW 2 (WS): Sl 1, k1, *p4, k2*; repeat from * to * to last
6 sts, p4, k2.

Repeat these 2 rows 7 times more.

ROW 17 (RS): Sl 1, p1, *k2, k2tog, p2*; repeat from * to
* to last 6 sts, k2, k2tog, p1, k1—37 sts.

ROW 18 AND ALL WS ROWS: Work sts as they
appear (knit the knit sts, purl the purl sts).

ROW 19: Sl 1, p1, *k3, p2*; repeat from * to * to last 5 sts,
k3, p1, k1.

Repeat rows 19 and 20 seven times more.

ROW 35: Sl 1, p1, *k1, k2tog, p2*; repeat from * to * to
last 5 sts, k1, k2tog, p1, k1—30 sts.

ROW 37: Sl 1, p1, *k2, p2*; repeat from * to * to last 4 sts,
k2, p1, k1.

Continue as established until piece measures about 25 (26,
27, 28)" from beginning. Bind off.

FINISHING

Sew Sleeves into Armholes. Sew side and Sleeve seams. Sew
the bind-off row of scarf to left side of the Neck. Starting from
the bottom of V-neck, leave 2½" (6cm) open on the right side
of the Neck, continue sewing side edge of the scarf to right
side of the Neck, across the Back, and down the left side of the
Neck until it meets the sewn part of scarf. Insert the remaining
of the scarf into opening on right side.

Weave in loose ends to WS.

SEAWEAVE TURTLENECK

It's the color and stitch pattern that give this sweater its unusual aquatic allure. The sea-green yarn, knit in a folded-ribbon stitch, evokes the movement of waves and creates a beautiful texture and dimensionality. The pattern is reversed and worked in mirror image from the center of each side.

SEAWEAVE TURTLENECK

SIZES
To fit S/M (L/XL). Directions given are for the smaller size, with the larger size in parentheses. If there is only one figure, it applies to both sizes.

KNITTED MEASUREMENTS
Bust: 34 (40)" [86 (101.5)cm]

Length: 23½ (25)" [60 (63.5)cm]

Upper arm: 11 (14)" [28 (35.5)cm]

MATERIALS
12 (15) balls Karabella Aurora 8 (100% extra fine merino wool; about 98 yds [90m] per 1¾ oz [50g] ball): color #43, Sea Green

Size 7 (4.5mm) needles, or size to obtain gauge

Size 7 (4.5mm) 16" [40.5cm] circular needles

GAUGE
23½ sts and 26 rows = 4" (10cm) over folded-ribbon patt (slightly stretched), using size 7 needles.

FOLDED-RIBBON STITCH
(MULTIPLE OF 9 STS + 3)
ROW 1 (WS): K3, p6, k3.

ROW 2 (RS): P3, k4, k2tog, yo, p3.

ROW 3: K3, yo, p1, p2tog, p3, k3.

ROW 4: P3, k2, k2tog, k2, yo, p3.

ROW 5: K3, yo, p3, p2tog, p1, k3.

ROW 6: P3, k2tog, k4, yo, p3.

ROW 7: Repeat Row 1.

ROW 8: P3, yo, ssk, k4, p3.

ROW 9: K3, p3, p2tog tbl, p1, yo, k3.

ROW 10: P3, yo, k2, ssk, k2, p3.

ROW 11: K3, p1, p2tog tbl, p3, yo, k3.

ROW 12: P3, yo, k4, ssk, p3.

Repeat rows 1–12.

Note: Folded-ribbon patt is reversed and worked mirror-image at center of each piece of this sweater.

BACK
Cast on 95 (113) sts.

ROW 1 (RS): K1, p3, (k4, k2tog, yo, p3) 5 (6) times, (yo, ssk, k4, p3) 5 (6) times, k1.

ROW 2 (WS): K4, (p3, p2tog tbl, p1, yo, k3) 5 (6) times, (yo, p1, p2tog, p3, k3) 5 (6) times, k1.

ROW 3: K1, p3, (k2, k2tog, k2, yo, p3) 5 (6) times, (yo, k2, ssk, k2, p3) 5 (6) times, k1.

ROW 4: K4, (p1, p2tog tbl, p3, yo, k3) 5 (6) times, (yo, p3, p2tog, p1, k3) 5 (6) times, k1.

ROW 5: K1, p3, (k2tog, k4, yo, p3) 5 (6) times, (yo, k4, ssk, p3) 5 (6) times, k1.

ROW 6: K4, (p6, k3) 10 (12) times, k1.

ROW 7: K1, p3, (yo, ssk, k4, p3) 5 (6) times, (k4, k2tog, yo, p3) 5 (6) times, k1.

ROW 8: K4, (yo, p1, p2tog, p3, k3) 5 (6) times, (p3, p2tog tbl, p1, yo, k3) 5 (6) times, k1.

ROW 9: K1, p3, (yo, k2, ssk, k2, p3) 5 (6) times, (k2, k2tog, k2, yo, p3) 5 (6) times, k1.

ROW 10: K4, (yo, p3, p2tog, p1, k3) 5 (6) times, (p1, p2tog tbl, p3, yo, k3) 5 (6) times, k1.

ROW 11: K1, p3, (yo, k4, ssk, p3) 5 (6) times, (k2tog, k4, yo, p3) 5 (6) times, k1.

ROW 12: K4, (p6, k3) 10 (12) times, k1.

ROWS 13–96: Repeat rows 1–12, increasing 1 st at beginning and end of row (after the first st and before last st and working new sts in Rev St st) on Rows 61 and 85—99 (117) sts.

ROWS 97–102: Repeat rows 1–6.

ARMHOLE SHAPING
ROW 103: Bind off 5 sts, ssk, k4, p3, (yo, ssk, k4, p3) 4 (5) times, (k4, k2tog, yo, p3) 4 (5) times, k4, k2tog, p5, k1—92 (110) sts.

ROW 104: Bind off 5 sts, p2tog, p3, k3, (yo, p1, p2tog, p3, k3) 4 (5) times, (p3, p2tog tbl, p1, yo, k3) 4 (5) times, p3, p2tog tbl, k1—85 (103) sts.

ROW 105: K1, ssk, k2, p3 (yo, k2, ssk, k2, p3) 4 (5) times, (k2, k2tog, k2, yo, p3) 4 (5) times, k2, k2tog, k1—83 (101) sts.

ROW 106: K1, p2tog, p1, k3, (yo, p3, p2tog, p1, k3) 4 (5) times, (p1, p2tog tbl, p3, yo, k3) 4 (5) times, p1, p2tog tbl, k1—81 (99) sts.

ROW 107: K1, ssk, p3, (yo, k4, ssk, p3) 4 (5) times, (k2tog, k4, yo, p3) 4 (5) times, k2tog, k1—79 (97) sts.

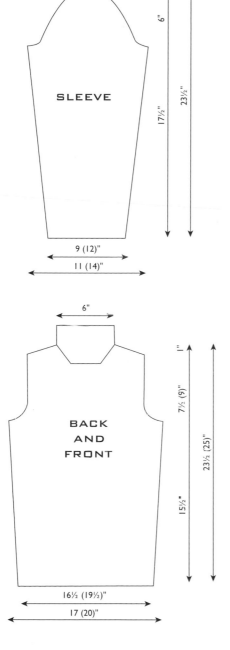

SLEEVE

2½ (5½)"

6"

17½"

23½"

9 (12)"

11 (14)"

6"

BACK
AND
FRONT

1"

7½ (9)"

23½ (25)"

15½"

16½ (19½)"

17 (20)"

ROW 112: K2, (p1, p2tog tbl, p3, yo, k3) 4 (5) times, (yo, p3, p2tog, p1, k3) 3 (4) times, yo, p3, p2tog, p1, k2.

ROW 113: K1, p1, (k2tog, k4, yo, p3) 4 (5) times, (yo, k4, ssk, p3) 3 (4) times, yo, k4, ssk, p1, k1.

ROW 114: K2, (p6, k3) 7 (9) times, p6, k2.

ROW 115: K1, p1, (yo, ssk, k4, p3) 4 (5) times, (k4, k2tog, yo, p3) 3 (4) times, k4, k2tog, yo, p1, k1.

ROW 116: K2, (yo, p1, p2tog, p3, k3) 4 (5) times, (p3, p2tog tbl, p1, yo, k3) 3 (4) times, p3, p2tog tbl, p1, yo, k2.

ROW 117: K1, p1, (yo, k2, ssk, k2, p3) 4 (5) times, (k2, k2tog, k2, yo, p3) 3 (4) times, k2, k2tog, k2, yo, p1, k1.

ROW 118: K2, (yo, p3, p2tog, p1, k3) 4 (5) times, (p1, p2tog tbl, p3, yo, k3) 3 (4) times, p1, p2tog tbl, p3, yo, k2.

ROW 119: K1, p1, (yo, k4, ssk, p3) 4 (5) times, (k2tog, k4, yo, p3) 3 (4) times, k2tog, k4, yo, p1, k1.

ROW 120: K2, (p6, k3) 7 (9) times, p6, k2.

ROW 121: K1, p1, (k4, k2 tog, yo, p3) 4 (5) times, (yo, ssk, k4, p3) 3 (4) times, yo, ssk, k4, p1, k1.

ROW 122: K2, (p3, p2tog tbl, p1, yo, k3) 4 (5) times, (yo, p1, p2tog, p3, k3) 3 (4) times, yo, p1, p2tog, p3, k2.

ROW 123: K1, p1, (k2, k2tog, k2, yo, p3) 4 (5) times, (yo, k2, ssk, k2, p3) 3 (4) times, yo, k2, ssk, k2, p1, k1.

ROW 124: K2, (p1, p2tog tbl, p3, yo, k3) 4 (5) times, (yo, p3, p2tog, p1, k3) 3 (4) times, yo, p3, p2tog, p1, k2.

ROW 125: K1, p1 (k2tog, k4, yo, p3) 4 (5) times, (yo, k4, ssk, p3) 3 (4) times, yo, k4, ssk, p1, k1.

ROW 126: K2, (p6, k3) 7 (9) times, p6, k2.

FOR SIZE SMALL/MEDIUM ONLY:
ROWS 127–150: Repeat rows (115–126) 2 times.

FOR SIZE LARGE/X-LARGE ONLY:
ROWS 127–162: Repeat rows (115–126) 3 times.

FOR BOTH SIZES: SHOULDER SHAPING
ROWS 151–156 (163–168): Continue in established patt, bind off 6 (9) sts at beginning of next 4 rows, then 7 (10) sts at beginning of next 2 rows. AT THE SAME TIME, on row 155 (167), place center 35 sts on stitch holder for Back Neck.

FRONT
Work same as for Back until row 143 (155).

ROW 143 (155): K1, p1, (yo, k4, ssk, p3) 2 (3) times, yo, k4, ssk, k1, place next 19 sts on holder for Front Neck, join second ball of yarn, k1, (k2tog, k4, yo, p3) 2 (3) times,

ROW 108: K1, p2tog, k2, (p6, k3) 8 (10) times, p6, k2, p2tog tbl, k1—77 (95) sts.

ROW 109: K1, p2tog, p1, (k4, k2tog, yo, p3) 4 (5) times, (yo, ssk, k4, p3) 3 (4) times, yo, ssk, k4, p1, p2tog, p1—75 (93) sts.

ROW 110: K1, p2tog, (p3, p2tog tbl, p1, yo, k3) 4 (5) times, (yo, p1, p2tog, p3, k3) 3 (4) times, yo, p1, p2tog, p3, p2tog tbl, k1—73 (91) sts.

ROW 111: K1, p1, (k2, k2tog, k2, yo, p3) 4 (5) times, (yo, k2, ssk, k2, p3) 3 (4) times, yo, k2, ssk, k2, p1, k1.

k2tog, k4, yo, p1—27 (36) sts each side. Work both sides at the same time.

ROW 144 (156): Right side: K2, (p6, k3) 2 (3) times, p6, k1. Left side: K1, (p6, k3) 2 (3) times, p6, k2.

ROW 145 (157): Left side: K1, p1, (k4, k2tog, yo, p3) 2 (3) times, k4, k2tog, k1. Right side: K1, ssk, k4, (p3, yo, ssk, k4) 2 (3) times, p1, k1—26 (35) sts each side.

ROW 146 (158): Right side: K2, (p3, p2tog tbl, p1, yo, k3) 2 (3) times, p3, p2tog tbl, k1. Left side: K1, p2tog, p3, (k3, yo, p1, p2tog, p3) 2 (3) times, k2—25 (34) sts each side.

ROW 147 (159): Left side: K1, p1, (k2, k2tog, k2, yo, p3) 2 (3) times, k2, k2tog, k1. Right side: K1, ssk, k2, (p3, yo, k2, ssk, k2) 2 (3) times, p1, k1—24 (33) sts each side.

ROW 148 (160): Right side: K2, (p1, p2tog tbl, p3, yo, k3) 2 (3) times, p1, p2tog tbl, k1. Left side: K1, p2tog, p1, (k3, yo, p3, p2tog, p1) 2 (3) times, k2—23 (32) sts each side.

ROW 149 (161): Left side: K1, p1, (k2tog, k4, yo, p3) 2 (3) times, k2tog, k1. Right side: K1, ssk, (p3, yo, k4, ssk) 2 (3) times, p1, k1—22 (31) sts each side.

ROW 150 (162): Right side: K2, (p6, k3) 2 (3) times, p2tog. Left side: P2tog tbl, (k3, p6) 2 (3) times, k2—21 (30) sts each side.

ROWS 151–156 (163–168): Continue working in established pattern, shape Shoulders as for back. AT THE SAME TIME, decrease 1 st at Neck edge twice every RS row on both sides.

SLEEVES

Cast on 53 (71) sts.

ROW 1 (RS): K1, (k4, k2tog, yo, p3) 3 (4) times, (yo, ssk, k4, p3) 2 (3) times, yo, ssk, k5.

ROW 2 (WS): K1, (p3, p2tog tbl, p1, yo, k3) 3 (4) times, (yo, p1, p2tog, p3, k3) 2 (3) times, yo, p1, p2tog, p3, k1.

ROW 3: K1, (k2, k2tog, k2, yo, p3) 3 (4) times, (yo, k2, ssk, k2, p3) 2 (3) times, yo, k2, ssk, k3.

ROW 4: K1, (p1, p2tog tbl, p3, yo, k3) 3 (4) times, (yo, p3, p2tog, p1, k3) 2 (3) times, yo, p3, p2tog, p1, k1.

ROW 5: K1, (k2tog, k4, yo, p3) 3 (4) times, (yo, k4, ssk, p3) 2 (3) times, yo, k4, ssk, k1.

ROW 6: K1, (p6, k3) 5 (7) times, p6, k1.

ROW 7: K1, (yo, ssk, k4, p3) 3 (4) times, (k4, k2tog, yo, p3) 2 (3) times, k4, k2tog, yo, k1.

ROW 8: K1, (yo, p1, p2tog, p3, k3) 3 (4) times, (p3, p2 tog tbl, p1, yo, k3) 2 (3) times, p3, p2tog tbl, p1, yo, k1.

ROW 9: K1, (yo, k2, ssk, k2, p3) 3 (4) times, (k2, k2tog, k2, yo, p3) 2 (3) times, k2, k2tog, k2, yo, k1.

ROW 10: K1, (yo, p3, p2tog, p1, k3) 3 (4) times, (p1, p2tog tbl, p3, yo, k3) 2 (3) times, p1, p2tog tbl, p3, yo, k1.

ROW 11: K1, (yo, k4, ssk, p3) 3 (4) times, (k2tog, k4, yo, p3) 2 (3) times, k2tog, k4, yo, k1.

ROW 12: K1, (p6, k3) 5 (7) times, p6, k1.

ROWS 13–108: Repeat rows 1–12. AT THE SAME TIME, increase 1 st each end (after the first st and before last st and working new sts in Rev St st) on rows 21, 41, 61, 81, and 101—63 (81) sts.

ROWS 109–114: Repeat rows 1–6.

CAP SHAPING

ROW 115: Bind off 5 sts, ssk, k4, p3 (yo, ssk, k4, p3) 2 (3) times, (k4, k2tog, yo, p3) 2 (3) times, k4, k2tog, p5, k1—56 (74) sts.

ROW 116: Bind off 5 sts, p2tog, p3, k3, (yo, p1, p2tog, p3, k3) 2 (3) times, (p3, p2tog tbl, p1, yo, k3) 2 (3) times, p3, p2tog tbl, k1—49 (67) sts.

ROW 117: K1, ssk, k2, p3, (yo, k2, ssk, k2, p3) 2 (3) times, (k2, k2tog, k2, yo, p3) 2 (3) times, k2, k2tog, k1—47 (65) sts.

ROW 118: K1, p2tog, p1, k3, (yo, p3, p2tog, p1, k3) 2 (3) times, (p1, p2tog tbl, p3, yo, k3) 2 (3) times, p1, p2tog tbl, k1—45 (63) sts.

ROW 119: K1, ssk, p3 (yo, k4, ssk, p3) 2 (3) times, (k2tog, k4, yo, p3) 2 (3) times, k2tog, k1—43 (61) sts.

ROW 120: K1, k2tog, k2, (p6, k3) 3 (5) times, p6, k2, ssk, k1—41 (59) sts.

ROW 121: K1, p3, (k4, k2tog, yo, p3) 2 (3) times, (yo, ssk, k4, p3) 2 (3) times, k1.

ROW 122: K4, (p3, p2tog tbl, p1, yo, k3) 2 (3) times, (yo, p1, p2tog, p3, k3) 2 (3) times, k1.

ROW 123: K1, p3, (k2, k2tog, k2, yo, p3) 2 (3) times, (yo, k2, ssk, k2, p3) 2 (3) times, k1.

ROW 124: K4, (p1, p2tog tbl, p3, yo, k3) 2 (3) times, (yo, p3, p2tog, p1, k3) 2 (3) times, k1.

ROW 125: K1, p3, (k2tog, k4, yo, p3) 2 (3) times, (yo, k4, ssk, p3) 2 (3) times, k1.

ROW 126: K4, (p6, k3) 4 (6) times, k1.

ROW 127: K1, p3, (yo, ssk, k4, p3) 2 (3) times, (k4, k2tog, yo, p3) 2 (3) times, k1.

ROW 128: K4, (yo, p1, p2tog, p3, k3) 2 (3) times, (p3, p2tog tbl, p1, yo, k3) 2 (3) times, k1.

ROW 129: K1, p3, (yo, k2, ssk, k2, p3) 2 (3) times, (k2, k2tog, k2, yo, p3) 2 (3) times, k1.

ROW 130: K4, (yo, p3, p2tog, p1, k3) 2 (3) times, (p1, p2tog tbl, p3, yo, k3) 2 (3) times, k1.

ROW 131: K1, p3, (yo, k4, ssk, p3) 2 (3) times, (k2tog, k4, yo, p3) 2 (3) times, k1.

ROW 132: K4, (p6, k3) 4 (6) times, k1.

ROWS 133–144: Repeat rows 121–132.

ROW 145: K1, p2tog, p1, k4, k2tog, (p3, k4, k2tog, yo) once (twice), p3, (yo, ssk, k4, p3) once (twice), ssk, k4, p1, p2tog, k1—37 (55) sts.

ROW 146: K1, k2tog, p3, p2tog tbl, (k3, p3, p2tog tbl, p1, yo) once (twice), k3, (yo, p1, p2tog, p3, k3) once (twice), p2tog, p3, k2tog—33 (51) sts.

ROW 147: K1, k2tog, k1, k2tog, (p3, k2, k2tog, k2, yo) once (twice), p3, (yo, k2, ssk, k2, p3) once (twice), ssk, k1, ssk, k1—29 (47) sts.

ROW 148: K1, p1, p2tog tbl, (k3, p1, p2tog tbl, p3, yo) once (twice), k3, (yo, p3, p2tog, p1, k3) once (twice), p1, p2tog, k1—27 (45) sts.

ROW 149: K1, k2tog, (p3, k2tog, k4, yo) once (twice), p3, (yo, k4, ssk, p3) once (twice), ssk, k1—25 (43) sts.

ROW 150: K1, p2tog, k2, (p6, k3) once (3 times), p6, k2, p2tog tbl, k1—23 (41) sts.

FOR SIZE SMALL/MEDIUM ONLY:

ROW 151: K1, ssk, p1, ssk, k4, p3, k4, k2tog, p1, k2tog, k1—19 sts.

ROW 152: K1, p2tog, p2tog, p3, k3, p3, p2tog tbl, p2tog tbl, k1—15 sts.
Bind off 15 sts.

FOR SIZE LARGE/X-LARGE ONLY:

ROW 151: K1, ssk, p1, ssk, k4, p3, yo, ssk, k4, p3, k4, k2tog, yo, p3, k4, k2tog, p1, k2tog, k1—37 sts.

ROW 152: K1, p2tog, p2tog, p3, k3, yo, p1, p2tog, p3, k3, p3, p2tog tbl, p1, yo, k3, p3, p2tog tbl, p2tog tbl, k1—33 sts.
Bind off 33 sts.

NECK

Sew Shoulder seams.

With RS facing, using circular needle, work 35 sts from back holder in pattern: P1, place marker, (k6, p3) 3 times, k6, p1, pick up and knit 9 sts from left side of Neck, work 19 sts from front holder in pattern: p2, k6, p3, k6, p2, pick up and knit 9 sts from right side of Neck—72 sts. Join and work in rounds as follows:

Note: The rnd will start after marker (after p1).

RND 1: *(K4, k2tog, yo, p3) 2 times, (yo, ssk, k4, p3) 2 times*; repeat from * to * once more.

RND 2: *(K3, k2tog, k1, yo, p3) 2 times, (yo, k1, ssk, k3, p3) 2 times*; repeat from * to * once more.

RND 3: *(K2, k2tog, k2, yo, p3) 2 times, (yo, k2, ssk, k2, p3) 2 times*; repeat from * to * once more.

RND 4: *(K1, k2tog, k3, yo, p3) 2 times, (yo, k3, ssk, k1, p3) 2 times*; repeat from * to * once more.

RND 5: *(K2tog, k4, yo, p3) 2 times, (yo, k4, ssk, p3) 2 times*; repeat from * to * once more.

RND 6: (K6, p3) 8 times.

RND 7: *(Yo, ssk, k4, p3) 2 times, (k4, k2tog, yo, p3) 2 times*; repeat from * to * once more.

RND 8: *(Yo, k1, ssk, k3, p3) 2 times, (k3, k2tog, k1, yo, p3) 2 times*; repeat from * to * once more.

RND 9: *(Yo, k2, ssk, k2, p3) 2 times, (k2, k2tog, k2, yo, p3) 2 times*; repeat * to * once more.

RND 10: *(Yo, k3, ssk, k1, p3) 2 times, (k1, k2tog, k3, yo, p3) 2 times*; repeat from * to * once more.

RND 11: *(Yo, k4, ssk, p3) 2 times, (k2tog, k4, yo, p3) 2 times*; repeat from * to * once more.

RND 12: (K6, p3) 8 times.
Bind off.

FINISHING

Sew Sleeves into Armholes. Sew side and Sleeve seams. Weave in loose ends to WS.

CASCADING PETAL SCARF

Drape yourself in an ethereal cascade of mohair lace petals. Knit in two pieces, this luxurious pale-green scarf has white sequins crocheted along the edge of the petals for some extra special sparkle.

CASCADING PETAL SCARF

SIZE
One size fits all.

FINISHED MEASUREMENTS
Length: 88" (224cm)

Width: 13" (33cm)

MATERIALS
2 balls Karabella Lace Mohair (61% super kid mohair, 8% wool, 31% polyester; about 540 yds [500m] per 1¾ oz [50g] ball): color #3234, Pale Green

1 spool Karabella Sequins (100% mohair with sequins; about 108 yds [100m] per 1¾ oz [50g] spool): White

Size 6 (4mm) needles

Size 1 (2.25mm) 24" [60cm] circular needle (holding needle)

Stitch holder

Crochet hook size G/6 (4mm)

GAUGE
18 sts and 24 rows = 4" (10cm) over St st, using size 6 needles.

PETALS
With lace mohair and size 6 needle, cast on 2 sts.

ROW 1 (RS): K1, m1, k1—3 sts.

ROW 2 (WS): P1, m1, p2—4 sts.

ROW 3: K3, m1, k1—5 sts.

ROW 4: P1, m1, p4—6 sts.

ROW 5: K5, m1, k1—7 sts.

ROW 6: P1, m1, p6—8 sts.

ROW 7: K7, m1, k1—9 sts.

ROWS 8, 10, AND 12: Purl.

ROWS 9 AND 11: Knit.

ROW 13: K6, k2tog, k1—8 sts.

ROW 14: P1, p2tog, p5—7 sts.

ROW 15: K4, k2tog, k1—6 sts.

ROW 16: P1, p2tog, p3—5 sts.

ROW 17: K2, k2tog, k1—4 sts.

ROW 18: P1, p2tog, p1—3 sts.

ROW 19: K1, k2tog—2 sts.

ROW 20: P2.

Repeat rows 1–20 three times more. Bind off.

SCARF
Note: For the neat scarf edges, sl the first st at the beginning of each row (excluding rows with petal connections).

Make Two Pieces as Follows:

Make 10 sets of petals first.

Take the first set of petals and using the size 1 holding needle pick up 60 sts evenly along the straight edge of the set. With RS of the petal set facing join lace mohair and using size 6 needles, work in St st (knit on RS, purl on WS) for 8 rows (body of the scarf).

Take the next set of petals and using holding needle pick up 60 sts evenly along the straight edge of the set. Place the set of petals over the body of the scarf with RS facing.

NEXT RS ROW (USING SIZE 6 NEEDLES): *Knit one petal st and one scarf st together*; repeat from * to * to end of row.

Work even in St st for 7 rows more. Attach next set of petals the same way as the previous one. Repeat from ** to ** until all 10 sets of petals are attached.

Work even in St st until scarf measures 44" (112cm), measuring from the tip of the first set of petals. Place all 60 sts on stitch holder. Work second piece the same.

With crochet hook and sequins yarn, work around the petals as follows: Begin at the right side edge of the top set of 4 petals, sc around the 1st petal, 2 sc together in the indentation between the 1st and the 2nd petal, sc around the 2nd petal, 2 sc together between the 2nd and the 3rd petal; repeat sc in same manner to the end of the 4th petal. With WS facing, sc along the side edge of the scarf to the next set of 4 petals, with WS of petals facing you sc around the 4 petals the same way as the previous set. With RS facing, sc along the side edge of scarf to the next set of 4 petals, work these petals on the RS, the same as the first set. Alternating these 2 rows of sc (sc 1 petal set of 4 on RS, then sc 1 petal set of 4 on WS), finish sc around all petal sets.

FINISHING
With RS facing, graft two scarf pieces together. Weave in loose ends.

SILKY
TURTLENECK

THE SUMPTUOUS ITALIAN SILK YARN USED TO
KNIT THIS PIECE GIVES THE LACE PATTERN A LUX-
URIOUS SHEEN AND EXCELLENT DRAPE, WHILE
THE TAUPE COLOR IS PERFECT FOR A SUMMER'S
AFTERNOON. SCALLOPED EDGING CONTRIBUTES
TO THE TOP'S FEMININE APPEAL.

SILKY TURTLENECK

SIZES

To fit S (M, L). Directions given are for the smallest size, with larger sizes in parentheses. If there is only one figure, it applies to all sizes.

KNITTED MEASUREMENTS

Bust: 33 (35, 39)" [84 (89, 99)cm]

Length: 22 (22½, 23)" [56 (57, 58.5)cm]

MATERIALS

9 (11, 13) balls Karabella Empire Silk (100% Italian silk about 90 yds [85m] per 1¾ oz [50g] ball): color #509, Taupe

Size 5 (3.75mm) needles

Size 5 (3.75mm) 16" [40cm] circular needle

Stitch holders

GAUGE

30 sts and 24 rows = 4" (10cm) over Lace patt, using size 5 needles.

LACE PATTERN
(MULTIPLE OF 23 STS)

ROW 1 (RS): *K1tbl, yo, (k1tbl, p1) twice, ssk, (k1tbl, p1) 4 times, k1tbl, k2tog, (p1, k1tbl) twice, yo, k1tbl *; repeat from * to *.

ROW 2 (WS): *P1 tbl, k1, yo, (p1 tbl, k1) twice, p2tog, (k1, p1 tbl) 3 times, k1, p2tog tbl, (k1, p1 tbl) twice, yo, k1, p1 tbl *; repeat from * to *.

ROW 3: *K1tbl, p1, k1tbl, yo, (k1tbl, p1) twice, ssk, (k1tbl, p1) twice, k1tbl, k2tog, (p1, k1tbl) twice, yo, k1tbl, p1, k1tbl *; repeat from * to *.

ROW 4: *(P1 tbl, k1) twice, yo, (p1 tbl, k1) twice, p2tog, k1, p1 tbl, k1, p2tog tbl, (k1, p1 tbl) twice, yo, (k1, p1 tbl) twice *; repeat from * to *.

ROW 5: *(K1tbl, p1) twice, k1tbl, yo, (k1tbl, p1) twice, ssk, k1tbl, k2tog, (p1, k1tbl) twice, yo, (k1tbl, p1) twice, k1tbl *; repeat from * to *.

ROW 6: *Yo, (p1 tbl, k1) 5 times, p3tog, (k1, p1 tbl) 5 times, yo.

Note: In working repeats of row 6, 2 yo's will be next to each other. To do this, wrap yarn around needle twice. On the next row, drop the one wrap and k in the front and the back of the remaining large yo.

Repeat rows 1–6 for lace patt.

BACK

Cast on 117 (125, 141) sts.

FOR SIZE SMALL ONLY:

ROW 1 (RS): K1, starting with row 1, repeat 23 sts of Lace patt 5 times, k1.

ROW 2 (WS): P1, working Row 2, repeat 23 sts of Lace patt 5 times, p1.

FOR SIZE MEDIUM ONLY:

ROW 1 (RS): K1, (k1, p1) twice (you just established 4 sts for 1x1 rib), starting with row 1 of Lace patt, repeat 23 sts of Lace patt 5 times, (p1, k1) twice, (you just established 4 sts for 1x1 rib), k1.

ROW 2 (WS): P1, (p1, k1) twice, working Row 2, repeat 23 sts of Lace patt 5 times, (k1, p1) twice, p1.

FOR SIZE LARGE ONLY:

ROW 1 (RS): K1, k1tbl, (p1, k1tbl) twice, k2tog, (p1, k1tbl) twice, yo, k1tbl, starting with row 1, repeat 23 sts of Lace patt 5 times, k1tbl, yo, (k1tbl, p1) twice, ssk, (k1tbl, p1) twice, k1tbl, k1.

ROW 2 (WS): P1, (p1 tbl, k1) twice, p2tog tbl, (k1, p1 tbl) twice, yo, k1, p1 tbl, working row 2, repeat 23 sts of Lace patt 5 times, p1 tbl, k1, yo, (p1 tbl, k1) twice, p2tog, (k1, p1 tbl) twice, p1.

ROW 3: K1, k1tbl, p1, k1tbl, k2tog, (p1, k1tbl) twice, yo, k1tbl, p1, k1tbl, working row 3 of Lace patt, repeat 23 sts of Lace patt 5 times, k1tbl, p1, k1tbl, yo, (k1tbl, p1) twice, ssk, k1tbl, p1, k1tbl, k1.

ROW 4: P1, p1 tbl, k1, p2tog tbl, (k1, p1 tbl) twice, yo, (k1, p1 tbl) twice, working row 4, repeat 23 sts of Lace patt 5 times, (p1 tbl, k1) twice, yo, (p1 tbl, k1) twice, p2tog, k1, p1 tbl, p1.

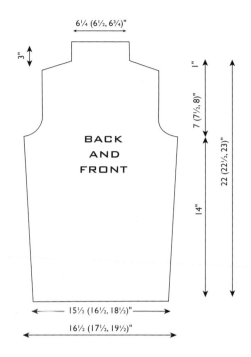

6¼ (6½, 6¾)"

3"

1"

7 (7½, 8)"

22 (22½, 23)"

14"

BACK
AND
FRONT

15½ (16½, 18½)"

16½ (17½, 19½)"

ROW 5: K1, k1tbl, k2tog, (p1, k1tbl) twice, yo, (k1tbl, p1) twice, k1tbl, working row 5, repeat 23 sts of Lace patt 5 times, (k1tbl, p1) twice, k1tbl, yo, (k1tbl, p1) twice, ssk, k1tbl, k1.

ROW 6: P1, p2tog tbl, (k1, p1 tbl) 5 times, yo, working row 6, repeat 23 sts of Lace patt 5 times, yo, (p1 tbl, k1) 5 times, p2tog, p1.

FOR ALL SIZES:

Continue as established, repeat 6 rows of Lace patt for 30 rows. Increase 1 st after the first and before the last st on row 31—119 (127, 143) sts. Work new sts in Rev St st.

Continue as established, increase 1 st after the first and before the last st of row 51—121 (129, 145) sts. Work new sts in St st.

Continue as established, increase 1 st after the first and before the last st of row 71—123 (131, 147) sts. Work new sts in Rev St st.

Continue as established for 84 rows total (piece measures about 14" [35.5cm] from beginning), ending with row 6 of Lace patt.

ARMHOLE SHAPING

ROW 1 (RS): Bind off 5 (7, 11) sts, k1, (p1, k1) 0 (1, 3) times, p1, k1tbl, p1, ssk, (k1tbl, p1) 4 times, k1tbl, k2tog, (p1, k1tbl) twice, yo, k1tbl, working row 1, repeat 23 sts of Lace patt 4 times, (p1, k1) 2 (4, 8) times—117 (123, 135) sts.

ROW 2 (WS): Bind off 6 (8, 12) sts, (p1, k1) 0 (1, 3) times,

(p1 tbl, k1) twice, p2tog, (k1, p1 tbl) 3 times, k1, p2tog tbl, (k1, p1 tbl) twice, yo, k1, p1 tbl, working row 2, repeat 23 sts of Lace patt 3 times, p1 tbl, k1, yo, (p1 tbl, k1) twice, p2tog, (k1, p1 tbl) 3 times, k1, p2tog tbl, k1, p1 tbl, k1, (p1, k1) 0 (1, 3) times, p1—109 (113, 121) sts.

ROW 3: Sl 1, (p1, k1) 0 (1, 3) times, p1, k1tbl, p1, ssk, (k1tbl, p1) twice, k1tbl, k2tog, (p1, k1tbl) twice, yo, k1tbl, p1, k1tbl, working row 3, repeat 23 sts of Lace patt 3 times, k1tbl, p1, k1tbl, yo, (k1tbl, p1) twice, ssk, (k1tbl, p1) twice, k1tbl, k2tog, p1, k1tbl, p1, (k1, p1) 0 (1, 3) times, k1—107 (111, 119) sts.

ROW 4: Sl 1, (k1, p1) 0 (1, 3) times, k1, p1 tbl, k1, p2tog, k1, p1 tbl, k1, p2tog tbl, (k1, p1 tbl) twice, yo, (k1, p1 tbl) twice, working row 4; repeat 23 sts of Lace patt 3 times, (p1 tbl, k1) twice, yo, (p1 tbl, k1) twice, p2tog, k1, p1 tbl, k1, p2tog tbl, k1, p1 tbl, k1, (p1, k1) 0 (1, 3) times, p1—105 (109, 117) sts.

ROW 5: Sl 1, (p1, k1) 0 (1, 3) times, p1, k1tbl, p1, ssk, k1tbl, k2tog, (p1, k1tbl) twice, yo, (k1tbl, p1) twice, k1tbl, working row 5, repeat 23 sts of Lace patt 3 times, (k1tbl, p1) twice, k1tbl, yo, (k1tbl, p1) twice, ssk, k1tbl, k2tog, p1, k1tbl, p1, (k1, p1) 0 (1, 3) times, k1—103 (107, 115) sts.

ROW 6: Sl 1, (k1, p1) 0 (1, 3) times, k1, p1tbl, k1, p3tog, (k1, p1 tbl) 5 times, yo, working row 6, rep 23 sts of Lace patt 3 times, yo, (p1 tbl, k1) 5 times, p3tog, k1, p1 tbl, k1, (p1, k1) 0 (1, 3) times, p1—101 (105, 113) sts.

ROW 7: Sl 1, (k1, p1) 0 (1, 3) times, ssk, (p1, k1tbl) 3 times, k2tog, (p1, k1tbl) twice, yo, k1tbl, working row 1, repeat 23 sts of Lace patt 3 times, k1tbl, yo, (k1tbl, p1) twice, ssk, (k1tbl, p1) 3 times, k2tog, (k1, p1) 0 (1, 3) times, k1—99 (103, 111) sts.

ROW 8: Sl 1, (k1, p1) 0 (1, 3) times, p2tog, (p1 tbl, k1) twice, p2tog tbl, (k1, p1 tbl) twice, yo, k1, p1 tbl, working row 2, repeat 23 sts of Lace patt 3 times, p1 tbl, k1, yo, (p1 tbl, k1) twice, p2tog, (k1, p1 tbl) twice, p2tog tbl, (p1, k1) 0 (1, 3) times, p1—97 (101, 109) sts.

ROW 9: Sl 1, (p1, k1) 0 (1, 3) times, ssk, p1, k1tbl, k2tog, (p1, k1tbl) twice, yo, k1tbl, p1, k1tbl, working row 3, repeat 23 sts of Lace patt 3 times, k1tbl, p1, k1tbl, yo, (k1tbl, p1) twice, ssk, k1tbl, p1, k2tog, (k1, p1) 0 (1, 3) times, k1—95 (99, 107) sts.

ROW 10: Sl 1, (k1, p1) 0 (1, 3) times, p1 tbl, k1, p2tog tbl, (k1, p1 tbl) twice, yo, (k1, p1 tbl) twice, working row 4, repeat 23 sts of Lace patt 3 times, (p1 tbl, k1) twice, yo, (p1 tbl, k1) twice, p2tog, k1, p1 tbl, (p1, k1) 0 (1, 3) times, p1—95 (99, 107) sts.

ROW 11: Sl 1, (p1, k1) 0 (1, 3) times, k1tbl, k2tog, (p1, k1tbl) twice, yo, (k1tbl, p1) twice, k1tbl, working row 5, repeat 23 sts of Lace patt 3 times, (k1tbl, p1) twice, k1tbl, yo, (k1tbl, p1) twice, ssk, k1tbl, (k1, p1) 0 (1, 3) times, k1.

ROW 12: Sl 1, (k1, p1) 0 (1, 3) times, p2tog tbl, (k1, p1 tbl) 5 times, yo, working row 6, repeat 23 sts of Lace patt 3 times, yo, (p1 tbl, k1) 5 times, p2tog, (p1, k1) 0 (1, 3) times, p1.

ROW 13: Sl 1, (k1, p1) 0 (1, 3) times, k1tbl, (p1, k1tbl) twice, k2tog, (p1, k1tbl) twice, yo, k1tbl, working row 1, repeat 23 sts of Lace patt 3 times, k1tbl, yo, (k1tbl, p1) twice, ssk, (k1tbl, p1) twice, k1tbl, (k1, p1) 0 (1, 3) times, k1.

ROW 14: Sl 1, (k1, p1) 0 (1, 3) times, (p1 tbl, k1) twice, p2tog tbl, (k1, p1 tbl) twice, yo, k1, p1 tbl, working row 2, repeat 23 sts of Lace patt 3 times, p1 tbl, k1, yo, (p1 tbl, k1) twice, p2tog, (k1, p1 tbl) twice, (p1, k1) 0 (1, 3) times, p1.
Repeat rows 9–14 until Armhole measures 7 (7½, 8)" [18 (19, 20)cm], ending with WS row and row 6 (4, 6) of Lace patt.

SHOULDER SHAPING
Bind off 7 (8, 10) sts at the beginning of next 2 rows—81 (83, 87) sts.
Bind off 8 (8, 10) sts at the beginning of next 2 rows—65 (67, 67) sts.
Bind off 8 (9, 9) sts at the beginning of next 2 rows—49 sts.
Place remaining 49 sts to stitch holder for Back Neck.

FRONT
Work as for Back.

NECK
Sew Shoulder seams. Place 49 sts from Back Neck stitch holder and 49 sts from Front Neck stitch holder to the circular needle—98 sts. With RS facing, join yarn at one Shoulder. Circular needle is used for ease in working around neckline but Neck is worked back and forth in rows.

FOR SIZE SMALL ONLY:
ROW 1 (RS): K1, *k1tbl, (p1, k1tbl) twice, k2tog, (p1, k1tbl) twice, yo, k1tbl, working row 1, repeat 23 sts of Lace patt, k1tbl, yo, (k1tbl, p1) twice, ssk, (k1tbl, p1) twice, k1tbl*, k2tog, repeat from * to * to last st, k1—97 sts.
ROW 2 (WS): P1, p1 tbl, *k1, p1tbl, k1, p2tog tbl, (k1, p1 tbl) twice, yo, k1, p1 tbl, working row 2, repeat 23 sts of Lace patt, p1 tbl, k1, yo, (p1 tbl, k1) twice, p2tog, k1, p1 tbl, k1*, p3tog, repeat from * to * to last 2 sts, p1 tbl, p1—95 sts.

ROW 3: K1, k1tbl, p1, k1tbl, k2tog, (p1, k1tbl) twice, yo, k1tbl, p1, k1tbl, working row 3, repeat 23 sts for Lace patt 3 times, k1tbl, p1, k1tbl, yo, (k1tbl, p1) twice, ssk, k1tbl, p1, k1tbl, k1.

ROW 4: P1, p1 tbl, k1, p2tog tbl, (k1, p1 tbl) twice, yo, (k1, p1 tbl) twice, working row 4, repeat 23 sts for Lace patt 3 times, (p1 tbl, k1) twice, yo, (p1 tbl, k1) twice, p2tog, k1, p1 tbl, p1.

ROW 5: K1, k1tbl, k2tog, (p1, k1tbl) twice, yo, (k1tbl, p1) twice, k1tbl, working Row 5, repeat 23 sts of Lace patt 3 times, (k1tbl, p1) twice, k1tbl, yo, (k1tbl, p1) twice, ssk, k1tbl, k1.

ROW 6: P1, p2tog tbl, (k1, p1 tbl) 5 times, yo, working row 6, repeat 23 sts of Lace patt 3 times, yo, (p1 tbl, k1) 5 times, p2tog, p1.

ROW 7: K1, k1tbl, (p1, k1tbl) twice, k2tog, (p1, k1tbl) twice, yo, k1tbl, working row 2, repeat 23 sts of Lace patt 3 times, k1tbl, yo, (k1tbl, p1) twice, ssk, (k1tbl, p1) twice, k1tbl, k1.

ROW 8: P1, (p1 tbl, k1) twice, p2tog tbl, (k1, p1 tbl) twice, yo, k1, p1 tbl, working row 3, repeat 23 sts for Lace patt (3 times, p1 tbl, k1, yo, (p1 tbl, k1) twice, p2tog, (k1, p1 tbl) twice, p1.
Repeat rows 3–8 until neck measures 3" (7.5cm). Bind off.

FOR SIZE MEDIUM ONLY:
ROW 1: K1, *k1tbl, k2tog, (p1, k1tbl) twice, yo, (k1tbl, p1) twice, k1tbl, working row 5, repeat 23 sts of Lace patt, (k1tbl, p1) twice, k1tbl, yo, (k1tbl, p1) twice, ssk, k1tbl*, k2tog, repeat from * to *, k1—97 sts.
ROW 2: P1, *p2tog tbl, (k1, p1 tbl) 5 times, yo, working row 6, repeat 23 sts of Lace patt, yo, (p1 tbl, k1) 5 times, p2tog, p1*, repeat from * to *—97 sts.
ROW 3: K1, *k1tbl, (p1, k1tbl) twice, k2tog, (p1, k1tbl) twice, yo, k1tbl, working row 1, repeat 23 sts for Lace patt, k1tbl, yo, (k1tbl, p1) twice, ssk, (k1tbl, p1) twice, k1tbl, k1*, repeat from * to *.
ROW 4: P1, *(p1 tbl, k1) twice, p2tog tbl, (k1, p1 tbl) twice, yo, k1, p1 tbl, working row 2, repeat 23 sts for Lace patt, p1 tbl, k1, yo, (p1 tbl, k1) twice, p2tog, (k1, p1 tbl) twice, p1*, repeat from * to *.
ROW 5: K1, *k1tbl, p1, k1tbl, k2tog, (p1, k1tbl) twice, yo, k1tbl, p1, k1tbl, working row 3, repeat 23 sts of Lace patt , k1tbl, p1, k1tbl, yo, (k1tbl, p1) twice, ssk, k1tbl, p1, k1tbl, k1*, repeat from * to *.
ROW 6: P1, *p1 tbl, k1, p2tog tbl, (k1, p1 tbl) twice, yo, (k1, p1 tbl) twice, working row 4, repeat 23 sts of Lace patt, (p1 tbl, k1) twice, yo, (p1 tbl, k1) twice, p2tog, k1, p1 tbl, p1*, repeat from * to *.

ROW 7: K1, *k1tbl, k2tog, (p1, k1tbl) twice, yo, (k1tbl, p1) twice, k1tbl, working row 5, repeat 23 sts of Lace patt, (k1tbl, p1) twice, k1tbl, yo, (k1tbl, p1) twice, ssk, k1tbl, k1*, repeat from * to *.

Repeat rows 2–7 until neck measures 3" (7.5cm). Bind off.

FOR SIZE LARGE ONLY:

ROW 1 (RS): K1, m1, *k1tbl, (p1, k1tbl) twice, k2tog, (p1, k1tbl) twice, yo, k1tbl, working row 1, repeat 23 sts of Lace patt, k1tbl, yo, (k1tbl, p1) twice, ssk, (k1tbl, p1) twice, k1tbl*, k1, m1, k1; repeat from * to *, m1, k1—101 sts.

ROW 2 (WS): P1, k1, *(p1 tbl, k1) twice, p2tog tbl, (k1, p1 tbl) twice, yo, k1, p1 tbl, working row 2, repeat 23 sts of Lace patt, p1 tbl, k1, yo, (p1 tbl, k1) twice, p2tog, (k1, p1 tbl) twice*, p1, k1, p1; repeat from * to *, k1, p1—101 sts.

ROW 3: K1, p1 *k1tbl, p1, k1tbl, k2tog, (p1, k1tbl) twice, yo, k1tbl, p1, k1tbl, working row 3, repeat 23 sts of Lace patt, k1tbl, p1, k1tbl, yo, (k1tbl, p1) twice, ssk, k1tbl, p1, k1tbl*, k1, p1, k1; repeat from * to *, p1, k1.

ROW 4: P1, k1, *p1 tbl, k1, p2tog tbl, (k1, p1 tbl) twice, yo, (k1, p1 tbl) twice, working row 4, repeat 23 sts of Lace patt, (p1 tbl, k1) twice, yo, (p1 tbl, k1) twice, p2tog, k1, p1 tbl*, p1, k1, p1; repeat from * to *, k1, p1.

ROW 5: K1, p1, *k1tbl, k2tog, (p1, k1tbl) twice, yo, (k1tbl, p1) twice, k1tbl, working Row 5, repeat 23 sts of Lace patt, (k1tbl, p1) twice, k1tbl, yo, (k1tbl, p1) twice, ssk, k1tbl*, k1, p1, k1; repeat from * to *, p1, k1.

ROW 6: P1, k1, *p2tog tbl, (k1, p1 tbl) 5 times, yo, working row 6, repeat 23 sts of Lace patt, yo, (p1 tbl, k1) 5 times, p2tog*, p1, k1, p1; repeat from * to *, k1, p1.

ROW 7: K1, p1, *k1tbl, (p1, k1tbl) twice, k2tog, (p1, k1tbl) twice, yo, k1tbl, working Row 1, repeat 23 sts of Lace patt, k1tbl, yo, (k1tbl, p1) twice, ssk, (k1tbl, p1) twice, k1tbl*, k1, p1, k1; repeat from * to *, p1, k1.

Repeat rows 2–7 until neck measures 3" (7.5cm). Bind off.
Sew side and Neck seams. Weave in loose ends.

FINISHING
Sew side and Neck seam. Weave in loose ends.

COZY MOSS SHRUG

This adorable shrug knits up quickly thanks to its simple construction. Its graceful curves flatter most figures, and its smart look complements outfits from dressy to casual. Nothing beats this sweater for its soft and cozy feel.

COZY MOSS SHRUG

SIZE
To fit S/M (L/XL). Directions given are for the smaller size, with the larger size in parentheses. If there is only one figure, it applies to both sizes.

FINISHED MEASUREMENTS
Bust: 34 (38)" [86 (96.5)cm]

Length: 20 (20½)" [51 (52)cm]

Sleeve width: 13 (14)" [33 (35.5)cm]

MATERIALS
7 (8) balls Karabella Puffy (100% merino wool; about 54 yds [50m] per 3½ oz [100g] ball): color #55, Moss Green

Size 15 (10mm) needles, or size to obtain gauge

GAUGE
10 sts and 12 rows = 4" (10cm) over 1×1 rib (k1, p1), using size 15 needles.

CARDIGAN
Note: This cardigan is worked in 1 piece from Right Sleeve to Left Sleeve.

Cast on 31 (33) sts.

Work 40 rows in 1x1 rib (k1, p1).

ROW 41 (RS): K1, m1, work in 1x1 rib to last st, m1, k1.
Cont working in patt, repeat same increases in rows 51, 55, 56, 57, 58, 59—45 (47) sts.

ROW 60: Work in patt, cast on 15 sts at end of row—60 (62) sts.

ROW 60: Work in patt, cast on 15 sts at end of row—75 (77) sts.

ROWS 62–67 (69): Work in patt.

ROW 68 (70): Work in patt to last 3 sts, decrease 1 st, k1—74 (76) sts.

ROW 69 (71): K1, decrease 1 st, work in patt to end—73 (75) sts.

ROW 70 (72): Work in patt to last 3 sts, decrease 1 st, k1, cast on 16 (18) sts—88 (92) sts.
Work in patt for 16 rows more—86 (88) rows.

ROW 87 (89): Bind off 44 (46) sts for front opening, work in patt 44 (46) sts for the back.

ROW 88 (90): Work 44 (46) sts in patt, cast on 44 (46) sts for front—88 (92) sts.
Work in patt for 16 rows more—104 (106) rows.

ROW 105 (107): Bind off 16 (18) sts, k1, m1, work in patt to end—73 (75) sts.

ROW 106 (108): Work in patt to last 2 sts, m1, k1—74 (76) sts.

ROW 107 (109): K1, m1, work in patt to end—75 (77) sts.

ROWS 108 (110) THROUGH 113 (115): Work in patt.

ROW 114 (116): Bind off 15 sts, work in patt—60 (62) sts.

ROW 115 (117): Bind off 15 sts, work in patt—45 (47) sts.

Continue working in patt, decreasing 1 st at beginning and end of next 5 rows—35 (37) sts.

Work in patt for 4 more rows.

ROWS 125 (127): Work in patt, decrease 1 st at beginning and end of next row—33 (35) sts

Work even in patt and repeating this decrease row in row 134 (136)—31 (33) sts.

Work in patt for 40 rows more.
Bind off.

BACK FINISHING
Pick up 40 (44) sts evenly along the bottom edge of the back and work in 1×1 rib for 16 rows. Bind off.

FRONT FINISHING
Sew Right Front Band to Right Front, connecting points A and B (see diagram at top right).
Sew Left Front Band to Left Front, connecting points C and D (see diagram at top right).
Sew side and Sleeve seams. Weave in loose ends.

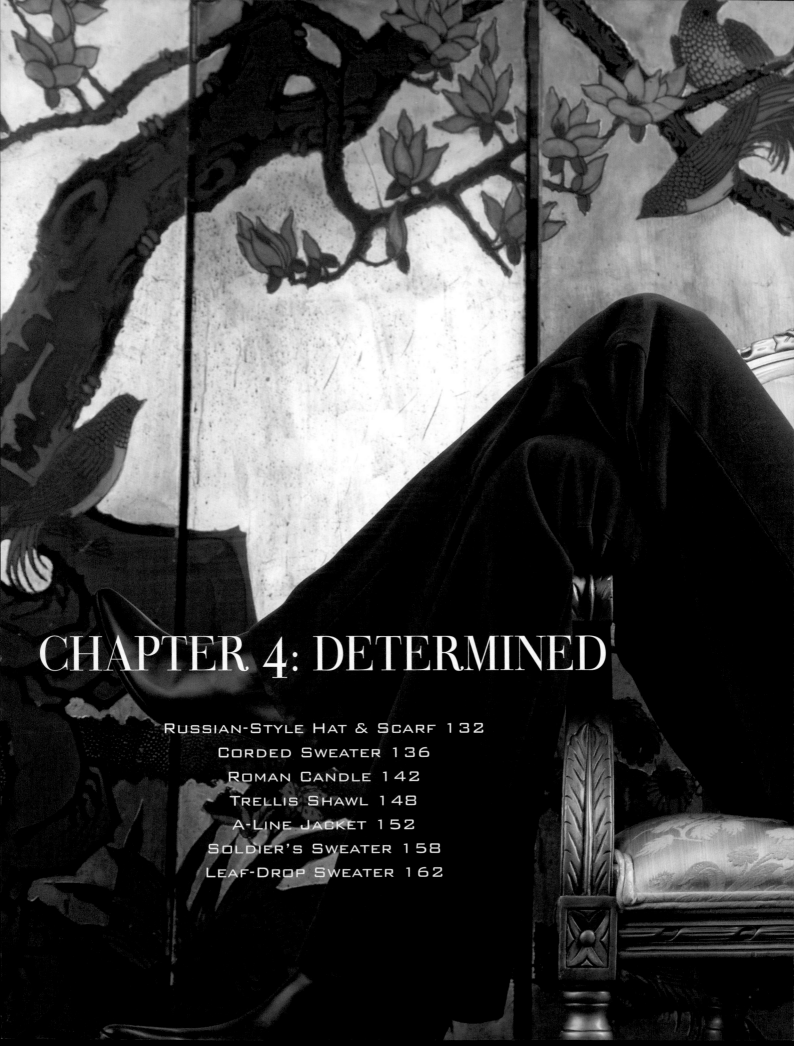

CHAPTER 4: DETERMINED

RUSSIAN-STYLE HAT & SCARF

Fashionable since the days of the czars, this Russian-style hat & petal-shaped scarf will keep you warm, even on the streets of Moscow. Knit in cashmere and trimmed with dark brown Karabella fur, the ensemble is perfect for those days when you simply refuse to sacrifice couture to the cold.

RUSSIAN-STYLE HAT & SCARF

SIZES

Hat: One size fits all.

Scarf: To fit S/M (L/XL). Directions are for the smaller size, with the larger size in parentheses. If there is only one set of figures, it applies to both sizes.

KNITTED MEASUREMENTS

Hat circumference: About 22" (56cm)

Scarf length: 35 (37)" [89 (94)cm]

Scarf width: 5" (12.5cm)

MATERIALS

Hat:

1 ball Karabella Supercashmere (100% cashmere; about 81 yds [75m] per 1¾ oz [50g] ball): color #75, Dark Brown

20 yds (19m) Karabella Fur (100% fur): color #4, Dark Brown

Scarf:

2 balls Karabella supercashmere, color #75 Dark Brown

9 yds (8m) Karabella Fur, color #4, Dark Brown

Size 10½ (6.5mm) needles, or size to obtain gauge

Size 9 (5.5mm) 16" [40cm] circular needle

Size 9 (5.5mm) double-pointed needles

Size 13 (9mm) 16" [40cm] circular needle

Size M/13 (9mm) crochet hook

Stitch marker

GAUGE

15 sts and 20 rows = 4" (10cm) over St st, using size 9 needles.

SCARF

With size 10½ needles, cast on 20 sts.

ROW 1 (RS): Sl 1, (k2, p2) 4 times, k3.

ROW 2 (WS): Sl 1, (p2, k2) 4 times, p2, k1.

Repeat rows 1 and 2 until there are 26 (32) rows total.

ROW 27 (33): Sl 1, k1, ssk, p1, (k2, p2) twice, k2, p1, k2tog, k2—18 sts.

ROWS 28 (34), 30 (36), 32 (38), 34 (40), 36 (42), AND 38 (44): Work sts as they appear (knit the knit sts, purl the purl sts).

ROW 29 (35): Sl 1, k1, ssk, (k2, p2) twice, k2, k2tog, k2—16 sts.

ROW 31 (37): Sl 1, k1, ssk, k1, p2, k2, p2, k1, k2tog, k2—14 sts.

ROW 33 (39): Sl 1, k1, ssk, p2, k2, p2, k2tog, k2—12 sts.

ROW 35 (41): Sl 1, k1, ssk, p1, k2, p1, k2tog, k2—10 sts.

ROW 37 (43): Sl 1, k1, ssk, k2, k2tog, k2—8 sts.

ROWS 39 (45) THROUGH 44 (50): Work even in St st.

ROW 45 (51): Sl 1, k2, m1, k2, m1, k3—10 sts.

ROW 46 (52): Sl 1, p2, k1, m1, p2, m1, k1, p3—12 sts.

ROW 47 (53): Sl 1, k2, p2, m1, k2, m1, p2, k3—14 sts.

ROW 48 (54): Sl 1, p2, k2, p1, m1, p2, m1, p1, k2, p3—16 sts.

ROW 49 (55): Sl 1, k2, p2, k2, m1, k2, m1, k2, p2, k3—18 sts.

ROW 50 (56): Sl 1, p2, k2, p2, k1, m1, p2, m1, k1, p2, k2, p3—20 sts

ROW 51 (57): Sl, k2, p2, k2, p2, m1, k2, m1, p2, k2, p2, k3—22 sts.

ROW 52 (58): Sl, p2, k2, p2, k2, p1, m1, p2, m1, p1, k2, p2, k2, p3—24 sts

ROW 53 (59): Sl 1, k1, ssk, p1, k2, p2, k2, m1, k2, m1, k2, p2, k2, p1, k2tog, k2—24 sts.

ROW 54 (60): Sl 1, p2, k1, p2, k2, p2, k1, p2, k1, p2, k2, p2, k1, p2, k1.

ROW 55 (61): Sl 1, k1, ssk, k2, p2, k2, p1, m1, k2, m1, p1, k2, p2, k2, k2tog, k2—24 sts.

ROW 56 (62): Sl 1, p4, (k2, p2) 3 times, k2, p4, k1.

ROW 57 (63): Sl 1, k1, ssk, k1, p2, k2, p2, m1, k2, m1, p2, k2, p2, k1, k2tog, k2—24 sts.

ROW 58 (64): Sl 1, p3, k2, p2, k2, p4, k2, p2, k2, p3, k1.

ROW 59 (65): Sl 1, k1, ssk, p2, k2, p2, k1, m1, k2, m1, k1, p2, k2, p2, k2tog, k2—24 sts.

ROW 60 (66): Sl 1, p2, k2, p2, k2, p6, k2, p2, k2, p2, k1.

ROW 61 (67): Sl 1, k1, ssk, p1, k2, p2, k2, m1, k2, m1, k2, p2, k2, p1, k2tog, k2—24 sts.

ROW 62 (68): Sl 1, p2, k1, p2, k2, p2, k1, p2, k1, p2, k2, p2, k1, p2, k1.

ROW 63 (69): Sl 1, k1, ssk, k2, p2, k2, p1, m1, k2, m1, p1, k2, p2, k2, k2tog, k2—24 sts.

ROW 64 (70): Sl 1, p4, (k2, p2) 3 times, k2, p4, k1.

ROW 65 (71): Sl 1, k1, ssk, k1, (p2, k2) 3 times, p2, k1, k2tog, k2—22 sts.

ROW 66 (72): Sl 1, p1, p2tog, (k2, p2) 3 times, k2, ssp, p1, k1—20 sts.

ROW 67 (73): Sl 1, k1, ssk, p1, (k2, p2) twice, k2, p1, k2tog, k2—18 sts.

ROW 68 (74): Sl 1, p1, p2tog, (p2, k2) twice, p2, ssp, p1, k1—16 sts.

ROW 69 (75): Sl 1, k1, ssk, k1, p2, k2, p2, k1, k2tog, k2—14 sts.

ROW 70 (76): Sl 1, p1, p2tog, k2, p2, k2, ssp, p1, k1—12 sts.

ROW 71 (77): Sl 1, k1, ssk, p1, k2, p1, k2tog, k2—10 sts.

ROW 72 (78): Sl 1, p1, p2tog, p2, ssp, p1, k1—8 sts.

ROW 73 (79): Sl 1, k1, ssk, k2tog, k2—6 sts.

ROW 74 (80): Sl 1, p2tog, ssp, k1—4 sts.

ROW 75 (81): Sl 1, ssk, k1—3 sts.

ROW 76 (82): P3tog. Fasten off.

Make 2 identical pieces and weave them together with kitchener stitch along the scarf Center Back (cast-on edges).

FUR FINISHING

With crochet hook and fur, work one row of single crochet around the edge of each leaf-shaped scarf end. Fasten fur ends. Weave in loose ends to WS.

HAT

With size 9 circular needle and cashmere, cast on 80 sts. Place marker and join sts in rnd (Note: Sl marker every rnd). Work 6 rnds in garter st (knit 1 rnd, purl 1 rnd).

NEXT RND: Change to fur and size 13 circular needle and k2tog around—40 sts.

Work in St st (knit each rnd) until all 20 yds of fur are used (about 8 rnds)—piece measures about 4½" (11cm) from CO edge.

NEXT RND: Change to cashmere and size 9 circular needle and (k1, m1) to end of rnd—80 sts.

CROWN SHAPING

Note: Change to double-pointed needles, when necessary. Work in St st for 1" (2.5cm).

NEXT RND: (K2tog, k14) 5 times—75 sts.

NEXT RND: (K2tog, k13) 5 times—70 sts.

NEXT RND: (K2tog, k12) 5 times—65 sts.

NEXT RND: (K2tog, k11) 5 times—60 sts.

Continue in this manner, making 5 decreases in each rnd, until there are 10 sts total.

NEXT RND: K2tog around—5 sts.

Cut yarn and draw yarn through remaining 5 sts and pull sts together to close top of hat.

Weave in loose ends to WS.

CORDED SWEATER

COMFORTABLE BUT SLEEK, THIS DRESSY SWEATER DERIVES ITS CHIC VERTICAL LINES FROM AN I-CORDLESS CORDING TECHNIQUE. THE NEUTRAL COLOR MAKES THIS SWEATER A PERFECT MATCH FOR ANYTHING IN YOUR WARDROBE.

CORDED SWEATER

SIZES

To fit XS (S, M, L, XL). Directions are for the smallest size, with the larger sizes in parentheses. If there is only one set of figures, it applies to all sizes.

KNITTED MEASUREMENTS

Bust: 32 (35, 38, 41, 44)" [81 (89, 96.5, 104, 112)cm]

Length: 21 (21½, 22, 22½, 23)" [53 (54.5, 56, 57, 58.5)cm]

Upper arm: 11 (12, 13, 14, 15)" [28 (30.5, 33, 35.5, 38)cm]

MATERIALS

10 (11, 12, 14, 15) balls Karabella Margrite Bulky (80% extra fine merino wool, 20% cashmere; about 77 yds [70m] per 1¾ oz [50g] ball): color #16, Putty

Size 10½ (6.5mm) needles, or size to obtain gauge

Size 10 (6mm) 16" [40cm] circular needle

Size 7 (4.5mm) 16" [40cm] circular needle

Cable needles

Stitch markers

Stitch holders

GAUGE

14 sts and 21 rows = 4" (10cm) over St st, using size 10½ needles.

3-STITCH SLANTED RIGHT CROSSING (3SLR)

Sl 2 sts on CN and hold to back, k1 from LH needle, k2 from CN.

3-STITCH SLANTED RIGHT CROSSING WITH DECREASE (3SLRD)

Sl 2 sts on CN and hold to back, k1 from LH needle, k2tog from CN.

3-STITCH SLANTED RIGHT CROSSING WITH INCREASE (3SLRI)

Sl 2 sts on CN and hold to back, k1 from LH needle, m1, k2 from CN.

3-STITCH SLANTED RIGHT CROSSING WITH DECREASE ON WS (3SLRPD)

Sl 1 st on CN and hold to back, p2tog from LH needle, p1 from CN.

3-STITCH SLANTED LEFT CROSSING (3SLL)

Sl 1 st on CN and hold to front, k2 from LH needle, k1 from CN.

3-STITCH SLANTED LEFT CROSSING WITH DECREASE (3SLLD)

Sl 1 st on CN and hold to front, ssk from LH needle, k1 from CN.

3-STITCH SLANTED LEFT CROSSING WITH INCREASE (3SLLI)

Sl 1 st on CN and hold to front, k2 from LH needle, m1, k1 from CN.

3-STITCH SLANTED LEFT CROSSING WITH DECREASE ON WS (3SLLPD)

Sl 2 sts on CN and hold to front, p1 from LH needle, p2tog from CN.

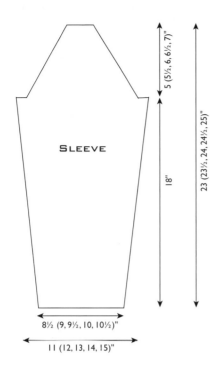

SLEEVE

5 (5½, 6, 6½, 7)"

18"

23 (23½, 24, 24½, 25)"

8½ (9, 9½, 10, 10½)"

11 (12, 13, 14, 15)"

4"

1"

FRONT & BACK

6½ (7, 7½, 8, 8½)"

13½"

21 (21½, 22, 22½, 23)"

14¾ (16¼, 17¾, 19¼, 20¾)"

16 (17½, 19, 20½, 22)"

4-STITCH CORD CROSSING (4CC)

Sl 3 sts on CN and hold to front, k1 from LH needle, return 2 sts from CN back to LH needle, leave last st on CN hold to back, k2 from LH needle, k1 from CN.

BACK

With size 10½ needles, cast on 65 (70, 75, 80, 85) sts.

ROW 1 (RS): K15 (17, 19, 21, 23), place marker, 4CC, k27 (28, 29, 30, 31), place marker, 4CC, k15 (17, 19, 21, 23).

Note: Sl markers in every row.

ROW 2 AND ALL WS ROWS: Purl.

ROWS 3, 7, AND 11: Knit to 1st marker, sl marker, 4CC, knit to 2nd marker, sl marker, 4CC, knit to end.

ROW 5: Knit to 3 sts before 1st marker, 3SLR, sl marker, 4CC, 3SLL, knit to 3 sts before 2nd marker, 3SLR, sl marker, 4CC, 3SLL, knit to end.

ROW 9: Knit to 3 sts before 1st marker, 3SLRD, sl marker, 4CC, 3SLLD, knit to 3 sts before 2nd marker, 3SLRD, sl marker, 4CC, 3SLLD, knit to end—61 (66, 71, 76, 81) sts.

ROW 12: Repeat row 2.

Next 16 rows: Repeat rows 5-12 twice more—53 (58, 63, 68, 73) sts.

ROWS 29 AND 33: Work as row 5.

ROWS 31 AND 35: Work as row 3.

ROW 37: Knit to 3 sts before 1st marker, 3SLRI, sl marker, 4CC, 3SLLI, knit to 3 sts before 2nd marker, 3SLRI, sl marker, 4CC, 3SLLI, knit to end—57 (62, 67, 72, 77) sts.

ROWS 39, 43, AND 47: Work same as row 3.

ROWS 41 AND 45: Work same as row 5.

Next 24 rows: Repeat rows 37-48 twice more—65 (70, 75, 80, 85) sts.

ROW 73: Work same as row 37—69 (74, 79, 84, 89) sts.

ROW 75: Work same as row 3.

ARMHOLE SHAPING

ROW 77: Bind off 3 (3, 3, 4, 4) sts, then work same as row 5—66 (71, 76, 80, 85) sts.

ROW 78 (WS): Bind off 3 (3, 3, 4, 4) sts, purl to end—63 (68, 73, 76, 81) sts.

All WS rows: Purl.

ROW 79: K2, ssk, knit to 1st marker, sl marker, 4CC, knit to 2nd marker, sl marker, 4CC, knit to last 4 sts, k2tog, k2—61 (66, 71, 74, 79) sts.

ROW 81: K2, ssk, knit to 3 sts before 1st marker, 3SLR, sl marker, 4CC, 3SLL, knit to 3 sts before 2nd marker, 3SLR, sl marker, 4CC, 3SLL, knit to last 4 sts, k2tog, k2—59 (64, 69, 72, 77) sts.

Repeat rows 79-82 1(1, 2, 2, 2) times more—55 (60, 61, 64, 69) sts.

NEXT RS ROW: Knit to marker, sl to 1st marker, 4CC,
knit to 2nd marker, sl marker, 4CC, knit to end.
NEXT WS ROW: Purl.
NEXT RS ROW: Knit to 3 sts before 1st marker, 3SLR, sl
marker, 4CC, 3SLL, knit to 3 sts before 2nd marker, 3SLR, sl
marker, 4CC, 3SLL, knit to end.
Repeat last 4 rows until Armhole measures $6\frac{1}{2}$ ($7\frac{1}{2}$, 8)"
[16.5 (19, 20)cm], start Shoulder shaping.

FOR SIZES SMALL/X-LARGE ONLY:
NEXT RS ROW: Work same as row 79—(58 [67] sts).
NEXT WS ROW: Purl.
NEXT RS ROW: Knit to 3 sts before 1st marker, 3SLR, sl
marker, 4CC, 3SLL, knit to 3 sts before 2nd marker, 3SLR, sl
marker, 4CC, 3SLL, knit to end.
NEXT WS ROW: Purl.
NEXT RS ROW: Knit to 1st marker, sl marker, 4CC, knit to
2nd marker, sl marker, 4CC, knit to end.
NEXT WS ROW: Purl.
Repeat last 4 rows until Armhole measures 7 ($8\frac{1}{2}$)" [18
(21.5)cm]. Start Shoulder shaping.

SHOULDER SHAPING
Bind off 6 (7, 7, 7, 8) sts at beg of next 2 rows, continue
as established.
Bind off 6 (6, 7, 7, 7) sts at beg of next 2 rows, continue
as established.
Bind off 6 (6, 6, 7, 7) sts at beg of next 2 rows, continue
as established.
Place remaining 19 (20, 21, 22, 23) sts on stitch holder for
Back Neck.

FRONT
Work as for Back until Armhole measures 5 ($5\frac{1}{2}$, 6, $6\frac{1}{2}$, 7)"
[12.5 (14, 15, 16.5, 18)cm]—55 (58, 61, 64, 67) sts remain.
NEXT RS ROW: Work 21 (22, 23, 24, 25) sts as established, k2tog, k1, place next 7 (8, 9, 10, 11) sts on stitch
holder for front, join second ball of yarn and work the other
side as follows: k1, ssk, work 21 (22, 23, 24, 25) sts as established to end—23 (24, 25, 26, 27) sts remain each side.
Work both sides at once.
Repeat this Neck edge decrease in every other row 5 times
more—18 (19, 20, 21, 22) sts on each side.

AT THE SAME TIME, when Armhole measures 6½ (7, 7½, 8, 8½)" [15 (16.5, 18, 20, 21.5)cm] shape Shoulders same as for Back, working the first BO row at Armhole edge of one Shoulder, and the second BO row at the Armhole edge of the other Shoulder.

NECK

Sew Shoulder seams.

With size 10 circular needle and RS facing, knit across 19 (20, 21, 22, 23) sts from Back Neck holder, pick up and knit 14 sts from Left Neck side, knit across 7 (8, 9, 10, 11) sts from front Neck holder, pick up and knit 14 sts from Right Neck side—54 (56, 58, 60, 62) sts. Join in rnd and work in St st (knit every row) for 4" (10cm).

Change to size 7 circular needle and purl next 2 rnds.

Bind off loosely.

SLEEVES

With size 10½ needles, cast on 33 (34, 35, 36, 37) sts.

Work in St st.

Increase 1 st at beginning and end of the following rows:

FOR SIZE X-SMALL ONLY:

Rows 31, 57, and 83—(39 sts).

FOR SIZE SMALL ONLY:

Rows 21, 41, 61, and 81—(42 sts).

FOR SIZE MEDIUM ONLY:

Rows 11, 27, 43, 59, and 75—(45 sts).

FOR SIZE LARGE ONLY:

Rows 11, 25, 39, 53, 67, and 81—(48 sts).

FOR SIZE X-LARGE ONLY:

Rows 11, 23, 35, 47, 59, 71, and 83—(51 sts).

Continue even in St st until piece measures 18" (46cm).

CAP SHAPING

Bind off 3 (3, 3, 4, 4) sts at the beginning of next 2 rows—33 (36, 39, 40, 43) sts.

ROW 3 (RS): K2, 3SLRD, knit to last 5 sts, 3SLLD, k2—31 (34, 37, 38, 41) sts.

Continuing in St st, repeat this decrease row in the following rows:

FOR SIZE X-SMALL ONLY:

Rows 7, 11, 15, and 19—(23 sts).

FOR SIZES SMALL AND MEDIUM ONLY:

Rows 7, 11, 15, 19, and 23—(24, 27 sts).

FOR SIZE LARGE ONLY:

Rows 7, 11, 15, 19, 23, and 27—(26 sts).

FOR SIZE X-LARGE ONLY:

Rows 7, 11, 15, 19, 23, 27, and 31—(27 sts).

ROWS 20, 22, AND 24: P2, 3SLLPD, purl to last 5 sts, 3SLRPD, p2.

ROWS 21, 23, AND 25: Repeat row 3—(11 sts).

FOR SIZE SMALL ONLY:

ROWS 24, 26, AND 28: P2, 3SLLPD, purl to last 5 sts, 3SLRPD, p2.

ROWS 25, 27, AND 29: Repeat row 3—(12 sts).

FOR SIZE MEDIUM ONLY:

ROWS 24, 26, 28, AND 30: P2, 3SLLPD, purl to last 5 sts, 3SLRPD, p2—(13 sts after row 30).

ROWS 25, 27, AND 29: Repeat row 3.

FOR SIZE LARGE ONLY:

ROWS 28, 30, AND 32: P2, 3SLLPD, purl to last 5 sts, 3SLRPD, p2.

ROWS 29, 31, AND 33: Repeat row 3—(14 sts).

FOR SIZE X-LARGE ONLY:

ROWS 32, 34, AND 36: P2, 3SLLPD, purl to last 5 sts, 3SLRPD, p2.

ROWS 33, 35, AND 37: Repeat row 3—(15 sts).

FOR ALL SIZES:

Bind off 11 (12, 13, 14, 15) sts

FINISHING

Sew Sleeves into the Armholes. Sew side and Sleeve seams. Weave in loose ends to WS.

ROMAN CANDLE

This basketweave sweater has a wonderful texture that stands out against the red of the yarn. Like its firework namesake, this supersoft turtleneck will attract lots of attention while you bask in the comfort and elegance of cashmere.

ROMAN CANDLE

SIZES
To fit S (M, L, XL). Directions are for the smallest size, with larger sizes in parentheses. If there is only one set of figures, it applies to all sizes.

KNITTED MEASUREMENTS
Bust: 33 (36, 39, 42)" [84 (91.5, 99, 106.5)cm]

Length: 22 (22½, 23, 23½)" [56 (57, 58.5, 59.5)cm]

Upper arm: 11 (12, 13, 14)" [28 (30.5, 33, 35.5)cm]

MATERIALS
6 (7, 7, 8) balls Karabella Boise (50% cashmere, 50% merino wool; about 163 yds [150m] per 1¾ oz [50g] ball): color #63, Burgundy

Size 8 (5mm) needles, or size to obtain gauge

Size 3 (3.25mm) needles

Size 4 (3.5mm) 16" [40cm] circular needle

Cable needle

Stitch holders

Stitch markers

GAUGE
32 sts and 24 rows = 4" (10cm) in Basket patt, using size 8 needles.

BASKET PATTERN 1
(OVER 6 STS +5)
ROW 1 (RS): K4, *sl 3 sts to CN and hold to front, k3, k3 from CN*; repeat from * to * to last st, k1.

ROW 2 AND ALL WS ROWS: Purl.

ROWS 3 AND 7: Knit.

ROW 5: K1, *sl 3 sts to CN and hold to back, k3, k3 from CN*; repeat from * to * to last 4 sts, k4.

ROW 8: Purl.

Repeat these 8 rows for patt.

BASKET PATTERN 2
(OVER 6 STS +5)
ROW 1 (RS): K1, *sl 3 sts to CN and hold to front, k3, k3 from CN*; repeat from * to * to last 4 sts, k4.

ROW 2 AND ALL WS ROWS: Purl.

ROWS 3 AND 7: Knit.

ROW 5: K4, *sl 3 sts to CN and hold to back, k3, k3 from CN*; repeat from * to * to last st, k1.

ROW 8: Purl

Repeat these 8 rows for patt.

BACK
With size 3 needles, cast on 102 (114, 126, 138) sts and work in 2x2 (k2, p2) rib as follows:

ROW 1: (RS) *K2, p2*; repeat from * to * to last 2 sts, k2.

ROW 2 (WS): P2, *k2, p2*; repeat from * to * to end of row.

Continue in rib for 6" (15cm), ending with WS row.

Change to size 8 needles and increase 29 sts evenly spaced as follows:

NEXT RS ROW FOR SIZE SMALL ONLY: K3, m1, *k3, m1, k4, m1*; repeat from * to * to last st, k1—131 sts.

NEXT RS ROW FOR SIZE MEDIUM ONLY: K1, m1, *k4, m1*; repeat from * to * to last st, k1—143 sts.

NEXT RS ROW FOR SIZE LARGE ONLY: (K5, m1) twice, *k4, m1*; repeat from * to * to last 16 sts, k5, m1, k6, m1, k5—155 sts.

NEXT RS ROW FOR SIZE X-LARGE ONLY: K6, m1, *k5, m1, k4, m1*; repeat from * to * to last 6 sts, k6—167 sts.

NEXT WS ROW (ALL SIZES): Purl.

Work in basket patt 1 for approx 7½" (19cm), ending with WS row (row 4 of patt).

ARMHOLE SHAPING
Bind off 6 sts at beginning of next 2 rows, continue in patt 1—119 (131, 143, 155) sts.

Bind off 3 sts at beginning of next 4 rows, continue in established patt—107 (119, 131, 143) sts.

Work even in Basket patt 1 until Armhole measures about 7½ (8, 8½, 9)" [19 (20, 31.5, 23)cm] from first bind off row, ending with WS row (row 4 of patt).

SHOULDER SHAPING

Bind off 11 (13, 14, 16) at beginning of next 4 rows, continue in established patt—63 (67, 75, 79) sts.
Bind off 10 (12, 13, 15) at beginning of next 2 rows, continue in patt—43 (43, 49, 49) sts.
Place remaining 43 (43, 49, 49) sts to stitch holder for Back Neck.

FRONT

Work as for Back until Armhole measures about 6½ (7, 7½, 8)" [16.5 (18, 19, 20)cm], ending with WS row (row 4 of patt)—107 (119, 131, 143) sts.

NECK SHAPING

ROW 1 (RS): K1, work row 5 of patt from * to * for 36 (42, 48, 54) sts, k4 (4, 1, 1), place next 25 (25, 31, 31) sts to stitch holder for Front Neck, join second ball of yarn and continue the other side as follows: k1 (1, 4, 4), work row 5 of patt from * to * for 36 (42, 42, 48) sts, to last 4 sts, k4. Continue working both sides at the same time.
ROWS 2, 4, AND 6 (WS): Purl to Neck edge; other side of Neck: bind off 3 sts, purl to end.
ROW 3 (RS): Knit to Neck edge; other side of Neck: bind off 3 sts, knit to end.
ROW 5: K4, work row 1 of patt from * to * to last 1 (1, 4, 4) sts, k1 (1, 4, 4); other side of Neck: bind off 3 sts, k4 (1, 4, 1) sts, work row 1 of patt from * to * to last 1 st, k1,
ROW 7: Work same as row 3.
Shape Shoulders as for back, BO stitches at beginning of Armhole sides only.

TURTLENECK

Sew Shoulder seams.
With RS facing and circular needle work in K2, p2 rib across 43 (43, 49, 49) sts from Back Neck holder, continuing in 2 x 2 rib pick up 16 sts along Neck side edge, work across 25 (25, 31, 31) sts from Front Neck holder, pick up 16 sts along other side of the Neck edge—100 (100, 112, 112) sts. Join in round and work for 5" (12.5cm) in rib. Bind off tightly.

SLEEVES

With size 3 needles, cast on 62 (66, 70, 74) sts and work in 2 × 2 rib (work same as lower body rib—Rows 1 and 2) for 8" (20cm), ending with WS row. In the next row change to size 8 needles and increase 21 (23, 25, 27) sts evenly spaced as follows:
NEXT RS ROW FOR SIZE SMALL: (K2, m1, k3, m1) 4 times, (k5, m1) 3 times, (k2, m1, k3, m1) 5 times, k2—83sts.
NEXT RS ROW FOR SIZE MEDIUM: (K3, m1, k2, m1) 5 times, (k5, m1) 2 times, (k3, m1, k2, m1) 5 times, k3, m1, k3—89 sts.
NEXT RS ROW FOR SIZE LARGE: (K3, m1, k2, m1) 5 times, (k5, m1) 2 times, (k3, m1, k2, m1) 6 times, k3, m1, k2—95 sts.
NEXT RS ROW FOR SIZE X-LARGE: (K3, m1, k2, m1) 6 times, (k5, m1) 2 times, (k3, m1, k2, m1) 6 times, k3, m1, k1—101sts.
NEXT WS ROW: Purl.
Start basket patt 1 and work 14 rows ending on WS row.
NEXT RS ROW (INCREASES): k1, m1, place marker, knit to last st, place marker, m1, k1—85 (91, 97, 103) sts.
Move markers in every row.
Repeat this increase row every 16th row (row 7 of basket patt 1) 2 times more—89 (95, 101, 107) sts.
Remove markers in the next WS row.
NEXT RS ROW: Start working basket patt 2 beginning with row 1.
Work in basket patt 2 until piece measures about 18" (46cm) from CO edge, ending with WS row (row 8 of patt).

CAP SHAPING

Bind off 6 sts at beginning of next 2 rows, continue in basket patt 2—77 (83, 89, 95) sts.
Bind off 3 sts at beginning of next 4 rows, continue in basket patt 2—65 (71, 77, 83) sts.
Work even as established until cap measures about 4½ (5, 5½, 6)" [11 (12.5, 14, 15)cm], ending with WS row.
Bind off 3 sts at beginning of next 8 rows, work the remaining sts in patt—41 (47, 53, 59) sts.
Bind off remaining sts.

FINISHING

Sew side and Sleeve seams. Weave in loose ends to WS of work.

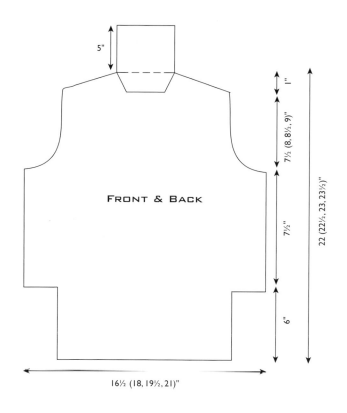

FRONT & BACK

5"

1"

7½ (8, 8½, 9)"

7½"

6"

22 (22½, 23, 23½)"

16½ (18, 19½, 21)"

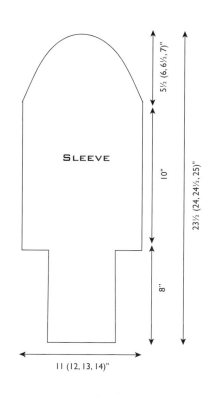

SLEEVE

5½ (6, 6½, 7)"

10"

8"

23½ (24, 24½, 25)"

11 (12, 13, 14)"

TRELLIS SHAWL

Flattering and oh-so-hip, this cozy shawl with sleeves always gets rave reviews. What's more, the lace pattern is very simple to make, and the blend of wool, cashmere, and mohair yarns creates a lightweight yet very warm covering.

TRELLIS SHAWL

SIZES
To fit S/M (L/XL). Directions are for the smaller size, with the larger size in parentheses. If there is only one set of figures, it applies to all sizes.

KNITTED MEASUREMENTS
Length: 20" (51cm)

Width: 70 (75)" [178 (191)cm]

MATERIALS
5 (6) balls Karabella Margrite (80% extra fine merino wool, 20% cashmere; 154 yds [140m] per 1¾ oz [50g] ball): color #4, Grey

3 (4) balls Karabella Mirage (72% kid mohair, 28% polyamide; 245 yds [225m] per 1¾ oz [50g] ball): color #50211, Beige

Size 8 (5mm) needles, or size to obtain gauge

Stitch markers

GAUGE
12½ sts and 22 rows = 4" (10cm) over trellis patt, using size 8 needles, and two strands held together (1 strand of each yarn).

VERTICAL LACE TRELLIS (ODD NUMBER OF STS)
ROW 1: (RS) Sl 1, k1, *yo, k2tog*; repeat from * to * to last st, k1.

ROWS 2 AND 4: Sl 1, purl to end.

ROW 3: Sl 1, *ssk, yo*; repeat from * to * to last 2 sts, k2. Repeat these 4 rows for patt.

BODY
With 1 strand of each yarn held together, cast on 63 sts and work in trellis patt for 70 (75)" [178 (191)cm]. Bind off.

SLEEVE
With 1 strand of each yarn held together, cast on 51 sts and work in trellis patt for 7" (18cm). Bind off.

FINISHING
With WS facing, fold both ends of the Body to the center. Sew Sleeves to each end of folded Body as shown on schematic (above right). Leave the rest of the Body unsewn. Sew Sleeve seams together.

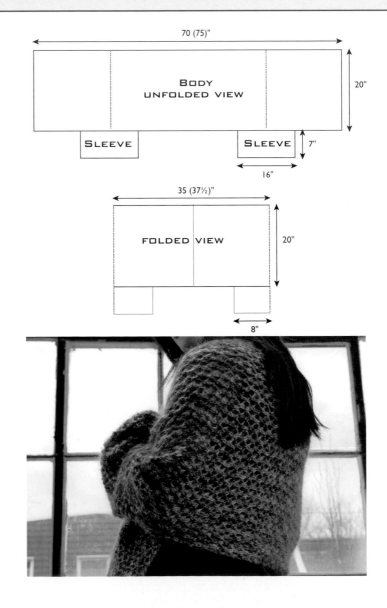

A-LINE JACKET

This quick-to-knit tweed jacket complements nearly every figure. With its
cropped sleeves, high collar, and over-
sized three-inch diameter buttons, it is
the perfect way take your work wardrobe
retro while still maintaining a profes-
sional look.

A-LINE JACKET

SIZES
To fit S (M, L, XL). Directions are for the smallest size, with larger sizes in parentheses. If there is only one set of figures, it applies to all sizes.

KNITTED MEASUREMENTS
Bust: 34 (38, 42, 46)" [86 (96.5, 106.5, 117)cm]

Length: 23½ (24, 24½, 25)" [60 (61, 62, 63.5)cm]

Upper arm: 15 (16, 17, 18)" [38 (40.5, 43, 46)cm]

MATERIALS
8 (9, 9, 10) balls Karabella Puffy multicolor (100% merino wool; about 54 yds [50m] per

3½ oz [100g] ball): color #7372, Black/Grey

Size 13 (9mm) needles, or size to obtain gauge

Size 13 (9mm) 16" (40cm) circular needle

Stitch markers

Stitch holders

Three 3" (7.5cm) diameter black buttons

GAUGE
8 sts and 13 rows = 4" (10cm) over St st, using size 13 needles.

FORMING THE BUTTONHOLE
RS ROW: Sl 1, p1, k3, bind off 2, continue as established to end.
WS ROW: Work sts as they appear to last 5 sts, cast on 2 sts, p3, k1, p1.

BODY
Note: Work this jacket as one piece up to Armhole shaping. With size 13 needles, cast on 98 (106, 114, 122) sts.
ROW 1 (RS): Sl 1, p1, k24 (26, 28, 30), place marker, k45 (49, 53, 57) sts, place marker, k25 (27, 29, 31), p1, k1.
Note: Sl markers every row.
ROW 2: Sl 1, purl to end.
ROWS 3–6: Work even in St st, slipping the first st in each row.
ROW 7 (RS) DECREASES: Sl 1, p1, (knit to 2 sts before marker, ssk, k1, k2tog) twice, knit to last 2 sts, p1, k1—94 (102, 110, 118) sts.
Continue working as established, repeat decreases between markers in rows 15, 23, 31, and 39—78 (86, 94, 102) sts.
Note: Remove both markers in row 39.
FORM THE 1ST BUTTONHOLE: For sizes Small and Large in Rows 17 and 18; for sizes Medium and X-Large in Rows 19 and 20.

FORM THE 2ND BUTTONHOLE: For size Small in Rows 37 and 38; for sizes Medium and Large in Rows 39 and 40 (please note that Row 39 is also a decrease row); for size X-Large in Rows 41 and 42.
ROW 43 (RS): Sl 1, p1, k20 (22, 24, 26) and place these 22 (24, 26, 28) sts on stitch holder for right front; bind off 2 sts, with 1 st on right needle from BO, knit the next 31 (35, 39, 43) for back, place next 22 (24, 26, 28) sts on stitch holder for Left Front. Turn work and continue working back piece on 32 (36, 40, 44) sts as follows:

BACK
ROW 44 (WS): Bind off 2 sts, purl to end—30 (34, 38, 42) sts. Continue working in St st.
ROW 47 (DECREASES): K2, ssk, knit to last 4 sts, k2tog, k2—28 (32, 36, 40) sts.
Repeat this decrease row every other RS row 5 (4, 4, 3) times more, and after that every RS row 4 (7, 8, 11) times more—10 (10, 12, 12) sts.
NEXT WS ROW: Purl.
Place remaining 10 (10, 12, 12) sts on st holder for Back Neck.

LEFT FRONT

ROW 43 (RS): Sl 22 Left Front stitches from stitch holder onto needle. Join a ball of yarn, bind off 2 sts, knit to last 2 sts, p1, k1—20 (22, 24, 26) sts.

ROW 44 AND ALL WS ROWS (UNTIL SPECIAL INSTRUCTIONS): Sl 1, k1, purl to end.

ROW 45 (RS) DECREASES: K2, k2tog, knit to last 2 sts, p1, k1—19 (21, 23, 25) sts.

Continue work as established repeating this decrease every other RS row 4 (3, 3, 2) times—15 (18, 20, 23) sts, and after that every RS row 0 (3, 4, 7) times more, ending with RS row 61 (63, 65, 67)—15 (15, 16, 16) sts remain.

NEXT WS ROW: Bind off 4 (4, 5, 5) sts, purl to end—11 sts.

NEXT RS ROW: K2, k2tog, knit to last 3 sts, ssk, k1—9 sts.

Next and all WS rows: Purl.

NEXT RS ROW: K2, k2tog, knit to last 3 sts, ssk, k1—7 sts.

NEXT RS ROW: K2, k2tog, ssk, k1—5 sts.

NEXT RS ROW: K2, k2tog, k1—4 sts.

NEXT RS ROW: K1, k2tog, k1—3 sts.

NEXT RS ROW: K3tog, cut yarn, and pull through remaining st to close.

RIGHT FRONT

Note: As you continue working Right Front instructions, make the 3rd buttonhole in the following rows: for size Small in Rows 57 and 58; for size Medium in Rows 59 and 60; for size Large in Rows 61 and 6; for size X-Large in Rows 63 and 64.

ROW 44 (WS): Sl 22 right front stitches from stitch holder onto needle. Join a ball of yarn, bind off 2 sts, purl to last 2 sts, k1, p1—20 (22, 24, 26) sts.

The rest of WS rows (until special instructions): Purl to last 2 sts, k1, p1.

ROW 45 (RS) DECREASES: Sl 1, p1, knit to last 4 sts, ssk, k2—19 (21, 23, 25) sts.

Continue work as established, repeat this decrease every other RS row 4 (3, 3, 2) times—15 (18, 20, 23) sts, and after that every RS row 0 (3, 4, 7) times more, ending with RS row 61 (63, 65, 67)—15 (15, 16, 16) sts.

NEXT WS ROW: Purl to last 2 sts, k1, p1.

NEXT RS ROW: Bind off 5 (5, 6, 6) sts, knit to last 4 sts, ssk, k2—9 sts.

NEXT AND ALL WS ROWS: Purl.

NEXT RS ROW: K1, k2tog, knit to last 4 sts, ssk, k2—7 sts.

NEXT RS ROW: K1, k2tog, ssk, k2—5 sts

NEXT RS ROW: K1, ssk, k2—4 sts

NEXT RS ROW: K1, ssk, k1—3 sts.

NEXT RS ROW: K3tog, cut yarn pull the yarn through to secure the st.

SLEEVES

With size 13 circular needle, cast on 34 (36, 38, 40) sts, place end of rnd marker, join in rnd.

RND 1: K16 (17, 18, 19), place marker, knit to end of rnd, sl marker.

RND 2: Knit to marker, sl marker, knit to end, sl marker. Repeat rnd 2 until there are 20 rnds total.

RND 21: Knit to 2 sts before marker, k2tog, sl marker, k2, ssk, knit to end, sl marker—32 (34, 36, 38) sts. Repeat rnd 2 until there are 34 rnds total.

RND 35: Repeat rnd 21—30 (32, 34, 36) sts. Repeat rnd 2 until there are 45 rnds total, remove end of rnd marker (leave the second marker in place).

Cap Shaping

Starting with row 46, work back and forth in rows as follows:

ROW 46 (WS): Bind off 2 sts, purl to marker, sl marker, purl to end—28 (30, 32, 34) sts.

ROW 47 (RS): Bind off 2 sts, knit to marker, move marker, knit to end—26 (28, 30, 32) sts.

ROW 48 AND ALL WS ROWS: Purl to marker, sl marker, purl to end.

ROW 49: K2, ssk, knit to marker, sl marker, knit to last 4 sts, k2tog, k2—24 (26, 28, 30) sts.

ROW 51: Knit to marker, sl marker, knit to end.

ROW 52: Purl to marker, sl marker, purl to end.

Next 12 rows: Repeat rows 49 to 52—18 (20, 22, 24) sts.

ROW 65: Same as row 49—16 (18, 20, 22) sts.

ROW 67: Knit to 2 sts before marker, k2tog, k2, ssk, knit to end—14 (16, 18, 20) sts.

NEXT 6 (8, 10, 12) ROWS: Repeat rows 67 and 68—8 sts.

NEXT RS ROW: Same as row 67—6 sts rem.

Right Sleeve (short rows)

NEXT WS ROW: P4, wrap next st, turn.

NEXT RS ROW: K4.

NEXT WS ROW: P2, wrap next st, turn.
NEXT RS ROW: K2.
Place all sts (6 sts including the 2 wraps) to stitch holder for
Right Sleeve.

LEFT SLEEVE
NEXT WS ROW: Purl to end.
NEXT RS ROW: K4, wrap next st, turn.
NEXT WS ROW: P4.
NEXT RS ROW: K2, wrap next st, turn.
NEXT WS: P2.
Place all sts (6 sts including the 2 wraps) to stitch holder for
Left Sleeve.

COLLAR
Sew Sleeves into Armholes.
With size 13 circular needle and RS facing, pick up 7 sts from
Right Front, starting at 2½ (2½, 3, 3)" [6 (6, 7.5, 7.5)cm]
from Right Center Front edge, knit all sts from Right Sleeve
stitch holder (knit the knit and wrap sts together), knit 10 (10,
12, 12) sts from Back Neck stitch holder, knit all sts from Left
Sleeve holder (knit the knit and wrap sts together), pick up 7
sts from Left Front, ending at 2½ (2½, 3, 3)" [6 (6, 7.5,
7.5)cm] before the Left Center Front edge—34 (34, 36, 36) sts.
NEXT WS ROW: Sl 1, k1, purl to last 2 sts, k1, p1.
NEXT RS ROW: Sl 1, p1, knit to last 2 sts, p1, k1.
Purl 1 row on RS side.
NEXT WS ROW: Sl 1, k1, purl to last 2 sts, k1, p1.
NEXT RS ROW: Sl 1, p1, knit to last 2 sts, p1, k1.
Next 7 rows: Repeat last 2 rows, ending with WS row.
Bind off loosely.

FINISHING
Fold the collar to WS and sew the bind-off row of the Collar to
the Neck edge of the jacket. Sew on buttons. Weave in loose
ends to WS.

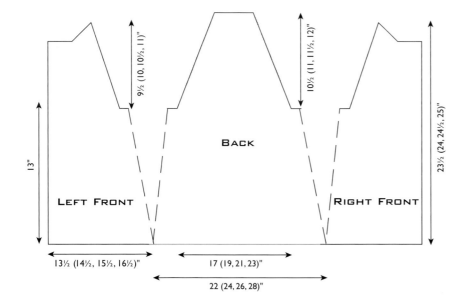

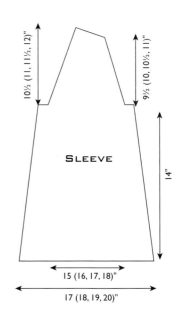

SOLDIER'S SWEATER

This charming sweater is sure to bring the troops to attention. A curved cutout below the button band brings out the sweater's girlish charm. The full-fashioned decrease technique used in this piece makes decreases visible, creating a flowing feeling to this figure-hugging sweater that will make them stand up and salute.

SOLDIER'S SWEATER

SIZES
To fit S (M, L, XL). Directions given are for the smallest size, with larger sizes in parentheses. If there is only one figure specified, it applies to all sizes.

KNITTED MEASUREMENTS
Bust: 33 (36, 39, 42)" [84 (91.5, 99, 106.5)cm]

Length: 18½ (19, 19½, 20)" [47 (48, 49.5, 51)cm]

Upper arm: 10½ (11¼, 12, 12¾)" [26.5 (28.5, 30.5, 32)cm]

MATERIALS
11 (12, 13, 14) balls Karabella Aurora 8 (100% extra fine merino wool; about 98 yds [90m] per 1¾ oz [50g] ball): color #276, Pale Green

Size 7 (4.5mm) needles

Size 6 (4mm) 40" [100cm] circular needles

Six 1" (2.5cm) diameter buttons

GAUGE
21 sts and 25 rows = 4" (10cm) over rib k1, p1 (slightly stretched) using size 7 needles.

RFFD (RIGHT FULL-FASHIONED DECREASE)
Sl next st knitwise to RH needle, sl next st purlwise to RH needle, knit both sts together (same as ssk), sl the resulting st back onto LH needle and k2tog (with the next stitch on LH needle).

LFFD (LEFT FULL-FASHIONED DECREASE)
Sl 1 st knitwise to RH needle, knit together the next 2 sts from left needle, then pass the slipped st over the resulting st from the k2tog.

BACK
With smaller needle, cast on 82 (90, 98, 106) sts.
ROW 1 (RS): *K2, p2*; repeat from * to * to end of row, k2.
ROW 2 (WS): *P2, k2*; repeat from * to * to end of row, p2.
Repeat these 2 rows until piece measures 2" (5cm) from CO (about 12 rows). Change to larger needle. On next row make a decrease at the end to balance patt as follows:
ROW 13 (RS): *K1, p1*; repeat from * to * to last 2 sts, k2tog—81 (89, 97, 105) sts.
ROW 14 (WS): *P1, k1*; repeat from * to * to last st, p1.
ROW 15: *K1, p1*; repeat from * to * to last st, k1.
Work in established patt until piece measures 11" (28cm) from CO, ending with WS row.

ARMHOLE SHAPING
NEXT RS ROW (DECREASES): K1, p1, k1, p1 then work RFFD, work in k1, p1 to last 7 sts, work LFFD, p1, k1, p1, k1—77 (85, 93, 101) sts. Repeat this decrease row every 4 rows 3 (4, 5, 6) times more—65 (69, 73, 77) sts. Work even until Armhole measures 7 (7½, 8, 8½)" [18 (19, 20, 21.5)cm].

SHOULDER SHAPING
Bind off 7 (8, 8, 9) sts at beginning of next 4 rows. Bind off remaining 37 (37, 41, 41) sts for Back Neck.

LEFT FRONT (AS WORN)
With larger needle, cast on 16 (20, 24, 28) sts.
ROW 1 (WS): P2, *k1, p1*; repeat from * to * to end of row.
ROW 2 (RS): *K1, p1; repeat from * to * to last 2 sts, yo, k2—17 (21, 25, 29) sts.
ROW 3: P2, k1 p1 into yo, (2 sts), *k1, p1*; repeat from * to * to end of row—18 (22, 26, 30) sts.
NEXT 28 ROWS: Repeat last 2 rows 14 times more 46 (50, 54, 58) sts.
Work even until piece measures 9" (23cm), ending with a WS row.

ARMHOLE AND NECK SHAPING
NEXT RS ROW: (decreases): K1, p1, k1, p1, work RFFD (for Armhole shaping), work in k1, p1 patt to the last 5 sts, LFFD (for Neck shaping), k2—42 (46, 50, 54) sts.
NEXT WS AND ALL WS ROWS: Work even in patt.
Repeat the RS decrease row every 4 rows 4 (4, 4, 5) times more—26 (30, 34, 34) sts.

Continue in patt and making LFFD at neckline only (no Armhole decreases) every 4 rows 6 (7, 9, 8) times—14 (16, 16, 18) sts. Work even in patt until Armhole measures 7 (7½, 8, 8½)" [18 (19, 20, 21.5)cm]. Shape shoulder: Bind off 7 (8, 8, 9) sts at beginning of next 2 rows.

RIGHT FRONT

Work as for Left Front, reversing all shaping.

SLEEVES

Cast on 43 (45, 47, 49) sts.

ROW 1 (RS): *K1, p1*; repeat from * to * to last st, k1.
ROW 2 (WS): *P1, k1*; repeat from * to * to last st, p1.
Repeat these 2 rows for 4" (10cm).

NEXT ROW (INCREASES): Working in patt as established, increase 1 st each side of row (after the first and before the last st)—45 (47, 49, 51) sts.
Repeat increase row every 12 (10, 10, 8) rows 5 (6, 7, 8) times more—55 (59, 63, 67) sts. Work even until piece measures 17" (43cm), ending with RS row.

CAP SHAPING

Decrease row (RS): K1, p1, k1, p1, work RFFD, work in patt to last 7 sts, work LFFD, p1, k1, p1, k1.
Repeat this decrease row every 4 rows 9 (10, 10, 11) times more—15 (15, 19, 19) sts.
Bind off.

BAND AND FRONT PANEL

Join Shoulder seams. Sew Sleeve caps into Armholes and sew Sleeves and side seams.

Place one marker at first decrease on Right Front Neck line and second marker 7" (18cm) (moving along toward the Shoulder line) from that marker, on the Right Front side of jacket.

With RS facing and smaller needle, beginning at the bottom of Right Front side, pick up 124 (126, 128, 130) sts along right half to Right Shoulder seam, 48 (48, 52, 52) sts from the back sts, 124 (126, 128, 130) sts from the Left Shoulder seam down left half to the bottom of the left half—296 (300, 308, 312) sts. Note: When distributing the above-mentioned sts, pick up more sts from curved bottom corners, than from the upper part of the fronts to create a better fit.

Next row (WS): *K2, p2*; repeat from * to * to end of row.
Work in k2, p2 rib for 2" ending with WS row.

NEXT RS ROW: Bind off sts up to second marker, work in patt to the first marker, place stitches between 1st and 2nd marker on stitch holder for central Panel (make sure you have an even number of sts here), bind off remaining sts to end of Left Front lower edge.

Join yarn, transfer sts from stitch holder to a needle and work in k2, p2 rib as follows: *Sl 1, work next st in established patt, then continue in established 2x2 rib to end of panel*. Repeat from * to * for 4½" (11cm). Bind off tightly.

FINISHING

Sew the bind-off edge of central Panel to opposite side. Sew 6 buttons to the central Panel, as shown in photo. Weave in loose ends to WS.

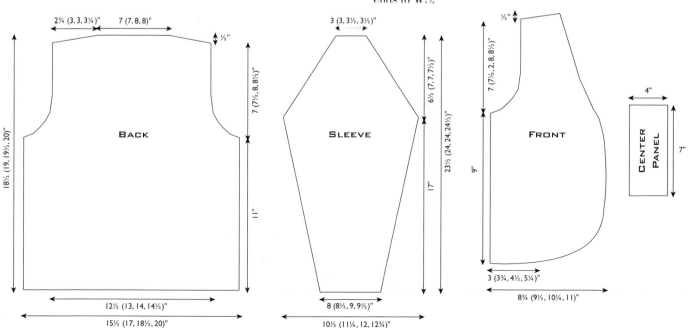

2¾ (3, 3, 3¼)"   7 (7, 8, 8)"

½"

7 (7½, 8, 8½)"

BACK

11"

18½ (19, 19½, 20)"

12½ (13, 14, 14½)"

15½ (17, 18½, 20)"

3 (3, 3½, 3½)"

6½ (7, 7, 7½)"

SLEEVE

17"

8 (8½, 9, 9½)"

10½ (11¼, 12, 12¾)"

½"

7 (7½, 2, 8, 8½)"

23½ (24, 24, 24½)"

9"

FRONT

3 (3¾, 4½, 5¼)"

8¾ (9½, 10¼, 11)"

4"

CENTER PANEL

7"

LEAF-DROP SWEATER

This sweater has an unusual jewel-shaped bottom with matching flared sleeves. Its classic V-neck and gracefully curved lines—done in a vertical waves pattern—flatter just about every figure, and the spring-green color will lift your spirits. Knitted in a luxuriously warm wool/cashmere blend, this sweater will electrify a straight black skirt and black tights for days at the office, travel to faraway locales, or a night on the town.

LEAF-DROP SWEATER

SIZES
To fit S (M, L, XL). Directions are for the smallest size, with larger sizes in parentheses. If there is only one figure, it applies to all sizes.

KNITTED MEASUREMENTS
Bust: 33 (35, 37½, 40)" [84 (89, 95, 101.5)cm]

Length: 22½ (23, 23½, 24)" [57 (58.5, 60, 61)cm]

Upper arm: 11 (12, 13, 14)" [28 (30.5, 33, 35.5)cm]

MATERIALS
7 (8, 9, 10) balls Karabella Boise (50% merino wool, 50% cashmere; about 163 yds [150m] per 1¾ oz [50g] ball: color #509, Lime Green

Size 6 (4mm) needles, or size to obtain gauge

Size 6 (4mm) 24" [60cm] circular needle, or size to obtain gauge

Size 4 (3.5mm) needles

Stitch holders

GAUGE
26 sts and 36 rows = 4" (10cm) over Vertical Waves patt.

VERTICAL WAVES PATTERN (12 STS + 3 OVER 8 ROWS)
ROW 1 (RS): K1, *p2, k3tog, (yo, k1) 3 times, yo, sl 1-k2tog-psso, p1*; repeat from * to * for patt, to last 2 sts, p1, k1.

ROW 2 AND ALL WS ROWS: Purl all yo from the previous row, work the rest of sts as they appear.

ROW 3: K1, *p2, k9, p1*; repeat from * to * for patt to last 2 sts, p1, k1.

ROW 5: K1, *(k1, yo) twice, sl 1-k2tog-psso, p3, k3tog, yo, k1, yo*; repeat from * to * for patt to last 2 sts, k2.

ROW 7: K1, *k5, p3, k4*; repeat from * to * for patt to last 2 sts, k2.

ROW 8: Repeat Row 2.

Repeat Rows 1–8 for pattern.

BACK
With size 6 needles, cast on 99 (107, 115, 123) sts.

ROW 1 (RS): K1, *k2, p2*; repeat from * to * to last 2 sts, k2.

ROW 2 (WS): P2, *k2, p2*; repeat from * to * to last st, p1.

Repeat Rows 1 and 2 two times more.

Begin Vertical Waves patt as follows:

FOR SIZES SMALL AND X-LARGE ONLY:
Work in Vertical Waves patt, repeating Rows 1–8 of the pattern until there are 70 rows total from CO.

FOR SIZE MEDIUM ONLY:
ROW 1 (RS): K2, yo, ssk, p1, (work Row 1 of patt from * to * for next 96 sts), p2, k2tog, yo, k2.

ROW 2 AND ALL WS ROWS: Purl all yo from the previous row, work the rest of sts as they appear.

ROW 3 (RS): K4, p1, (work Row 3 of patt from * to * for next 96 sts), p2, k4.

ROW 5: K1, k3tog, yo, k1, yo, (work Row 5 of patt from * to * for next 96 sts), (k1, yo) twice, sl 1-k2tog-psso, k1.

ROW 7: K5, (work Row 7 of patt from * to * for next 96 sts), k6.
Continue working as established, repeating Rows 1–8 until there are 70 rows total from CO.

FOR SIZE LARGE ONLY:
ROW 1: K4, yo, k1, yo, sl 1-k2tog-psso, p1, (work Row 1 of patt from * to * for next 96 sts), p2, k3tog, yo, k1, yo, k4.

ROW 2 AND ALL WS ROWS: Purl all yo from the previous row, work the rest of sts as they appear.

ROW 3: K8, p1, (work Row 3 of patt from * to * for next 96 sts), p2, k8.

ROW 5: K2, p3, k3tog, yo, k1, yo, (work Row 5 of patt from * to * for next 96 sts), (k1, yo) twice, sl 1-k2tog-psso, p3, k2.

ROW 7: K2, p3, k4, (work Row 7 of patt from * to * for next 96 sts), k4, p3, k2.
Continue working as established repeating Rows 1–8 until there are 70 rows total from CO.

FOR ALL SIZES:

Continue in Vertical Waves patt as established, add 1 st after the first and before the last st of rows 71, 85, and 99—105 (113, 121, 129) sts. Work new sts as St sts (knit on RS, purl on WS) at side edges.

Continue as established until there are 126 rows total from CO (piece measures about 14" [35.5cm]), ending with Row 8 of patt and begin Armhole shaping.

ARMHOLE SHAPING

FOR SIZE SMALL ONLY:

ROW 127 (RS): Bind off 5 sts, k3tog, (yo, k1) 3 times, yo, sl 1-k2tog-psso, p1, (work Row 1 of patt from * to * for next 84 sts), p1, k4—100 sts.

ROW 128 (WS): Bind off 5 sts, purl all yo from the previous row, work the rest of sts as they appear—95 sts.

ROW 129: K1, ssk, k7, p1, (work Row 3 of patt from * to * for next 72 sts), p2, k7, k2tog, k1—93 sts.

ROW 130 AND ALL WS ROWS: Work sts as they appear.

ROW 131: K1, ssk, p3, k3tog, yo, k1, yo, (work Row 5 of patt from * to * for next 72 sts), (k1, yo) twice, sl 1-k2tog-psso, p3, k2tog, k1—91 sts.

ROW 133: K1, ssk, p3, k4, (work Row 7 of patt from * to * for next 72 sts), k5, p2, k2tog, k1—89 sts.

ROW 135: K1, ssk, yo, k1, yo, sl 1-k2tog-psso, p1, (work Row 1 of patt from " to " for next 72 sts), p2, k3tog, yo, k1, yo, k2tog, k1—87 sts.

ROW 137: K1, ssk, k3, p1, (work Row 3 of patt from * to * for next 72 sts), p2, k3, k2tog, k1—85 sts.

ROW 139: K1, ssk, k3, (work Row 5 of patt from * to * for next 72 sts), k4, k2tog, k1—83 sts.

ROW 141: K5, (work Row 7 of patt from * to * for next 72 sts), k6—83 sts.

ROW 143: K4, p1, (work Row 1 of patt from * to * for next 72 sts), p2, k4.

ROW 145: K4, p1, (work Row 3 of patt from * to * for next 72 sts), p2, k4.

ROW 147: K5, (work Row 5 of patt from * to * for next 72 sts), k6.

ROW 149: K5, (work Row 7 of patt from * to * for next 72 sts), k6.

ROW 150: Work sts as they appear.

Repeat rows 143–150 until Armhole measures 7½" (19cm). Begin Shoulder shaping.

FOR SIZE MEDIUM ONLY:

ROW 127 (RS): Bind off 6 sts, p1, (work Row 1 of patt from * to * for next 96 sts), p2, k2tog, yo, k5—107 sts.

ROW 128 (WS): Bind off 6 sts, purl all yo from the previous row, work the rest of sts as they appear—101 sts.

ROW 129: K1, ssk, p1, k9, p1, for patt (work Row 3 of patt from * to * for next 84 sts), k2tog, k1—99 sts.

ROW 130 AND ALL WS ROWS: Work sts as they appear.

ROW 131: K1, ssk, k3, p3, k3tog, yo, k1, yo, (work Row 5 of patt from * to * for next 72 sts), (k1, yo) twice, sl 1-k2tog-psso, p3, k3, k2tog, k1—97 sts.

ROW 133: K1, ssk, k2, p3, k4, (work Row 7 of patt from * to * for next 72 sts), k5, p3, k2, k2tog, k1—95 sts.

ROW 135: K1, ssk, k3, yo, k1, yo, sl 1-k2tog-psso, p1, (work Row 1 of patt from * to * for next 72 sts), p2, k3tog, yo, k1, yo, k3, k2tog, k1—93 sts.

ROW 137: K1, ssk, k6, p1, (work Row 3 of patt from * to * for next 72 sts), p2, k6, k2tog, k1— 91 sts.

ROW 139: K1, ssk, p2, k3tog, yo, k1, yo, (work Row 5 of patt from " to " for next 72 sts), (k1, yo) twice, sl 1-k2tog-psso, p2, k2tog, k1—89 sts.

ROW 141: K1, ssk, p1, k4, (work Row 7 of patt from * to * for next 72 sts), k5, p1, k2tog, k1—87 sts.

ROW 143: K1, ssk, k3, p1, (work Row 1 of patt from * to * for next 72 sts), p2, k3, k2tog, k1—85 sts.

ROW 145: K5, p1, (work Row 3 of patt from * to * for next 72 sts), p2, k5—85 sts.

ROW 147: K1, p1, k3tog, yo, k1, yo, (work Row 5 of patt from * to * for next 72 sts), (k1, yo) twice, sl 1-k2tog-psso, p1, k1.

ROW 149: K1, p1, k4, (work Row 7 of patt from * to * for next 72 sts), k5, p1, k1.

ROW 151: K5, p1, (work Row 1 of patt from * to * for next 72 sts), p2, k5.

ROW 152: Work sts as they appear.

Repeat Rows 145–152 until Armhole measures 8" (20cm). Begin Shoulder shaping.

FOR SIZE LARGE ONLY:

ROW 127 (RS): Bind off 6 sts, yo, k1, yo, sl 1-k2tog-psso, p1, (work Row 1 of patt from * to * for next 96 sts), p2, k3tog, yo, k1, yo, k7—115 sts.

ROW 128 (WS): Bind off 6 sts, purl all yo from the previous row, work the rest of sts as they appear—109 sts.

ROW 129: K1, ssk, k2, p1, (work Row 3 of patt from * to * for next 96 sts), p2, k2, k2tog, k1—107 sts.

ROW 130 AND ALL WS ROWS: Work sts as they appear.

ROW 131: K1, ssk, k2, (work Row 5 of patt from * to * for next 96 sts), k3, k2tog, k1—105 sts.

ROW 133: K1, ssk, k1, (work Row 7 of patt from * to * for next 96 sts), k2, k2tog, k1—103 sts.

ROW 135: K1, ssk, (work Row 1 of patt from * to * for next 96 sts), p1, k2tog, k1—101 sts.

ROW 137: K1, ssk, p1, k9, p1, (work Row 3 of patt from * to * for next 84 sts), k2tog, k1—99 sts.

ROW 139: K1, ssk, k3, p3, k3tog, yo, k1, yo, (work Row 5 of patt from * to * for next 72 sts), (k1, yo) twice, sl 1-k2tog-psso, p3, k3, k2tog, k1—97 sts.

ROW 141: K1, ssk, k2, p3, k4, (work Row 7 of patt from * to * for next 72 sts), k5, p3, k2, k2tog, k1—95 sts.

ROW 143: K1, ssk, k3, yo, k1, yo, sl 1-k2tog-psso, p1, (work Row 1 of patt from * to * for next 72 sts), p2, k3tog, yo, k1, yo, k3, k2tog, k1—93 sts.

ROW 145: K1, ssk, k6, p1, (work Row 3 of patt from * to * for next 72 sts), p2, k6, k2tog, k1—91 sts.

ROW 147: K1, ssk, p2, k3tog, yo, k1, yo, (work Row 5 of patt from * to * for next 72 sts), (k1, yo) twice, sl 1-k2tog-psso, p2, k2tog, k1—89 sts.

ROW 149: K2, p2, k4, (work Row 7 of patt from * to * for next 72 sts), k5, p2, k2.

ROW 151: K3, yo, k1, yo, sl 1-k2tog-psso, p1, (work Row 1 of patt from * to * for next 72 sts), p2, k3tog, yo, k1, yo, k3.

ROW 153: K7, p1, (work Row 3 of patt from * to * for next 72 sts), p2, k7.

ROW 155: K2, p2, k3tog, yo, k1, yo, (work Row 5 of patt from * to * for next 72 sts), (k1, yo) twice, sl 1-k2tog-psso, p2, k2.

ROW 156: Work sts as they appear.

Repeat rows 149-156 until Armhole measures 8½" (21.5cm). Begin Shoulder shaping.

FOR SIZE X-LARGE ONLY:

ROW 127 (RS): Bind off 9 sts, k1, yo, k1, yo, sl 1-k2tog-psso, p1, (work Row 1 of patt from * to * for next 108 sts), p1, k4—120 sts.

ROW 128 (WS): Bind off 9 sts, purl all yo from the previous row, work the rest of sts as they appear—111 sts.

ROW 129: K1, ssk, k3, p1, (work Row 3 of patt from * to * for next 96 sts), p2, k3, k2tog, k1—109 sts.

ROW 130 AND ALL WS ROWS: Work sts as they appear.

ROW 131: K1, ssk, k3, (work Row 5 of patt from * to * for next 96 sts), k4, k2tog, k1—107 sts.

ROW 133: K1, ssk, k2, (work Row 7 of patt from * to * for next 96 sts), k3, k2tog, k1—105 sts.

ROW 135: K1, ssk, p1, (work Row 1 of patt from * to * for next 96 sts), p2, k2tog, k1—103 sts.

ROW 137: K1, ssk, (work Row 3 of patt from * to * for next 96 sts), p1, k2tog, k1—101 sts.

ROW 139: K1, ssk, yo, k1, yo, sl 1-k2tog-psso, p3, k3tog, yo, k1, yo, (work Row 5 of patt from * to * for next 84 sts), k2tog, k1—99 sts.

ROW 141: K1, ssk, k3, p3, k4, (work Row 7 of patt from * to * for next 72 sts), k5, p3, k3, k2tog, k1—97 sts.

ROW 143: K1, ssk, k4, yo, k1, yo, sl 1-k2tog-psso, p1, (work Row 1 of patt from * to * for next 72 sts), p2, k3tog, yo, k1, yo, k4, k2tog, k1—95 sts.

ROW 145: K1, ssk, k7, p1, (work Row 3 of patt from * to * for next 72 sts), p2, k7, k2tog, k1—93 sts.

ROW 147: K1, ssk, p3, k3tog, yo, k1, yo, (work Row 5 of patt from * to * for next 72 sts), (k1, yo) twice, sl 1-k2tog-psso, p3, k2tog, k1—91 sts.

ROW 149: K2, p3, k4, (work Row 7 of patt from * to * for next 72 sts), k5, p3, k2.

ROW 151: K4, yo, k1, yo, sl 1-k2tog-psso, p1, (work Row 1 of patt from * to * for next 72 sts), p2, k3tog, yo, k1, yo, k4.

ROW 153: K8, p1, (work Row 3 of patt from * to * for next 72 sts), p2, k8.

ROW 155: K2, p3, k3tog, yo, k1, yo, (work Row 5 of patt from * to * for next 72 sts), (k1, yo) twice, sl 1-k2tog-psso, p3, k2.

ROW 156: Work sts as they appear.

Repeat rows 149–156 until Armhole measures 9" (23cm). Begin Shoulder shaping.

SHOULDER SHAPING (ALL SIZES)

Bind off 6 (7, 7, 7) sts at beginning of next 2 rows—71 (71, 75, 77) sts.

Bind off 6 (6, 7, 7) sts at beginning of next 2 rows—59 (59, 61, 61) sts.

Bind off 6 (6, 6, 7) sts at beginning of next 2 rows—47 (47, 49, 49) sts.

Place remaining 47 (47, 49, 49) sts on stitch holder for Back Neck.

FRONT

The Front is started as two separate pieces, which are connected in one piece in the middle. Start working the Front from the right side as described.

RIGHT SIDE (AS WORN):

With size 6 needles, cast on 51 (55, 59, 63) sts.

ROW 1 (RS): K1, *k2, p2*; repeat from * to * to last 2 sts, k2.

ROW 2 (WS): P2, *k2, p2*; repeat from * to * to last st, p1.

Repeat rows 1 and 2 two times more.

Begin working in Vertical Waves patt as follows:

FOR SIZES SMALL/X-LARGE ONLY:

Work in Vertical Waves patt, repeating Rows 1–8 of the pattern until there are 70 rows total from CO.

FOR SIZE MEDIUM ONLY:

ROW 1 (RS): K1, (work Row 1 of patt from * to * for next 48 sts), p2, k2tog, yo, k2.

ROW 2 AND ALL WS ROWS: Purl all yo from the previous row, work the rest of sts as they appear.

ROW 3 (RS): K1, (work Row 3 of patt from * to * for next 48 sts), p2, k4.

ROW 5 (RS): K1, (work Row 5 of patt from * to * for next 48 sts), (k1, yo) twice, sl 1-k2tog-psso, k1.

ROW 7 (RS): k1, (work Row 7 of patt from * to * for next 48 sts), k6.

Work in Vertical Waves patt, repeating rows 1–8 of the pattern until there are 70 rows total from CO.

FOR SIZE LARGE ONLY:

ROW 1 (RS): K1, (work Row 1 of patt from * to * for next 48 sts), p2, k3tog, yo, k1, yo, k4.

ROW 2 AND ALL WS ROWS: Purl all yo from the previous row, work the rest of sts as they appear.

ROW 3 (RS): K1, (work Row 3 of patt from * to * for next 48 sts), p2, k8.

ROW 5 (RS): K1, (work Row 5 of patt from * to * for next 48 sts), (k1, yo) twice, sl 1-k2tog-psso, p3, k2.

ROW 7 (RS): K1, (work Row 7 of patt from * to * for next 48 sts), k5, p3, k2.

Work in Vertical Waves patt, repeating Rows 1–8 of the pattern until there are 70 rows total from CO.

FOR ALL SIZES:

Continuing as established, add 1 st before the last st of row 71—52 (56, 60, 64) sts. Work new sts as St sts (knit on RS, purl on WS).

Continue as established for 7 rows more, ending with row 78 (Row 8 of patt).

Place 52 (56, 60, 64) sts on stitch holder and start working the Left Side.

LEFT SIDE (AS WORN)

With size 6 needles, cast on 51 (55, 59, 63) sts.

ROW 1 (RS): K1, *k2, p2*; repeat from * to * to last 2 sts, k2.

ROW 2 (WS): P2, *k2, p2*; repeat from * to * to last st, p1.

Repeat Rows 1 and 2 two times more.

Begin working in the Vertical Waves patt as follows:

FOR SIZES SMALL/X-LARGE ONLY:

Work in Vertical Waves pattern, repeating Rows 1–8 of the pattern until there are 70 rows total from CO.

FOR SIZE MEDIUM ONLY:

ROW 1 (RS): K2, yo, ssk, p1, (work Row 1 of patt from * to * for next 48 sts), p1, k1.

ROW 2 AND ALL WS ROWS: Purl all yo from the previous row, work the rest of sts as they appear.

ROW 3 (RS): K4, p1, (work Row 3 of patt from * to * for next 48 sts), p1, k1.

ROW 5 (RS): K1, k3tog, yo, k1, yo, (work Row 5 of patt from * to * for next 48 sts), k2.

ROW 7 (RS): K5, (work Row 7 of patt from * to * for next 48 sts), k2.

Work in Vertical Waves patt, repeating Rows 1–8 of the pattern until there are 70 rows total from CO.

FOR SIZE LARGE ONLY:

ROW 1 (RS): K4, yo, k1, yo, sl 1 k2tog psso, p1, (work Row 1 of patt from * to * for next 48 sts), p1, k1.

ROW 2 AND ALL WS ROWS: Purl all yo from the previous row, work the rest of sts as they appear.

ROW 3 (RS): K8, p1, (work Row 3 of patt from * to * for next 48 sts), p1, k1.

ROW 5 (RS): K2, p3, k3tog, yo, k1, yo, (work Row 5 of patt from * to * for next 48 sts), k2.

ROW 7 (RS): K2, p3, k4, (work Row 7 of patt from * to * for next 48 sts), k2.

ROW 8: Work same as row 2.

Work in Vertical Waves patt, repeating Rows 1–8 of the pattern until there are 70 rows total from CO.

FOR ALL SIZES:

Continue as established, add 1 st after the first st of Row 71—52 (56, 60, 64) sts. Work new sts as St sts (knit on RS, purl on WS).

Continue as established for 7 rows more, ending with Row 78 (Row 8 of patt).

FRONT BODY

Place 52 (56, 60, 64) sts of right side and 52 (56, 60, 64) sts of left side on one needle. With RS facing left side sts first, and right side sts after them—104 (112, 120, 128) sts.

ROW 79 (RS; ROW 1 OF PATT): Work 51 (55, 59, 63) sts as established, p2tog, work 51 (55, 59, 63) sts as established—103 (111, 119, 127) sts.

ROW 81 (ROW 3 OF PATT): Work 51 (55, 59, 63) sts in patt as established, p2tog, work 50 (54, 58, 62) sts as established—102 (110, 118, 126) sts.

ROW 83 (ROW 5 OF PATT): Work 50 (54, 58, 62) sts as established, k2tog, work 50 (54, 58, 62) sts as established—101 (109, 117, 125) sts.

Continue in patt as established, adding 1 st after the first and before the last st of Rows 85 and 99—105 (113, 121, 129) sts. Work new sts as St sts (knit on RS, purl on WS).

Continue as established for 31 rows more, ending with Row 114 (Row 4 of patt).

V-NECK SHAPING

ROW 115 (RS) ROW 5 OF PATT: Left side: Work 40 (44, 48, 52) sts as established, (ending with yo stitch), (k1, yo) twice, sl 1-k2tog-psso, p3, k3tog, yo, k1—51 (55, 59, 63) sts; join the second ball of yarn and continue for the right side as follows: k2tog (to balance uneven number of sts for left and right sides), yo, sl 1-k2tog-psso, p3, k3tog, yo, k1, yo, work 40 (44, 48, 52) sts as established—51 (55, 59, 63) sts.

Note: Continue working both sides of neck at once, decreasing at V-neck side as described below. AT THE SAME TIME, starting from Row 127, shape Armholes as for Back, and AT THE SAME TIME when Armhole measures 7½ (8, 8½, 9)" [19 (20, 21½, 23)cm] shape Shoulders as for back.

ROWS 117, 121, 125, 129, 133, 137, 141, 145, 149, 153, 157, AND 161: Work each side as established.

ROW 119: Left side: Work as established to last 11 sts, p2, k3tog, (yo, k1) twice, k1, k2tog, k1; Right side: k1, ssk, k1, (k1, yo) twice, sl 1-k2tog-psso, p1, continue as established

ROW 123: Left side: Work as established to last 10 sts, (k1, yo) twice, sl 1-k2tog-psso, p2, k2tog, k1; Right side: k1, ssk, p2, k3tog, yo, k1, yo, continue as established.

ROW 127 (BEGIN ARMHOLE SHAPING): Left side: Work as established to last 9 sts, p2, k3tog, yo, k1, yo, k2tog, k1; Right side: k1, ssk, yo, k1, yo, sl 1-k2tog-psso, p1, continue as established.

ROW 131: Left side: Work as established to last 8 sts, (k1, yo) twice, sl 1-k2tog-psso, k2tog, k1; Right side: k1, ssk, k3tog, yo, k1, yo, continue as established.

ROW 135: Left side: Work as established to last 7 sts, p2, k3tog, yo, k2; Right side: k2, yo, sl 1-k2tog-psso, p1, continue as established.

ROW 139: Left side: Work as established to last 6 sts, k3, k2tog, k1; Right side: k1, ssk, k2, continue as established.

ROW 143: Left side: Work as established to last 5 sts, p2, k2tog, k1; Right side: k1, ssk, p1, continue as established.

ROW 147: Left side: work as established to last 4 sts, k1, k2tog, k1; Right side: k1, ssk, continue as established.

ROW 151: Left side: Work as established to last 3 sts, k2tog, p1; Right side: p1, ssk, p1, k3tog, (yo, k1) 3 times, yo, sl 1-k2tog-psso, p1, continue as established.

ROW 155: Left side: Work as established to last 6 sts, k3tog, yo, k3; Right side: k3, yo, sl 1-k2tog-psso, p1, continue as established.

ROW 159: Left side: Work as established to last 13 sts, p2, k3tog, yo, k1, yo, k4, k2tog, p1; Right side: p1, k2tog, k4, yo, k1, yo, sl 1-k2tog-psso, p1, continue as established.

ROW 163: Left side: Work as established to last 12 sts, (k1, yo) twice, sl 1-k2tog-psso, p3, k3tog, yo, k1; Right side: k1, yo, sl 1-k2tog-psso, p3, k3tog, yo, k1, yo, continue as established.

ROW 164: Work each side as established.

FOR SIZES SMALL/MEDIUM ONLY:
Repeat Rows 117–156.

FOR SIZES LARGE/X-LARGE ONLY:
Repeat Rows 117–160.

FOR ALL SIZES:
Continue even at V-neck edges, if needed, until desired length.

FRONT LEAF
With size 4 needles, cast on 3 sts.

ROW 1 (RS): K1, m1, k1 (center st), m1, k1—5 sts.

ROW 2 (WS): P1, k1, m1, p1 (center st), m1, k1, p1—7 sts.

ROW 3: K1, p1, k1, m1, k1 (center st), m1, k1, p1, k1—9 sts.

ROW 4: P1, k1, p1, k1, m1, p1 (center st), m1, k1, p1, k1, p1—11 sts

ROW 5: K1, p1, k1, p1, k1, m1, k1 (center st), m1, k1, p1, k1, p1, k1—13 sts.

Continue working in this manner, increasing 1 st on each side from the center st in every row and working new sts into 1×1 rib (knit 1, purl 1) until there are 51 sts in total, ending with Row 24.

Continue increasing 1 st on each side from the center st on WS rows only and working new sts into 1×1 rib. Beginning with Row 25, decrease 1 st on each edge of the leaf in every RS and WS rows, omitting decreases in Rows 28, 30, and 35. Work decreases as follows:

RS ROW DECREASE: K1, ssk, work as established in 1×1 to the center st, k1, work as established in 1×1 rib to the last 3 sts, k2tog, k1.

WS ROW DECREASE: K1, p2tog, work as established to the center st, m1, p1, m1, work as established to last 3 sts, p2tog tbl, k1.

Continue working in this manner for 74 rows total.

ROW 75: K1, ssk, k1, k2tog, k1.

ROW 76: P1, k1, p1, k1, p1.

ROW 77: K1, k3tog, k1.

ROW 78: P3tog.

SLEEVES
Sleeves are worked the same way as the Front, starting from two separate pieces, which are connected in one piece in the middle. Start working the Sleeve from the Right Sleeve side as described.

RIGHT SLEEVE SIDE
With size 6 needles, cast on 27 (28, 29, 30) sts.

ROW 1 (RS): P2, *K2, p2*; repeat from * to * to last 1 (2, 3, 0) st(s), k1 (k2, k3, k0) st(s).

ROW 2 (WS): P1 (p2, p3, p0), *k2, p2*; repeat from * to * to last 2 sts, k2.

Repeat Rows 1 and 2 two times more.

Begin the Vertical Waves pattern as follows:

ROW 1 (RS): K1, (work Row 1 of patt from * to * for next 24 sts), p1, k0 (p1, p1, p1), k0 (k0, k1, k1), k0 (k0, k0, k1), k1.

ROW 2 AND ALL WS ROWS: Purl all yo from the previous row, work the rest of sts as they appear.

ROW 3 (RS): K1, (work Row 3 of patt from * to * for next 24 sts), p1, k0 (p1, p1, p1), k0 (k0, k1, k1), k0 (k0, k0, k1), k1.

ROW 5 (RS): K1, (work Row 5 of patt from * to * for next 24 sts), p1, k0 (k1, k1, k1), k0 (k0, k1, k1), k0 (k0, k0, k1), k1.

ROW 7 (RS): K1, (work Row 7 of patt from * to * for next 24 sts), p1, k0 (k1, k1, k1), k0 (k0, k1, k1), k0 (k0, k0, k1), k1.

ROW 8: Repeat Row 2.

Continue working as established, repeating Rows 1–8 seven times more, and after that Rows 1–4 once more, ending with Row 74 (Row 4 of patt), counting from CO.

Add 1 st before the last st of the row (working the new st in patt when possible) in the following rows:

FOR SIZE MEDIUM ONLY:
Row 73.

FOR SIZE LARGE ONLY:
Rows 57, 65, and 73.

FOR SIZE X-LARGE ONLY:
Rows 41, 49, 57, 65, and 73.
Place 27 (29, 32, 35) sts on stitch holder and start working the Left Sleeve side.

LEFT SLEEVE SIDE
With size 6 needles, cast on 27 (28, 29, 30) sts.

ROW 1 (RS): K1 (k2, k3, k0), *p2, k2*; repeat from * to * to last 2 sts, p2.

ROW 2 (WS): K2, *p2, k2*; repeat from * to * to last 1 (2, 3, 0) sts, p1 (p2, p3, p0).

Repeat Rows 1 and 2 two times more.

Start working in the Vertical Waves patt as follows:

ROW 1 (RS): K1, k0 (k0, k0, k1), k0 (k0, k1, k1), k0 (p1, p1, p1), (work Row 1 of patt from * to * for next 24 sts), p1, k1.

ROW 2 AND ALL WS ROWS: Purl all yo from the previous row, work the rest of sts as they appear.

ROW 3 (RS): K1, k0 (k0, k0, k1), k0 (k0, k1, k1), k0 (p1, p1, p1), (work Row 3 of patt from * to * for next 24 sts), p1, k1.

ROW 5 (RS): K1, k0 (k0, k0, k1), k0 (k0, k1, k1), k0 (k1, k1, k1), (work Row 5 of patt from * to * for next 24 sts), k2.

ROW 7 (RS): K1, k0 (k0, k0, k1), k0 (k0, k1, k1), k0 (k1, k1, k1), (work Row 7 of patt from * to * for next 24 sts), k2.

ROW 8: Repeat Row 2.

Continue working as established, repeating Rows 1–8 seven times more, and after that Rows 1–4 once more, ending with row 74 (Row 4 of pattern), counting from CO.

Add 1 st after the first st of the row (working the new st in patt, when possible) in the following rows:

FOR SIZE SMALL ONLY:
None—27 sts.

FOR SIZE MEDIUM ONLY:
Row 73—29 sts.

FOR SIZE LARGE ONLY:
Rows 57, 65, and 73—32 sts.

FOR SIZE X-LARGE ONLY:
Rows 41, 49, 57, 65, and 73—35 sts.

SLEEVE BODY
Note: Add 1 st after the first st of the row and 1 st before the last st of the row (working the new st in patt, when possible) in the following rows:

In Row 81, for sizes Medium, Large, and X-Large only, and after that every 8 rows for all sizes (in Rows 89, 97, 105, 113, 121, and so on) until there are 71 (77, 83, 89) sts in a Sleeve. Place 27 (29, 32, 35) sts of Right Sleeve side and 27 (29, 32, 35) sts of Left Sleeve side on one needle. With RS facing left side sts first, and right side sts after them—54 (58, 64, 70) sts.

ROW 75 (RS): Work Row 5 of patt as follows: work 26 (28, 31, 34) sts as established, k2tog, work 26 (28, 31, 34) sts as established—53 (57, 63, 69) sts.

ROW 77 (ROW 7 OF PATT): Work 26 (28, 31, 34) sts as established, k2tog, work 25 (27, 30, 33) sts as established—52 (56, 62, 68) sts.

ROW 79 (ROW 1 OF PATT): Work 25 (27, 30, 33) sts as established, p2tog, work 25 (27, 30, 33) sts as established—51 (55, 61, 67) sts.

Continue in patt as established (working increase rows as specified above), until there are 158 rows total (piece measures about 17½" [44.5cm]), counting from CO and ending with Row 8 of Vertical Waves patt—71 (77, 83, 89) sts.

CAP SHAPING
FOR SIZE SMALL ONLY:
ROW 1 (RS): Bind off 5 sts, yo, k1, yo, sl 1-k2tog-psso, p1, (work Row 1 of patt from * to * for next 48 sts), p2, k3tog, (yo, k1) three times, yo, sl 1-k2tog-psso, k1—66 sts.

ROW 2 (WS): Bind off 5 sts, purl all yo from the previous row, work the rest of sts as they appear— 61 sts.

ROW 3: Bind off 2 sts, k2, p1, (work Row 3 of patt from * to * for next 48 sts), p2, k5—59 sts.

ROW 4: Bind off 2 sts, work the rest of sts as they appear— 57 sts.

ROW 5: Bind off 2 sts, k1, (work Row 5 of patt from * to * for next 48 sts), k5—55 sts.

ROW 6: Bind off 2 sts, purl all yo from the previous row, work the rest of sts as they appear—53 sts.

ROW 7: Bind off 1 st, (work Row 7 of patt from * to * for next 48 sts), k3—52 sts.

ROW 8: Bind off 1 st, work the rest of sts as they appear— 51 sts.

Continue working 51 sts in Vertical Waves patt (from Row 1 of patt) for 34 rows more, ending with Row 2 of patt.

FOR SIZE MEDIUM ONLY:
ROW 1 (RS): Bind off 6 sts, k2, yo, k1, yo, sl 1-k2tog-psso, p1, (work Row 1 of patt from * to * for next 60 sts), p2, k1—71 sts.

ROW 2 (WS): Bind off 6 sts, purl all yo from the previous row, work the rest of sts as they appear—65 sts.

ROW 3: Bind off 3 sts, k3, p1, (work Row 3 of patt from * to * for next 48 sts), p2, k7—62 sts.

ROW 4: Bind off 3 sts, work the rest of sts as they appear— 59 sts.

ROW 5: Bind off 2 sts, k2, (work Row 5 of patt from * to * for next 48 sts), k6—57 sts.

ROW 6: Bind off 2 sts, purl all yo from the previous row, work the rest of sts as they appear—55 sts.

ROW 7: Bind off 1 st, k1, (work Row 7 of patt from * to * for next 48 sts), k4—54 sts.

ROW 8: Bind off 1 st, work the rest of sts as they appear—53 sts.

ROW 9: Bind off 1 st, (work Row 1 of patt from * to * for next 48 sts), p2, k1—52 sts.

ROW 10: Bind off 1 st, purl all yo's from the previous row, work the rest of sts as they appear—51 sts.

Continue working 51 sts in Vertical Waves patt (from Row 3 of patt) for 36 rows more, ending with Row 6 of patt.

FOR SIZES LARGE/X-LARGE ONLY:

ROW 1 (RS): Bind off 6 (9) sts, k3tog, (yo, k1) three times, yo, sl 1-k2tog-psso, p1, (work Row 1 of patt from * to * for next 60 sts), p2, k4 (7)—77 (80) sts.

ROW 2 (WS): Bind off 6 (9) sts, purl all yo from the previous row, work the rest of sts as they appear—71 sts.

ROW 3: Bind off 3 sts, k6, p1, (work Row 3 of patt from * to * for next 60 sts)—68 sts.

ROW 4: Bind off 3 sts, work the rest of sts as they appear—65 sts.

ROW 5: Bind off 2 sts, p1, k4, (work Row 5 of patt from * to * for next 48 sts), (k1, yo) twice, sl 1-k2tog-psso, p3, k1—63 sts.

ROW 6: Bind off 2 sts, purl all yo from the previous row, work the rest of sts as they appear—61 sts.

ROW 7: Bind off 2 sts, k3, (work Row 7 of patt from * to * for next 48 sts), k5, p1, k1—59 sts.

ROW 8: Bind off 2 sts, work the rest of sts as they appear—57 sts.

ROW 9: Bind off 1 st, k1, p1, (work Row 1 of patt from * to * for next 48 sts), p2, k3—56 sts.

ROW 10: Bind off 1 st, purl all yo from the previous row, work the rest of sts as they appear—55 sts.

ROW 11: Bind off 1 st, p1, (work Row 3 of patt from * to * for next 48 sts), p2, k2—54 sts.

ROW 12: Bind off 1 st, work the rest of sts as they appear—53 sts.

ROW 13: Bind off 1 st, (work Row 5 of patt from * to * for next 48 sts), k3—52 sts.

ROW 14: Bind off 1 st, purl all yo from the previous row, work the rest of sts as they appear—51 sts.

Continue working 51 sts in Vertical Waves patt (from Row 7 of patt) for 36 (40) rows more, ending with Row 2 (6) of patt.

FOR ALL SIZES:

Bind off 2 sts at beginning of next 2 rows, continue as established to end—47 sts.

NEXT RS ROW: Bind off 2 sts, k1, p1, [work Row 5 (1, 5, 1) of patt from * to * for next 36 sts], p2, k4—45 sts.

NEXT WS ROW: Bind off 2 sts, work the rest of sts as they appear—43 sts.

NEXT RS ROW: Bind off 3 sts, p1, k9, p1, [work Row 7 (3, 7, 3) of patt from * to * for next 24 sts], p2, k2— 40 sts.

NEXT WS ROW: Bind off 3 st, work the rest of sts as they appear—37 sts.

NEXT RS ROW: Bind off 5 sts, p2, k3tog, yo, k1, yo, [work Row 1 (5, 1, 5) of patt from * to * for next 24 sts], k1—32 sts.

NEXT WS ROW: Bind off 5 sts, work the rest of sts as they appear—27 sts

Bind off remaining 27 sts.

SLEEVE LEAF

With size 4 needles, cast on 3 sts.

ROW 1 (RS): K1, m1, k1 (center st), m1, k1—5 sts.

ROW 2 (WS): P1, k1, m1, p1 (center st), m1, k1, p1—7 sts.

ROW 3: K1, p1, k1, m1, k1 (center st), m1, k1, p1, k1—9 sts.

ROW 4: P1, k1, p1, k1, m1, p1 (center st), m1, k1, p1, k1, p1—11 sts.

ROW 5: K1, p1, k1, p1, k1, m1, k1 (center st), m1, k1, p1, k1, p1, k1—13 sts.

Continue working in this manner, increasing 1 st on each side of the center st in every row and working new sts into 1×1 rib (knit 1, purl 1) until there are 31 sts in total, ending with Row 14.

On WS rows only, continue increasing 1 st on each side of the center st and working new sts into 1×1 rib. AT THE SAME TIME, beginning with row 15, decrease 1 st on each edge of the leaf in every RS and WS row as follows:

RS decrease: K1, ssk, work as established in 1×1 to the center st, k1, work as established in 1×1 rib to the last 3 sts, k2tog, k1.

WS DECREASE: K1, p2tog, work as established to the center st, m1, p1, m1, work as established to last 3 sts, p2tog tbl, k1.

Omit decreases in rows 16, 19, 23, 27, 31, 35, 39, 43, 47, 51, 55, 59, 62, 64, 68, and 70.

Continue working in this manner for 70 rows total from CO.

ROW 71: K1, ssk, k1, k2tog, k1.

ROW 72: P1, k1, p1, k1, p1.

ROW 73: K1, k3tog, k1.

ROW 74: P3tog.

NECK

Sew Shoulder seams.

With circular needle, pick up and knit 55 (57, 63, 65) sts evenly along Right Neck side, pick up and knit 1 st at bottom of V-neck, pick up and knit 55 (57, 63, 65) sts along left neck side, work 44 (44, 48, 48) sts from Back Neck holder in 2_2 rib (knit 2 sts, purl 2 sts), then work remaining Back Neck sts as k1, k2tog (k2tog, increase 1 as knit st, increase 1 as knit st), join in round—157 (161, 177, 181) sts.

RND 1: *P2, k2*; repeat from * to * to 3 (1, 3, 1) sts before V-neck st, p2 (p0, p2, p0), slip 2 sts to right hand needle, k1, pass 2 slipped sts over, k0 (k2, k0, k2), *p2, k2*; repeat from * to * to the end of rnd.

RNDS 2, 4, AND 6: Work sts as they appear.

RND 3: *P2, k2*; repeat from * to * to 2 (4, 2, 4) sts before V-neck st, p1 (p2, p1, p2), k0 (k1, k0, k1), slip 2 sts to right hand needle, k1, pass 2 slipped sts over, p1 (p0, p1, p0), k2 (k1, k2, k1), *p2, k2*; repeat from * to * to the end of rnd.

RND 5: *P2, k2*; repeat from * to * to 1 (3, 1, 3) sts before V-neck st, p0 (p2, p0, p2), slip 2 sts to right-hand needle, k1, pass 2 slipped sts over, k2 (k0, k2, k0), *p2, k2*; repeat from * to * to the end of rnd.

RND 7: *P2, k2*; repeat from * to * to 4 (2, 4, 2) sts before V-neck st, p2 (p1, p2, p1), k1 (k0, k1, k0), slip 2 sts to right-hand needle, k1, pass 2 slipped sts over, p0 (p1, p0, p1), k1 (k2, k1, k2), *p2, k2*; repeat from * to * to the end of rnd.

RND 8: Work sts as they appear. Bind off firmly.

FINISHING

Sew side and Sleeve seams. Sew Front Leaf into the Front opening. Sew Sleeve Leafs into the openings on both Sleeves. Weave in loose ends to WS.

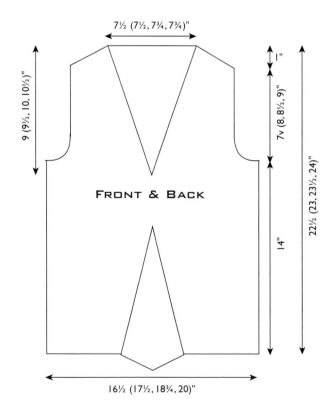

7½ (7½, 7¾, 7¾)"

9 (9½, 10, 10½)"

1"

7v (8, 8½, 9)"

22½ (23, 23½, 24)"

14"

FRONT & BACK

16½ (17½, 18¾, 20)"

ABBREVIATIONS

BACKWARD LOOP (E) INCREASE: *Wrap the working yarn around left thumb in a clockwise direction so the yarn coming from the needle is on top of the yarn circled around the thumb; insert the right needle under the yarn circle to the outside thumb, then slip the new stitch to right needle. Repeat from * for each increase.

BO: Bind off/bind-off

CN: Cable needle

CO: Cast on/cast-on

DPN: Double-pointed needles

K: Knit stitch

K1TBL: Knit 1 stitch through the back loop

K2TOG: Knit 2 stitches together

K3TOG: Knit 3 stitches together

LFFD: Left full-fashioned decrease

LH: Left-hand needle

M1: Make 1. Please see *backward loop (e) increase.*

P: Purl stitch

P1TBL: Purl one st through the back loop

P2TOG: Purl 2 stitches together

P2TOG TBL: Turn the work over slightly and insert the needle from the left-hand side into the back loops of the second and the first stitches, in that order, then wrap the yarn around the needle in front to complete the purl stitch

P3TOG: Purl 3 stitches together

PATT: Pattern

REV ST ST: Reverse Stockinette stitch (purl on right side, knit on wrong side)

RFFD: Right full-fashioned decrease

RND: Round

RS: Right side

SC: Single crochet

SK2P: Slip 1, k2tog, pass slipped stitch over (2 sts decreased)

SL: Slip

SL 1: Slip 1 st

SL 1-K2TOG-PSSO: Slip 1 stitch knitwise, knit 2 stitches together, pass slipped stitch over.

SL 2-K1-P2SSO: Slip 2 stitches knitwise, knit 1 stitch, pass two slipped stitches over

SSK: Slip 2 sts knitwise, one at a time, onto the right needle, insert left needle tip through both front loops and knit the two slipped sts together from this position

SSP: Slip 2 sts knitwise, one at a time, onto the right-hand needle, return both sts back to the left-hand needle in the twisted position, then purl both sts together through back loops

ST(S): Stitch(es)

ST ST: Stockinette stitch (knit on RS, purl on WS)

TBL: Through the back loop

WS: Wrong side

YO: Yarn over

YARN SUBSTITUTION GUIDE

Karabella yarns are available at fine yarn stores across the country. Knitters can also purchase Karabella yarns online at www.karabellayarns.com.

   The following guide lists all the Karabella yarns called for in this book and is organized by yarn weight should you wish to make substitutions. As always, if you're not sure whether a particular yarn can be used as a substitute, try knitting a swatch first—does the gauge match? The fabric should also be similar in drape, texture, and appearance. The amount of yarn per skein varies, so be sure you base your substitution on the total yardage called for rather than the number of skeins.

(1) SUPER FINE Lace Mohair: Any comparable fingering-weight, mohair-blend yarn

(2) FINE Aurora 4: Any comparable sport-weight, plied wool yarn

Vintage Cotton: Any comparable sport-weight, fine cotton yarn

(3) LIGHT Aurora 8: Any comparable worsted-weight, premium wool yarn

Boise: Any comparable DK-weight, fuzzy, cashmere-wool-blend yarn

Empire Silk: Any comparable worsted-weight, smooth, silk yarn

Marble: Any comparable worsted-weight, soft, loosely plied, wool-alpaca-blend yarn

Margrite: Any comparable DK-weight, wool-cashmere-blend yarn

Zodiac: Any comparable worsted-weight, plied cotton yarn with a sheen

(5) BULKY Margrite Bulky: Any comparable wool-cashmere-blend yarn

Aurora Bulky: Any comparable wool yarn

Supercashmere: Any comparable, supersoft cashmere yarn

Superyak: Any comparable, woven yak-wool-blend yarn

Sequins: Any comparable mohair yarn with sequins

(6) SUPER BULKY Puffy: Any comparable, fluffy, bouclé wool yarn

Puffy multicolor: Any comparable fluffy, chunky, variegated wool yarn with bouclé texture

INDEX